Fender
THE INSIDE STORY

BY FORREST WHITE

Early Years Vice President
and General Manager

GPI BOOKS
An Imprint of

*Miller Freeman Books*

San Francisco

Published by Miller Freeman Books
600 Harrison Street, San Francisco, CA 94107
Publishers of GPI Books and *Guitar Player* magazine
A member of the United Newspapers Group

Distributed to the book trade in the U.S. and Canada by
Publishers Group West, P.O. Box 8843, Emeryville, CA 94662

Distributed to the music trade in the U.S. and Canada by
Hal Leonard Publishing, P.O. Box 13819, Milwaukee, WI 53213

Cover design: Deborah Chusid
Text design: Brad Greene, Greene Design
Cover photo of Leo Fender ©1991 by Jon Sievert

ISBN 0-87930-309-3

Printed in the United States of America
98   5 4 3

DEDICATIONS

This book is deservedly dedicated to more than one:

To Clarence Leo Fender, a true legend in his time, my friend and former employer... the man who made it possible for me to become involved in the wonderful world of music, thereby changing the course of my life.

To William Schultz, President, Fender Musical Instruments, the man who saved the Fender name when it seemed headed for certain oblivion and restored the company to its former leadership recognition.

To my wife, Joan, who put up with my long working hours during the rapid growth years of the Fender Electric Instrument Co. and, along the way, presented me with our son, Curtis.

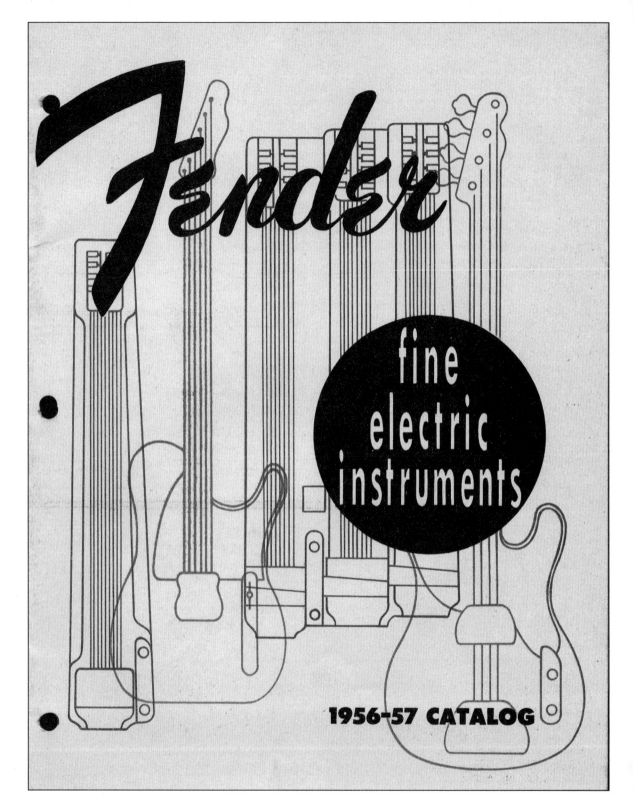

Fender

fine electric instruments

1956-57 CATALOG

CONTENTS

PART II — IN RETROSPECT

ACKNOWLEDGMENTS

It was impossible to remember the names of all of the friends I should thank for their contributions through the years, which enabled me to reach back in my memory for material to write this book.

There were those I agreed with, and I was pleased to learn that our thinking on most subjects ran along parallel lines. There were others, I am sorry to say, I disagreed with on many issues. However, this fact did not detract from their right to an opinion, and there were many times when I found that they were right and I was wrong. No one knows all of the answers, though I am sure most of us have met those who would have us believe they are the exception.

Tom Wheeler, the former editor of *Guitar Player* magazine who is now a journalism professor at the University of Oregon, recently paid a great tribute to Leo Fender by inaugurating *Guitar Player*'s annual "Leo Award" for innovation in guitar equipment design and manufacturing. Tom has been a long-time friend and I was pleased that he named another one of my long-time friends, Ted McCarty, as the first Leo Award recipient. Ted was the president of Gibson during the Fender early years, and he designed some of Gibson's solid-body electric guitars that are considered classics today. Ted acquired Paul Bigsby's business in 1965 and is still the president and owner of Bigsby Accessories, Inc. My congratulations to Ted and thank you, Tom, for the honor you bestowed on Leo Fender. I hope the *Guitar Player* Leo Award will gain proper recognition and prestige through the coming years.

I deeply appreciate the remarks made in the book by some of my long-time friends: Donald D. Randall, President, early years Fender Sales,

Inc.; Charlie Hayes, Sales Representative, early years Fender Sales, Inc.; Fred Martin, Chairman, C. F. Martin & Co. Inc.; Jerry Byrd and Speedy West, two of the best steel guitar players I have ever heard play; Merle Travis, great songwriter, guitar player, and pioneer contributor of ideas for the development of the solid-body standard guitar; Jimmy Wakely, one of the great singing cowboys of the silver screen; Bob Wills, the King of Western Swing, and a loyal user of Fender products through the years; and Brian T. Majeski, Editor, *The Music Trades* magazine.

My thanks and heartfelt gratitude to the early years employees for their hard work and dedication in helping to make Fender a name that will be known and respected by millions for countless years to come. Leo Fender would agree with me that they were the best group of people to work with that any company could ever hope to have.

I wish I had the space to thank all of the many dealers, musicians, and entertainers for their friendship and loyalty to Fender during the most wonderful years of my life.

This book would not have been written if it had not been that my dear friend and employer Clarence Leo Fender asked me to write it, and I have complied with his request to "tell it just like it happened." He said there were certain things he wanted people to know.

And last, but not least, my special thanks to Bill Schultz, president of Fender Musical Instruments, for saving the name of Fender from that period of time when there was a problem of quality control. Bill solved the quality problem and then proceeded to elevate the name of Fender to an even higher level of prominence in the manufacturing and distribution of musical instrument products. He has my highest respect for the outstanding job he has done to preserve the name Fender, which has such a personal meaning to me.

Forrest White

FOREWORD

This is the true *inside story* of the Fender early years—just the way it happened—authorized by my friend and former employer Leo Fender. Leo gave me permission to write this book because he felt that our many friends should know what *really* happened during the early years at Fender. He told me I should be the one to write it in my own words and that I should tell the truth without any feeling of intimidation. I didn't have to worry about research for material accuracy or look into a crystal ball, because I was there when it happened, serving as vice president and general manager. I did not require a ghost writer to put the facts on paper.

Some critics may not like the style I used in writing the book, but the true story is the important part. It is written in the way Leo Fender would want it to be—plain, down to earth, no fancy frills. I tried to write it in the same manner that would be used in telling the story verbally.

You will be able to read between the lines as you turn the pages of the book. You will find humor, sadness, scheming, deceptiveness, egotism, ineptitude, hardship, prosperity, stubborness, frustrations... but, above all, you will see how Leo Fender was able, with help, to overcome all of those obstacles on a rough road to phenomenal success. He truly became a legend in his lifetime.

You will be able to retrace steps from the Radio & Television Equipment Co., through Fender's Radio Service, K&F, Fender Electric Instrument Co., Fender Sales, Rickenbacker, CBS Musical Instruments, CLF Research, Music Man Inc., G & L, and Fender Musical Instruments.

Leo Fender, Charlie Hayes (Fender's first salesman), and Freddie Tavares (Leo's right-hand man in research and development) told me what happened before I was employed at Fender. I was there from May 1954 until December 1967, after the company had been sold to CBS.

The information I will give you in this book on purchase orders and production runs is taken from my personal records. If any writer disputes the information, just ask them where they were when it happened.

You will find some facts that differ from what you may have read elsewhere. Some writers seemingly feel it isn't necessary to check for facts when they write about Fender, and I resent the stories that have been written without evidence of much effort to substantiate the material—particularly some in recent years about the origins of the Stratocaster. You will find that the Strat was *absolutely not* designed for any one person, and it wasn't designed entirely *by* one person either. You will find that Bill Carson, whom I hired in 1957, who is my good friend and still one of Fender's most valuable employees, was never a plant manager or director of marketing, as was written in a special Stratocaster sales document. And there was absolutely *never* any intention on the part of Leo Fender or Don Randall to discontinue the Telecaster and Stratocaster. Not at any time. Period. The written statement that it was considered is ridiculous. It is a good example of someone's imagination for what I call "Fender fiction." I'm sure that my friends Bill Carson, Leo Fender, Don Randall, and many others who were involved in the true story of Fender would be pleased that these and other erroneous accounts will be cleared up.

I have great respect for the following writers, who are my friends, and when you read anything they have written you can believe they have researched their material: Tony Bacon, author of *The Ultimate Guitar Book* and *The Fender Book*; Rich Kienzle, senior editor of *The Journal* and a writer for *Country Music* magazine; Richard Smith, author of *The Complete History of Rickenbacker Guitars*; Tom Wheeler, consulting editor for *Guitar Player* magazine and author of *The Guitar Book* and *American Guitars*; and Walter Carter, co-writer (with George Gruhn) of *Acoustic Guitars and Other Fretted Instruments* and *Gruhn's Guide to Vintage Guitars*. Of course, there are many other writers who are very conscientious about their work, and I certainly meant no offense to them.

Recently my long-time friend Chet Atkins appeared in concert at the McCallum Theatre in Palm Desert, near Palm Springs, California. Chet and Paul Yandell, his guitarist friend in the band, were using small Music Man amplifiers. Needless to say, it made me feel very proud that these two musicians, second to none, chose amplifiers manufactured by the company that Leo Fender helped me form a few short years ago. Chet and Paul can well afford to use any amplifiers they feel would best showcase their talent. In reality, it was a continuation of the world famous Fender amplifier sound. The guitar-playing talent of Chet Atkins through an amplifier made possible by the genius of Leo Fender—what an incomparable combination.

How well I remember when Leo told me he knew I was the best friend he had in this world. Now there may be some who will try to tell you this is not true, that someone else deserves this honor. Well, I did not put those words in his mouth, and I darn sure did not fabricate his comment to impress anyone. I am proud of my association with him, and even more proud to say that Leo Fender was my dear friend as well as my employer.

Forrest White

INTRODUCTION
TO LEO FENDER
THE MAN

Much has been written about Leo Fender, the man, and the small operation he formed in 1945, the Fender Electric Instrument Co. Little did Leo know then that the humble beginning in Fullerton, California, would eventually become one of the greatest success stories in the history of the musical instrument business.

Leo Fender. What kind of a person was this man who became a legend in his lifetime? I can tell you he was not the easiest person to work for. I know, because I happened to be the only manager he had in those early years. Please understand that my friend Leo did not cause me problems intentionally. For him, research and development was the name of the game. If it couldn't be fixed with a screwdriver or a pair of pliers, then it wasn't all that important, and the manager could look out for himself. He did not really care to become involved with everyday management problems; sadly enough, he helped to *create* management problems, but remember what I said—unintentionally. Careful now, I am not trying to criticize my friend. I will explain more later on.

Leo could have been called a workaholic. He had a compulsive drive to work and a dogged determination to build the best darn amplifiers and musical instruments possible. He had seemingly set his mind to being successful with an "I'll show you" attitude, which may have been formed back in his high school days.

One Saturday afternoon, in the late summer of 1954, I was driving past his parents' home in Anaheim, California. I saw his father out in the front yard and stopped to say hello and visit awhile. We were making small talk about the weather and nothing in particular when he brought up the subject of Leo. He said, "You know, Leo's mother and I never did think he would amount to much. He always seemed so unconcerned, with no sense of direction. We only had enough money for one college education so we sent his sister, Wilda, because she seemed to be more serious and intelligent than Leo." At this point in time, things were looking much better at the factory, so I asked his father what opinion he had of Leo now. He said, "Well, I'll have to admit, he sure surprised us."

There was another thing that happened in Leo's childhood which must have had a great deal to do with his attitude toward life. He lost the sight in one eye through an accident at home. He never mentioned this to me. However, I was told that he thought his parents could have done more to save his injured eye.

Then, of course, Leo and his first wife, Esther, were married August 1, 1934, so he had added responsibility. They never had any children.

It is my opinion that Leo's lack of a complete college education, his loss of sight in one eye, and his added marriage responsibility were the basic reasons for his determination to show he had what it takes to succeed, despite the sorrow and disappointments he may have suffered along the way. He must have known that his parents didn't have much confidence in his ability. Again, please understand, this is only speculation on my part. Leo settled for the two years in junior college provided by the state, majoring in accounting, and made out very well regardless, thank you very much.

Perhaps there is something else I should tell you so that you will have a better understanding of Leo Fender, the man. Many were the evenings, after working hours, that we would talk about the events of the day. He would be relaxed then, and he seemed like a different person than when at work, which he tackled as though he were fighting fire. He told me, more than once, that he had the feeling that God was at his side, guiding and directing him, from the time he first made the decision to go into business for himself. It was at times like this when I would think, thank God I am associated with Leo Fender.

But then, I confess, I told him many times that I had never met a man before who could make me as angry so quickly as he could. I remember, so well, how he would laugh when I told him that. I think it is only human nature that we are so easily offended when someone we care about says or does something to hurt our feelings. In his defense, I must tell you, he would bend over backwards to try to make amends for anything he might have said or done to upset me—that is, if he felt he may have been wrong.

This, then, was but a brief look at the complex nature of the man who changed the course of and had the greatest influence on my life.

Forrest White

"Leo treated me like a son. Out of everything we did together our most monumental achievements were my upside-down backwards Stratocaster and my Showman amp. After burning and blowing up over 40 experimental amps and speakers, the 'Fender Dual Showman' was born, and with it was born Dick Dale, 'King of the Surf Guitar'."

—*Dick Dale*

Part I

FENDER EARLY YEARS HISTORY

CHAPTER 1

THE EARLY
FENDER
YEARS

Clarence Leo Fender told me he was born August 10, 1909, in a barn on a farm that his parents owned in an unincorporated area located between Anaheim and Fullerton, California. The barn was the only building on the property. They lived on one side, a hay pile was in the middle, and their horses were on the other side. They didn't build their first home until the following year. Leo lived in the Anaheim and Fullerton area for all but three years of his life.

Leo never learned to play the guitar, or even how to tune one, but he always liked music—Hawaiian music in particular. He said he heard a lot of Hawaiian music in the early 1920s because a steamship company had just built the Royal Hawaiian Hotel in Honolulu, which they promoted with the music. He took piano and saxophone lessons and played saxophone in the high school band, but he liked the sound of stringed instruments much better than horns. With stringed instruments, he said, you get all of the even and odd harmonics. With horns you only get the odd harmonics. You can't prove this by me; I'm only telling you what he said. I learned very soon not to argue with him, because he usually won.

Not long after I began working for him, I asked him how he got started, and he said, "I began tinkering with radios in 1922, while I was still in grammar school, before they even had regular radio stations in Southern California. It was then that I built my first crystal radio, which I listened to with a pair of earphones. All we had to listen to then was the radio communication between Catalina Island and the mainland. I thought it was great to be listening in on those conversations. The first broadcast stations in California were built a few years later."

He grew up in a time when electricity and its applications were still new and exciting. "My uncle owned an auto-electric store in Santa Maria, California," he said. "He manufactured storage batteries and some radio equipment. He used to give me magazines and books that had radio and electronic experiments in them. This is how I think I became interested in what I am doing now."

By the time Leo graduated from high school in 1928, he was hooked on electronics. He had an amateur "ham" radio station with the call letters W-6-DOE. Electrical amplification was still in its infancy but he was already involved in the business. "I was building amplifiers and PA systems, which I rented to dance bands, political rallies, baseball games and entertainment events," he said. "In electronics, 1928 was an important year. That was when the first AC vacuum tubes were available, making it feasible to build a practical tube amplifier. Before then, the only power source you could use was a heavy 'B' battery which went dead quickly and cost a fortune. Also, the first efficient speaker had just been invented by Paul Jensen. Because of these breakthroughs, I could build amplifiers that had 15 watts with what were, at the time, considered efficient speakers, fitted to sheet metal trumpets. Not much compared to today's standards, but a heck of a lot more than nothing."

Leo built three complete PA systems, which he rented between 1930 to 1947. "Renting the amplifiers and PA systems was only a part-time job," he said, "but I did pretty well at it. When I rented them for ball games, many times the teams would not have the money to pay me. I would sell time to the local merchants so that they could broadcast advertisements between innings."

I asked Leo why he seemed so obsessed with having so many tools. "Well, as far back as I can remember, I always had tools around. On a farm you have a lot of them. I like tools. Always have. Though my dad was a farmer, I was more interested in electronics and design, so I decided to pursue that sort of a course." Perhaps this was one of the reasons his father decided to send Leo's younger sister Wilda to college rather than him. (Again, this is pure speculation on my part.)

After graduating from high school, Leo studied accounting in junior college for two years, courtesy of the state of California. He passed a civil service exam around 1930. In 1932 and 1933 he was employed by the California Department of Motor Vehicles in the accounting department.

Leo married Esther Klotzky on August 1, 1934, when he was 25 and she was 20. Around seven years earlier, he had met her through his younger sister Wilda. Esther's family had moved into the Fenders' neighborhood when she was in the eighth grade. She and Wilda were good friends all the way through Fullerton High School, and they visited each other's homes frequently. Leo and Esther moved to San Luis Obispo in 1935 when Leo found a job as an accountant in the Highway Department for the State of California. They lived there through most of 1938. When he decided to open his own business, they moved back to Fullerton.

CHAPTER 2

FENDER'S
RADIO
SERVICE

Leo opened Fender's Radio Service in the latter part of 1938. He rented space at a Golden Eagle service station located on the corner of Spadra (now called Harbor Blvd.) and Santa Fe in Fullerton. "For the first three weeks I went from house to house looking for work," he told me. "After that, I had so many radios to repair I never had to look anymore."

Leo Fender had arrived as an entrepreneur, and business growth soon demanded a larger facility. He moved a few doors away to 112 South Spadra Blvd. It's hard to believe that his telephone number back then was just plain number 6. No area code. Not even an "exchange," as they used to call the prefix. He also started selling phonograph records from his new location.

Musicians began bringing their amplifiers to Leo for repair, and the more he worked on them, the more he became interested in musical instrument amplification. He did not like what he found in the circuitry of the majority of these amplifiers. Gradually he began to build amplifiers on a custom-order basis, and the musicians liked the sound he gave them.

Leo was interested in anything that was mechanical or electronic, and that included phonograph record changers that customers brought in

STATEMENT

FULLERTON, CALIF., ..., 194......

M...

IN ACCOUNT WITH

FENDER'S RADIO SERVICE
107 SO. SPADRA, FULLERTON
Phone 6

Date	Item	Charge	Credit	Balance

NOTICE: Balance Due Over 30 Days Subject to 2% Interest

1935 statement from Fender's Radio Service, Leo's first business.

for repair. He found that design problems were often the cause of the trouble in these units, and, as he thought about an improved design, the wheels started to turn.

Now, Doc Kauffman entered the picture. Doc would have talked your leg off if you gave him half the chance, but his talk was certainly not boring. Leo, being interested in everything, had been working on musical instrument magnetic pickups and had started to replace a few on some of the musicians' guitars, but there is a good chance he would never have built any electric musical instruments if he hadn't met Doc. Doc said that one day he took an amplifier into Fender's Radio Service for repair, and he saw Leo talking to some musician about a pickup. So he introduced himself and discovered he and Leo had many of the same interests. Before too long they decided to team up and form a company called K&F (Kauffman & Fender) Manufacturing Corp.

I asked Leo why he would have considered taking on a partner, and he said, "Well, I sort of knew who he was. I had seen him around town many times. He was a musician and seemed to know quite a lot about pickups and musical instruments. I thought it might be helpful to have his input."

Leo knew Doc had worked some with Paul Barth and George Beauchamp, who were both knowledgeable about musical instruments and electronics. Leo said George Beauchamp has been credited for the design of the first good magnetic guitar pickup. He said he thought Beauchamp had applied for a patent in 1934 but he didn't think it had been approved until around 1937. I would bet Leo knew exactly what the details were about that patent. Actually, it was filed June 2, 1934, and was granted August 10, 1937. The pickup was designed around two horseshoe magnets with legs approximately ⅛" thick and 1¼" wide. The legs of the magnets faced each other, overlapping the top and bottom of the magnet wire coil. There was a small gap between the magnets' legs, and they were charged with opposing magnetic fields. A coil of wire, into which individual pole-pieces were inserted, was placed between the legs of the magnets, and the guitar strings then passed between the upper legs of the magnets and the pole-pieces. The pickup was first used on what was called the Rickenbacker Frying Pan lap model steel guitar. The pickup gave the guitar a heck of a good tone with a great sustaining quality.

I mentioned that Leo had been servicing phonograph record changers and found they were not very reliable, having many mechanical problems. Well, he and Doc Kauffman decided they could design and build a better changer, so they started to work. After many hours of labor they had what they considered to be the answer to all changer problems. You know, they may have been right. They set it up in Leo's store window for a demonstration and let it run 24 hours a day for almost two months without any sign of trouble. But here is the sad part. Leo told me he and Doc really didn't have the money to follow through with patent protection. They sold their rights to the changer for only $5,000. It ended up as the forerunner of the famous little RCA 45-rpm changer. He said they sure made a mistake in selling their idea for such a small amount of money, because RCA must have sold a million of those changers when sales of 45-rpm "singles" picked up in the early 1950s.

In 1943, Leo and Doc designed a new pickup with the strings passing *through* the wound magnet wire coil. Every other pickup that I know of has the coil located under the strings. Leo said they built their first guitar to test the new pickup. The guitar body was very narrow, like a lap model Hawaiian steel guitar. When I asked Leo why they made it so narrow, he laughed and said, "Because it was the biggest piece of wood Doc could find." It was a standard 6-string solid-body guitar, however, with a fretted neck. It played real well, the sound was great, and when some of the musicians found out about the guitar, they wanted to rent it. Leo said he had names on a waiting list of those wanting to try it out. He and Doc filed for a patent on the pickup September 26, 1944; and the patent, #2,455,575, was granted December 7, 1948.

This first guitar was later given to our friend Roy Acuff for display in his museum, which was originally located across the street from Ernest Tubb's Record Shop on Broadway in Nashville, Tennessee. Roy later moved his museum to Opryland. The guitar is still on display, along with the letter of explanation which I wrote and Leo signed.

A growing business again demanded more room, so Leo and Doc moved just a few doors away to 107 South Spadra. The partners made progress during the year 1945. They built the first six K&F lap model Hawaiian steel guitars, along with their newly designed amplifiers, which they sold as sets. There were three different K&F model amplifiers, equipped with an 8", 10", or 12" speaker. Through 1945, all K&F amplifiers and guitars were sold through Coast Wholesale or Pacific Music Supply, or else sold direct to the customer by Leo.

By this time, Leo had really become dedicated to working with electric guitars and amplifiers. He just knew that this endeavor had to be

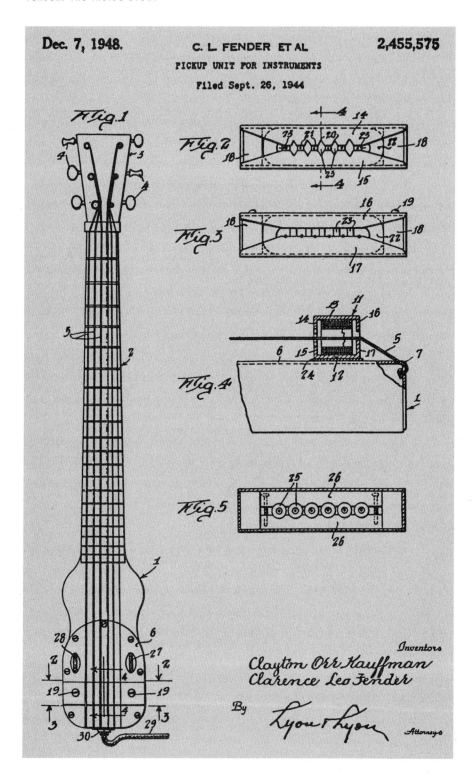

much more profitable than radio servicing. He told Doc they had to have more space because the business was growing. Doc was apprehensive about investing more money in this as yet unproven venture. Leo said, "Doc was scared because he had a little real estate in Oklahoma which he didn't want to lose, so rather than take the risk, he left."

The separation agreement was made during the latter part of 1945, although Doc didn't leave until early in 1946. It was a friendly separation, with no hard feelings from either partner. And here, friend, Leo Fender probably made the best deal of his lifetime. He traded Doc Kauffman a small punch press for his interest in the company. Doc didn't do too much of interest after the separation agreement with Leo, until Leo became successful a few years later. It would seem that Doc had second thoughts then about the monetary possibilities of guitar manufacturing, because in the 1960s he began to make what he called Doc Kauffman's Kremo-Kustom Guitars. I never did ask Doc if the punch press Leo traded him for his interest in K&F had a place of honor in his workshop. I think it should have, because it turned out to be one heck of an expensive power tool.

Leo's first business partner died June 26, 1990, in Fullerton, California. He was 89 years old.

Now that Leo was the sole owner of the operation, he renamed it the Fender Electric Instrument Co.

CHAPTER **3**

FENDER ELECTRIC INSTRUMENT CO. 1945

Leo made a few K&F guitars after Doc left, and he also kept working in his radio service shop until the end of 1947. At that time he turned over supervision of the shop to his employee Dale Hyatt, who had been working there since 1946. For some reason, however, Fender's Radio Service closed its doors forever in 1951.

Through the year 1945, Leo bought electronic parts for his radio service from Radio & Television Equipment Co. in Santa Ana. The company was owned by Francis Hall. (He preferred to be called F.C. Hall, so from now on, we will honor that preference.) Don Randall was the general sales manager, and he was the one who made sales calls on Leo. I was told that Don became interested in what Leo and Doc were doing with the amplifiers and guitars, and he encouraged Leo to go full-steam ahead with manufacturing. In addition, I was told Don promoted the deal to have the Radio & Television Equipment Co. serve as the exclusive distributor for all of Leo's future products. Leo and F.C. Hall must have thought Don's idea was a good one, because in 1946 Radio & Television Equipment Co. became the distributor for the Fender Electric Instrument Co.

During the time the distributorship was being decided, Leo was in the process of having two sheet metal buildings, 30' x 60', built on Santa Fe Avenue in Fullerton. When they were completed he moved his manufacturing operation. Now he had two new buildings and a new distributor, all in 1946.

The first Fender buildings on Santa Fe Ave. in Fullerton, 1946. (photo: Leo Fender)

Leo said when he moved into those two buildings, he had never seen so much space before in his life. They seemed absolutely huge to him. The facilities within the new buildings were not the best, however. Everyone had to walk across the street and then up a block or two to the Santa Fe Railroad Station to use the restrooms. That certainly was not very pleasant during the winter rainy season.

Now, the working conditions were no better than the toilet facilities in those sheet metal buildings. Just imagine how hot they became in the summertime and how cold in winter. In recounting those conditions, Leo revealed that they could also be dangerous. He said, "Around 1949, we started to put an acetate finish on the lap model Hawaiian steel guitar bodies; and to keep the acetate warm, we kept it near an open gas flame. I guess if anything ever happened [he meant explosion, but didn't say it], we would have blown that building over the moon. Actually, it was so bad that when the fire inspector came, he just looked in the door and ran off to call us at the nearest pay phone, he was so scared."

(Upper) The first guitar made by Leo Fender. (Lower) One of the first production guitars. (photo: Fender)

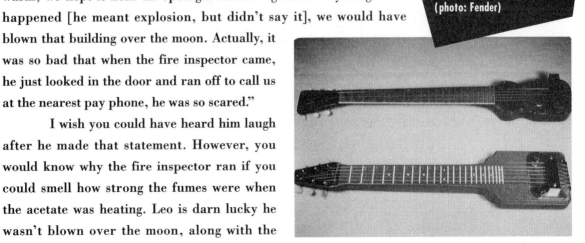

I wish you could have heard him laugh after he made that statement. However, you would know why the fire inspector ran if you could smell how strong the fumes were when the acetate was heating. Leo is darn lucky he wasn't blown over the moon, along with the

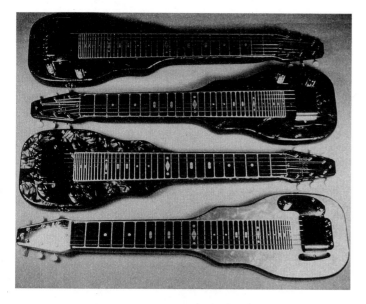

Early Fender lap model steel guitars. (photo: Fender)

building and anyone else in the area. You had the feeling you were standing next to a time bomb, believe me.

I'm sure that Leo's comments about the acetate finish will be confusing to some. This is the process he was describing: The acetate, a plastic material with a simulated pearl finish, came in large sheets. You would cut it to the proper size, depending on the shape of the wooden guitar body. When you heated the acetate, it became very pliable and you could wrap it over the top, the sides, and bottom, stretching and pressing it onto the wood body. You may be surprised to know that the acetate would fit like a glove. Then you would trim off the excess material by cutting all around the bottom about an inch-and-a-half from the edge. You would then glue a cut piece of felt on the bottom. Now you had a nice-looking guitar body ready for your next assembly operations. I know this because they were still doing it this way when I visited with Leo in 1951.

Leo never told me why he started using the dangerous acetate material, but I did hear of one possible reason. We all know they have been making darn good furniture out of oak wood for years. Well, Leo made several guitar bodies out of oak. I don't know what kind of oak, but after they were sold and had been used for awhile, the problems began. The secretion, or sap if you prefer, from the wood absolutely destroyed the chrome-plated parts on the guitars. I saw one of them in 1951 and it was a mess. There was a big bonfire when all those instruments were returned.

The next few years were not the best for Leo. For one thing, he was trying his best to keep his head above water and remain solvent. He was trying to keep the shop going, along with trying to produce new models of amplifiers and guitars. And don't forget, he had a new distributor waiting for product to sell to the dealers.

Leo did not exactly approve of the association with his new distributor. In fact, he was just plain unhappy. He said: "Those years were absolute hell. I think I worked from six in the morning 'til midnight every day of the week. A new trademark is a hard thing to get accepted. With no advertising, no one knew who we were and there was nothing to pep up sales. It took every penny I could get my hands on to keep things together. I was unhappy with our distributor [F. C. Hall], who was a former shipping clerk and never advertised."

During the latter part of 1946 Leo was producing what he called Deluxe single-neck Hawaiian steel guitars, available with six or eight strings. In early 1947 he made what sales literature called the first Dual 8 Professional steel guitar, and it went to a great steel guitar player, Noel Boggs. Noel, who played with Bob Wills and His Texas Playboys, was the first well-known musician to get on the Fender bandwagon. I mean, he was completely sold on the sound and performance of Leo's new Dual steel guitar and his new amplifier. How do I know? Noel told me so after I started to work for Leo.

These double-neck jewels (and they were just that in appearance and sound) were available as the Dual 6 or Dual 8, referring to, of course, the number of strings on each neck. They were equipped with Leo's strings-through-the-coil pickups (Leo called them Direct String pickups), and had the best darn sound and sustain you ever heard. As far as I'm concerned, they were the best sounding pickups Leo ever made for steel guitars.

I was so carried away with the guitar, I forgot to tell you about the new amplifiers. By early 1947, Leo had produced two new models: the Pro Amp with a 15" heavy-duty Jensen speaker and the Dual Professional amplifier with two 10" heavy-duty Jensen speakers. These were designed for professional musicians, and they were covered with a tweed material. They also were the first amplifiers to use Leo's new idea, a top-mounted chassis. This idea was great because now the controls were located on top of the amplifier for the musician's easy access. At first, some competitors were skeptical about this crazy way of mounting the chassis, with the tubes hanging upside down. As time went by, they found that there was nothing to worry about, and they all started building their amplifiers the same way. Many manufacturers of musical instruments, as well as amplifiers, would copy Leo's ideas through the coming years.

We must not forget to keep the record straight. (So many things happened in the early years that it is difficult to stay on the same subject.) Leo was building his first hardwood amplifiers from about the middle part of 1946 through the middle of 1948. These amplifiers had plain wooden cabinets with different stained finishes. Leo said they were fastened with angle iron. Even so, the cabinets were not nearly as strong as those with dove-tailed corners provided on the Pro Amp and Dual Professional.

Before I go on, just a word to my rock & roll musicians and fans: There ain't no such thing as that sound yet, man! This is still 1947, and the Telecaster is only a twinkle in Leo Fender's eye. So be patient while I tell some of your elders about the guys who entertained us.

As I said before, Noel Boggs, more than any other musician, was the first to light Leo Fender's "fire." Noel's boss, Bob Wills, would not allow another make of amplifier on stage after Noel had him try Leo's new professional model amps. Noel also played steel with Spade Cooley's band, at the time Leo was getting under steam. He would later be a regular on Jimmy Wakely's CBS network radio show. For some of you who are younger, I might mention that Jimmy was one of the singing movie cowboys. The Jimmy Wakely Trio sang on Gene Autry's *Melody Ranch* radio show Sunday nights on CBS for many years. (Jimmy Wakely and I became very good friends through the years and I was one of the first to be called to serve as a pallbearer when Jimmy passed away a few years ago.) Here is what Jimmy wrote about Noel several years ago:

> Noel Boggs is without doubt the most imitated steel player in the world today... and for two very good reasons. First, the big sound he gets from this hard-to-play instrument and, second, the fact that this is one artist whose talents cover various styles of music.
>
> Noel was born in Oklahoma City and his first professional breaks were with hillbilly dance bands. During his break-in period in radio on WKY in Oklahoma City, Noel was regularly playing in jam sessions

around town. Not satisfied with just "making a buck," Boggs wanted to improve on his favorite instrument and prove that the steel guitar was not a limited instrument...not just for Hawaiians or country bands. This made it tough for this talented artist as he had made so much headway that he made records with Bob Wills, Spade Cooley and other country artists, including this writer. Classification was a natural following and Boggs was typed, as they say in show business.

To beat off this terrible feeling of being "typed" and limited, Noel organized a small group and appeared in various night clubs, including the Plaza Hotel in Hollywood 17 weeks a year and the rest of the time in Reno, Las Vegas and Tahoe.

Meanwhile, the magic style of Noel Boggs was used in several movie sound tracks, including the award winning sound for Paramount's *War of the Worlds*.

You will agree, I am certain, that Noel Boggs has taken the steel guitar a long, long way since he left Oklahoma City.

Jimmy Wakely

Leo Fender appreciated the great amount of help Noel Boggs gave him during the rough days in those early years. I am sure that Leo would have wanted me to give Noel credit for his contribution to the success of Fender.

As Jimmy Wakely mentioned, Noel had helped with the sound track to *War of the Worlds*. Well, the next time you watch that movie, just remember, that is not the sound of the Martian ray guns you hear. That was Noel, sliding the bar back and forth on the strings of his great big Fender steel guitar.

By the end of 1947, Leo Fender was still not too happy with the name of his twin-10" speaker amplifier, so he changed it from Dual Professional to Super Amp.

Leo was not too happy with his distributor, Radio & Television Equipment Co., either. "During this time, they didn't sell hardly any of our guitars. They just sat there in this garage, and termites got into them and

The first advertisement for
a solid-body guitar: the
Broadcaster, in 1950.

ate through the bodies. We never found out about the termites until dealers started calling us about holes in the guitars. We ended up taking back 500 guitars and had to burn them all. On top of that, I was being sued by four people simultaneously [he never told me who], and I had to get an extra building because there wasn't enough space left in the radio shop."

I have thought a lot about what Leo said regarding the termites. In all fairness, there is probably more to that story than what he stated. I have a hunch that some of the 500 guitar bodies he burned were some of those oak-bodied "bombshell" guitars he had to take back. I really don't think you have trouble with termites after finish has been applied to the

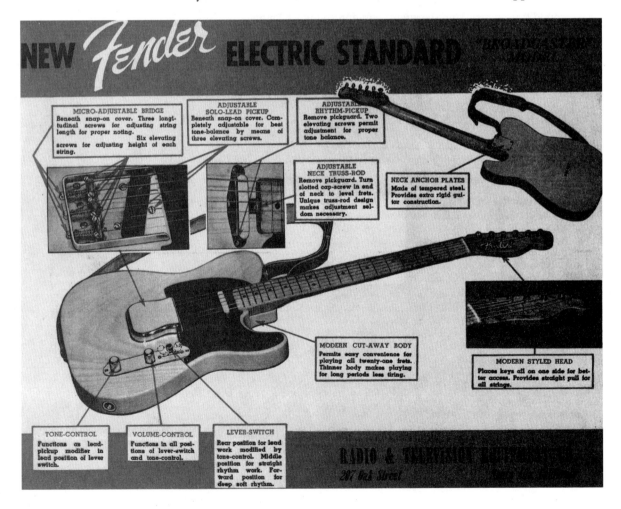

bodies. If you do, then the termites were probably already in the wood before it was processed. I say this based on experience. I have actually seen sawdust (I guess you would call it termite dust) in guitar cases right under a little hole where the termite had eaten its way out of the guitar body. I have seen this happen more than once. I did not make this statement to say Leo was wrong about the guitar bodies he burned. I do know, however, he was embarrassed about those oak wood bodies he had to take back. He said very little about that problem. Just understand, Leo was a proud man—not vain or self-centered, but proud.

This will give you a little insight into what Leo was thinking when he designed a new product. "In working as a repairman, and being preoccupied with the problems of others," he said, "I was always able to see the defects in the design of an instrument which overlooked completely the need of its maintenance. If something is easy to repair, it is easy to construct. The design of each element should be thought out in order to be easy to make and easy to repair." This was the way Leo thought about designing any product he made. I would like for you to remember his statement because I will remind you of it later on. It was the reason I resigned from CBS Musical Instruments.

The year 1948 proved to be a very important one in Fender history. This was the year that Leo first produced the tweed-covered Champion 800, Princeton, and Deluxe model amplifiers. This was also the year that he started to work on the design of his first solid-body standard electric guitar, which he would call the Broadcaster, and then change the name to Telecaster. This was the year Leo hired George Fullerton to work in production. Later on George would play an important part in the inside story of Fender. And this is the part that is so important to me: This was the year I first met Leo Fender. Little did I know then that he would be more influential in the course of my life than anyone else I would meet through the years.

CHAPTER **4**

ORIGIN OF
THE JAZZMASTER
GUITAR

I have been asked many times how I met and eventually became associated with Leo. To tell that part of the story, I must go back to the beginning of my story, to my first homemade guitar.

My father, C. F. White, was a general building contractor in Akron, Ohio. He had a small one-story building that was full of all kinds of power woodworking tools. I used to make all of the kitchen cabinet doors and other millwork for the houses he built.

In 1938, I decided I would try to build an electric solid woodbody steel guitar. Now, the body of the guitar was no problem, because I had all of my father's tools at my disposal. But making the pickup was an entirely different problem. I knew it would require a magnet of some kind, and a coil made from magnet wire. That was the limit of my knowledge of guitar pickups. I had no source for buying the acceptable size of the magnets. I did not have the slightest idea what the gauge of the magnet wire should be, and I did not know that the kind of magnet wire coating was important.

I finally found an old V-shaped magnet that had been salvaged from a Model T Ford and decided to mount the pickup on one of the magnet legs. I made the top and bottom pieces for the coil form out of wood. Then I drilled six holes in the top and bottom pieces, and inserted #8 X 1" round-head machine screws through the holes. I made sure that the screws extended through the bottom so they would touch the magnet. The finished coil form looked halfway decent.

I had purchased a spool of #38 gauge magnet wire, and now I was ready for the tedious winding operation. I first tried to wind the coil by hand, and that proved to be out of the question. I then removed the wheel from a hand-operated emery wheel (it would be called a grinding wheel today, I guess). I mounted the coil form on the mandrel, where the wheel had been, and then I was in business. There was an 8-to-1 ratio, so every time I turned the handle, the mandrel revolved eight times. This sure was a lot better than the one-on-one hand-winding method. I guess I must have wound a dozen coils through the later part of 1938 and 1939, whenever I could find the time, but with no luck.

I built a test neck that allowed plenty of room to slide a pickup in and out from under the strings, even when mounted on the leg of the big V-shaped magnet. I had a small PA amplifier, maybe 20 watts at most, made by a company called Bell. The amp had absolutely no humming sound when it was turned on. You could be standing next to it, with the volume turned up, and still not be able to hear it. And you darn sure could not hear the sound of the pickups I made during that period of time.

One day, in 1939, I decided to wrap a layer of tape around the exposed screw threads, between the top and bottom of the coil form, before I wound the magnet wire coil. I positioned the wound coil under the strings next to the bridge. I turned the amplifier on and the volume way up. I was sitting on a stool next to my workbench with the speaker on the bench next to my ear. Well, I just knew there would be no sound out of this latest darn pickup because all of the others had failed. So I strummed across the strings with great gusto, and disgust, and almost got knocked off the stool. Friend, I had just wound my first successful pickup and it came through like a ton of bricks.

It was obvious now what had happened with my earlier pickups. The screw threads had been cutting through the coating of the magnet wire and this caused a short in the coil winding. The layer of tape around the screw threads had made the difference. You live and learn. From the year 1938 through September of 1939, I made a single-neck, double-neck, and a four-neck steel guitar—all with six strings on each neck. Right after I tested my first successful pickup I found a source in Chicago for magnets $\frac{3}{16}$" in diameter by 1" long. That took care of a serious problem, because I could not make a decent looking guitar using one leg of a V-magnet.

Oh! The four-neck steel I made? Forget it. It was so heavy it required a crane to lift it. I tore it down after the first time I tried to lift it. Besides the weight, what kind of tunings would you use on a four-neck six-stringed steel?

During the month of September, 1939, I started to work in the Aircraft Assembly Training Dept. (the old Kelley-Springfield building) for Goodyear Aircraft in Akron, Ohio, and then disaster struck for yours truly. I came home after my first day at work, and became quite ill by evening. I was in the hospital by 8:00 p.m. and operated on soon after that. I had acute pancreatitis and, I can tell you, that ain't good. I was sick as the devil. This, of course, put an end to my guitar-making hobby for awhile. Around the first part of December, I was able to go back to work, and very soon I became an instructor in the training department teaching aircraft assembly methods and blueprint reading.

In November 1941, I went to see Alvino Rey and his Orchestra with the King Sisters, at the Paramont Theatre in Akron. I had been a fan of Alvino's for some time and it was a thrill to be able to see him in person. A song called "Guitar Boogie" was very popular at that time and, of course, he featured it, playing his big Gibson acoustic-body electric standard guitar. Alvino had his guitar mounted on a stand in playing position, so that he could go back and forth from playing the guitar to leading the orchestra.

One thing bothered me about his guitar. When he changed from his solo part to playing rhythm with the orchestra, he would have to fool around with the control knobs for the proper tone and volume settings. This did not make sense to me. He should have been able to just flip a switch for presetting between rhythm and lead positions. I went home and the next day I started working on a solid-body electric standard guitar with a preset circuit, to be used with a switch, so a musician would not have to mess with his control knobs. This doesn't seem like much now because almost everyone makes standard electric guitars with the switch arrangement. However, no commercially made guitar had this feature back in 1941. I completed the guitar in 1942, and the sound and switch action were great.

There was a problem with my guitar though. I had taken the neck off of an acoustic guitar, the body of which was split down its complete length on one side. This had been a very cheap guitar, and the frets were square and sharp as the dickens. It was torture to try to play the thing with that darn neck (I eventually destroyed the guitar for that reason), but my preset circuit was very successful. Little did I know then that the first commercially made solid-body electric standard guitar to use my idea would be the Fender Jazzmaster in 1958. I had a heck of a time talking Leo into using the idea, but I will tell you about it a little later on. I didn't know there was anyone by the name of Leo Fender in the year 1942.

I had made a solid-body electric standard guitar because it was much easier to make than an acoustic-body to test my preset circuitry. But, what was so great about the fact that I had made a solid-body electric standard guitar? If the strings and pickup sounded good on a solid-body steel guitar, then why shouldn't the sound be as good on a solid-body standard guitar? Quite honestly, I didn't think it was anything to brag about when I made mine. Les Paul said he made his first solid-body in 1941. Well, I had the idea in 1941, but I didn't complete my guitar until 1942. Merle Travis told me that Paul Bigsby made his around July 1947. Through the years, Les Paul, Merle Travis, and Paul Bigsby would become friends of mine. I still don't think it's a big deal about when or who made the first solid-body electric standard guitar. One thing we do know is that Leo Fender was the first one to mass-produce them.

My hobby was making guitars, but that was not by any means the only experience I had that qualified me to work for Leo Fender. There was also the work I did at Goodyear. In February 1943, I was in the standards and methods department (industrial engineering section). (I had been turned down by the military services because of my pancreatitis operation and the fact that I was on a strict diet.) My boss, Mel Hood, called me into his office and asked me if I had ever been to California. I told him, no, I hadn't, and I had never even thought about it. He told me Goodyear Aircraft had been awarded a contract to build the empennage (tail section) for the Lockheed P-38 fighter plane, and he wanted me to go to California to get the information the company needed. I would have to go to Los Angeles and to Fresno, where they had started to build the units.

My assignment was to write the operational breakdown and description of Pre, Sub, and Final assemblies, from blueprints or observation. (He said Lockheed did not have anything in writing.) I would have to estimate the standard time for each operation, determine the personnel requirements for the complete contract, list all of the jigs and tooling that would be required for each operation, show the flow from each preassembly through final assembly, obtain all part numbers and descriptions of same, and determine the amount of floor space required for the complete contract. I completed the assignment within six weeks.

I left for California by train the first part of March 1944, scheduled to arrive in Los Angeles on the 7th. I had to change trains in Chicago and there was a layover of six hours. They were having a heck of a blizzard, and the wind coming across the lake almost froze you on the spot. Then, three days later I was blessed with the warm California sunshine. It made quite an impression on this boy coming from the cold Midwest. Los Angeles in March 1944 was fantastic. There was no smog and the sky was a beautiful blue. The only tall building was the City Hall. And the traffic congestion was no big deal at that time. This seemed like Utopia. Reservations had been made for me at the Mayflower Hotel, near Pershing Square, in downtown Los Angeles.

After I had finished my assignment at Lockheed, I was granted a couple of days to recuperate. I had been working 16 hours a day for two weeks because they needed the information as soon as possible back at home base. I had written so much, for long hours at a time, that I could only make a straight line with my pen when I started to work in the mornings. A nurse had to put my hand under a red heat lamp for treatment each day so that I could continue to write.

Anyhow, on my first day off I called Hugh Farr, who played the fiddle and sang bass with the original Sons of the Pioneers. I had never met Hugh before. However, when I told him I made guitars as a hobby and that I was a fan of the Pioneers, this seemed to take care of the formalities. Hugh took me over to Republic Studios in North Hollywood where Roy Rogers was filming *The Yellow Rose of Texas*. I met Roy, Bob Nolan, and the rest of the Pioneers, along with Gabby Hayes. I was in the studio when the Pioneers were recording their songs for the sound tracks of *The Yellow Rose of Texas* and another Roy Rogers film, *Song of Nevada*.

Hugh Farr and I were walking down the middle of the street in this old western town movie set when we saw Gabby Hayes approaching. There was no mistaking who it was, the way he walked. He talked and acted the same in person as he did on the screen.

Hugh drove me around Hollywood for a little while before I had to get back to the hotel because I had to leave for Akron and Goodyear the next day. I really didn't get to see too much of California during my brief stay, because I was working inside most of the time. But, please believe me, I had seen enough to know that I would be coming back with my beautiful wife, Jean, even if it was just for a visit.

I traveled by train back to Akron and arrived there in the latter part of April. Remember, this was in 1944 and there was no way you could obtain plane reservations then because of the war priorities. I had plenty of time to think about my guitar-building hobby while on the train, and I decided to start work on a 10-string single-neck steel guitar as soon as I had some spare time.

I told you I had found a source for magnets in Chicago, so I placed the order for 10 pieces. By this time, I had also started to use #40 gauge magnet wire, but I did not know yet that the kind of coating was so important. (Leo taught me that later on.) I could not have done anything about the kind of coating anyhow, because I had to buy whatever the radio parts store had for sale.

Now the work began on the wood body. I selected a choice piece of maple, 2" thick, cut it to size, and routed out for the keys (Leo later told me they were called patent heads) and the area for the controls and pickup. I also routed out areas where I would place square inlays of oak wood on top, at all four corners, and for oak trim around the top and bottom edges. The fingerboard area was also raised approximately ½" and bound with oak trim.

Now this is the important part, and why I am explaining the making of the guitar in detail. The circuitry was the same as I had on the solid-body electric standard I made in 1942 (and later destroyed because of the impossible fret problems on the neck). Now, there is no reason in God's world, that I know of at least, to have a switch arrangement for presetting the tone and volume for rhythm and lead on a steel guitar, since it is never used for rhythm parts. The only reason I did it was to preserve the idea I had for the switching arrangement.

The 10-string. Note the switch at the upper end of the pickup. There is a slot in the metal control plate at the left of the switch. A finger lever moved in that slot to control a "doo-wah" sound that was not heard on commercially made instruments until many years later, with a foot pedal. (photo: Richard Smith)

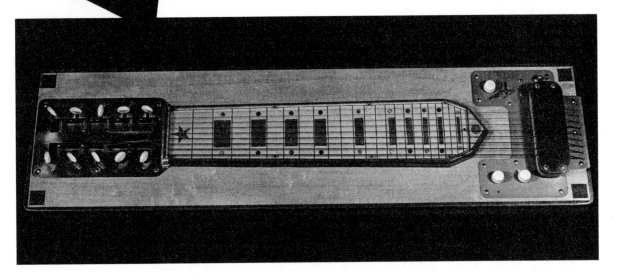

Another feature on this guitar is the locking nut. The locking nut was my own idea and I did not consider it a big deal. It's a popular feature of guitars today, but nobody had one then.

And last, but not least, it has a "doo-wah" effect lever near the tone and volume control knobs that you can control with your little finger. The lever was connected to a volume control (not to a tone control, like the "wah-wah" effect), and it was my idea to use it in this manner because you could pick the strings and have your little finger on the lever for the sound effect at the same time. You don't need a foot pedal for the effect, but to this day I've never seen this on an instrument.

Remember, this is a single-neck steel guitar with 10 strings, locking nut, switched presetting circuitry for rhythm and lead, and a "doo-wah" effect lever. And the guitar was made in 1944. I still have it, and a picture of it is in this book. Needless to say, I was proud of the completed guitar, because these features had not been used on commercially made instruments up through 1944.

In February 1949, I wrote to Jerry Byrd, one of the most talented steel guitar players I have ever heard, to tell him about my guitar and to ask for his opinion. I had started listening to Jerry in the early 1940s when he was on radio station WJR in Detroit. He had moved to WLW in Cincinnati when I wrote him. Here is what he had to say:

WLW

The Nation's Station

CROSLEY SQUARE   140 WEST NINTH ST.   CINCINNATI 2, OHIO

Monday P.M.
March 7, 1949

Dear Friend:

Your very fine letter was gratefully received and I will answer today and try to supply you with the information that you wanted.

I use a 6 string, 1938 model Rickenbacker and, as you say, keep my tuning secret for reasons too lengthy and numerous to explain here.

I have no idea of any 10 string tuning to give you, as I do not have any use for that many strings. I think it is too much guitar for all practical playing purposes. It's not how many necks, or strings, you have but what you can do with what you do have. No guitar, or number of strings, has ever made a player. It's up to the player to make something come forth from what he has, or it is, after all is said and done, valueless!

My new records, solo work of my own, are on Mercury records. My 1st release will be coming out March 15th. It's called "Steelin' The Blues" with "Drowsy Waters."

Thanks for your letter and I'll be waiting to hear from you.

Your friend,
Jerry

Well, it is pretty obvious that Jerry Byrd didn't think too much of my 10-string steel guitar idea. However, I thought some of my pickin' friends might appreciate words of wisdom from the master of steel guitar style and tone.

For many years, this same radio station WLW also had a show called the *Boone County Jamboree*. They would broadcast songs and bits of humor each weekday morning and tell their many listeners where selected artists and groups would be making personal appearances. One morning the announcer said a group would be appearing at the Armory in Akron on a weekend in early March 1947. The entertainers would include Merle Travis & the Drifting Pioneers, Cowboy Copas with his band, comedian Hank Penny, and a few others whose names escape me. I went to see the show, mainly because I liked to hear Merle Travis play his guitar.

Cowboy Copas was on the first part of the program. When his band began to play I almost jumped out of my seat. The steel guitar had the most beautiful clear sound that I had ever heard. I was sitting in the second row, near center stage. I could see the steel guitar was blond-colored and had a chrome diamond thing near each end on the front. I had no idea what kind of a guitar it was and could hardly wait to go backstage after the show to find out.

Finally the show was over, and backstage I went to meet that steel guitar player. He introduced himself as Bob Foster. And yes, he would show me his guitar. I found out the name was Fender. I asked him why it was called that and he said that was the name of the man who made it in a place called Fullerton, California, not far from Los Angeles.

That did it. Now I knew I had to go back to California just to meet the guy who made that guitar.

Then Bob Foster said, "I think the guitar sounds as good as it does because of this amplifier." I now saw the amplifier for the first time because it had not been visible from my seat in the audience. The little nameplate said "Fender, Fullerton, California." Bob said it was called Pro Amp and had a heavy-duty 15" Jensen speaker. I told him it sounded good but that I had never seen an amplifier with the chassis mounted that way, with the knobs on top and the tubes hanging down. He said Leo Fender was going to make all of his amplifiers that way. That is how I found out that there was a person named Fender and, needless to say, I was very much impressed. And I'll say it again, I had to meet that guy, Leo Fender.

CHAPTER **5**

WESTWARD HO! TO MEET LEO FENDER

The time had finally arrived. It was on Saturday morning, June 12, 1948, when we turned the nose of our car toward the place I wanted to visit again. I was finally on my way to meet the man who had made the guitar and amplifier I admired so much. My wife, Joan, was almost as excited as I was because she had not been to California and she was anxious to see what I had been raving about. Of course, half of my bragging on California was meant to get her interested so I would have more of a chance to return to meet Leo Fender.

We drove from Akron to St. Louis, Missouri, where we picked up the famous Route 66, which originates in Chicago and heads toward the West, through Springfield (Missouri), Oklahoma City, Amarillo, Albuquerque, Flagstaff, and on into the promised land of California. We followed Route 66 on to the city of Monrovia, just out of Los Angeles. We checked into, of all places, Motel 66. The motel was owned by friends of ours and would be our vacation home base.

I had purchased a Premier amplifier the previous year from my friend Mac at the Akron Music Center. It was a small store then, located on a side street. He was not a Fender dealer at the time, so I had no way of knowing there was an amp called the Pro Amp which was far superior to the Premier. The Akron Music Center is a Fender dealer now with several stores in the Akron area, and they advertise in *Guitar Player* magazine. I am so glad they are a part of the Fender family of dealers because I bought the first guitar Mac sold, a Martin D-28 flat top, when he opened his store in the early 1940s.

Anyhow, I had brought the Premier amp with me because I wanted to show it to Leo. I was not at all impressed with the amp, and I didn't even know the name of the manufacturer. I wanted to find out what Leo's impression was, so I put it in my car and headed for Fullerton.

It didn't take long because, as I mentioned before, there wasn't so much traffic back then in Los Angeles. I looked in the phone book and found Fender's Radio Service, located at 107 South Spadra. I found the store and walked in, expecting to find a man with a halo above his head. The store was not at all impressive. There was a man sitting beside a display rack containing phonograph records. He didn't look all that friendly—and he darn sure didn't have a halo. I introduced myself and said I was looking for Leo Fender, and was he Mr. Fender. He curtly told me, "No I'm not, I'm Dale Hyatt, and Mr. Fender isn't here." I asked him if he could tell me where I could find him. His answer was just as curt: "He's over at the factory." Well, I said, could you tell me where the factory is? Not much more friendly, he told me it was there in Fullerton, on Santa Fe Avenue near the corner of Pomona Street. Now that we really had a conversation going, I asked him about the names of some of the musicians he might know. The first name he mentioned was Noel Boggs, and I really don't remember who the two or three other names were. I thanked him, left the store, and was sort of relieved that he had not been Leo Fender. I did not know then that Dale and I would become friends later on and that it was just his nature to be direct and not waste words. There was one thing for certain—you never had to guess if Dale liked you or not.

It didn't take me long to find the factory, because Fullerton was not all that big back then. And still isn't. I told you that Fender's Radio Service was not all that impressive. It was great, though, compared to the two sheet metal buildings I was looking at. It was hard to imagine how musical products that sounded so good could come out of a place that looked so bad. I walked up to the door of the first building and asked to see Mr. Fender. I was told that they would have to find him and to just wait a few minutes. Well, I guess around 15 minutes can be considered a few. It was at least that long before an unimpressive looking person introduced himself as Leo Fender. He asked me how he could help me and all I could think of, at the time, was to say "I just wanted to meet you." Hey! Remember, I had just met "the man."

He did not look at all like I thought he would—more like a janitor than a man who could create such wonderful musical instrument products. He acted like he was awful busy, and that you should apologize for even thinking of bothering him. Then, I think I made the magic statement. "I build electric guitars as a hobby back in Akron, Ohio." His expression changed immediately from pure impatience to deep interest. And then the questions started. "What kind of electric guitars do you build, steel or standard?" I told him that I had made both kinds.

He said, "Look, it's almost lunch time, wait until I check a couple of things and then we can go get a sandwich and talk. Why don't you just look around until I get back. I'll only be a couple of minutes." His couple of minutes were more like an hour. It gave me a chance to look at the operation, and I was really amazed that he could manufacture anything, as congested as it was. To be more exact, it looked like a mess. They were covering guitar bodies with a plastic material (it was the acetate) in one of the buildings and the odor was terrible.

I noticed something that was only of mild interest to me at the time. There was a guitar body lying on one of the workbenches. It was made of solid wood and didn't look like anyone had worked on it for a while because it was covered with dust. As I said, it really didn't impress me, because I had made a solid-body electric before—so what! I didn't know at the time, of course, that what I saw that day would be the beginning of something big in the musical instrument business. It had to be the prototype of the Broadcaster. About that time, Leo showed up and we were on our way to lunch. I did not mention that I had seen the solid guitar body on the workbench because, as I said, it didn't seem important to me at the time.

I was really impressed with Leo Fender. He was so down to earth, no sign that he thought he was anyone special. One thing was obvious though. The man was really inquisitive. He picked my brain by asking me all that I knew about building guitars, which wasn't much, I admit, at the time. I told him I had a Premier amplifier with me and asked if he had ever heard the name. He said he was not familiar with the amplifier but that he would like to see it if I didn't mind.

I can tell you, it didn't take him very long to consume his hamburger. It seemed that he wanted that unimportant part over with in a hurry so that he could ask questions. Then, all too soon for me, it was time to leave. Even though we were only together a short time, it seemed like I had known him for ages.

I got the amplifier out of my car and took it into one of the buildings for Leo to see. He really looked it over and he hinted that he would like to take the chassis out to check it. Ha! I thought, this is the time. So I said "Leo, I have to get back to the motel. Why don't I trade you this amp for one of your Pro Amps even up?" I couldn't believe it; he jumped at the chance. This was my lucky day. I became the proud owner of one of Leo Fender's fabulous Pro Amps with a Jensen 15" heavy-duty speaker. I think Leo was almost as happy about the trade as I was because now he could check out an amplifier made by one of his competitors.

One of two rare photos of Paul Bigsby. Here he is outside his workshop, showing his latest Merle Travis-designed guitar. (photo: White)

A fellow by the name of Ray Massey was there when Leo and I made our trade. Ray was very good with electronics and he had been helping Leo. Leo had to leave for a little while to check on something, and while he was gone Ray invited me to follow him over to Downey (near Los Angeles) to see Paul Bigsby. Well, this seemed almost too good to be true. I had heard about Bigsby and the custom guitars he had been making. To meet two celebrities like Leo Fender

Merle Travis and Speedy West. (photo: Bigsby)

and Paul Bigsby on the same day would be almost unbelievable for someone like me. I thanked Leo for his courtesy of the day and for the trade he made with me on the amplifier, and then Ray and I were on our way to Downey.

Paul's workshop was in back of his home at 8114 East Phlox Street in Downey. He and Ray Massey were good friends, and the fact that I was with Ray seemed good enough for him. He was very friendly and he took me for a complete tour of his shop. I noticed that Ray did not tell Paul we had just come from Leo Fender's factory, and I found out why a little later. It was evident that Paul did not care for the fact that Leo was building steel guitars, too. Leo's steel guitars were mass-produced, however, and Paul just made his guitars on a custom special-order basis. Paul told me he had made a solid-body electric standard guitar for Merle Travis in 1947 which Merle had designed. Then, he showed me a guitar that was similar to Merle's which he had just finished. I asked Paul if there was anyone working with him at his shop and he said absolutely not. I asked him why he didn't train someone so they could carry on when he retired. He said there was no way he would consider that.

Ray told me later on that Paul was a loner, and he was quite surprised that Paul was so free in showing me his shop. I was the first one that he ever saw Paul give the grand tour. I was pleased to hear that. I took a couple of pictures of Paul with a solid-body electric standard guitar he had just finished. He also showed me a pedal steel guitar he had just finished for a musician by the name of Wayne Burdick.

Paul had been a pattern maker by trade and he was a terrific mechanic. He not only worked with wood and steel, he could make the wooden pattern molds to have parts made with cast iron. He was just plain good at what he did and the quality of his workmanship was excellent. He made his first custom steel guitar for a great musician by the name of Joaquin Murphy, but it had no pedals. The second steel he made had both foot and knee pedals. It was finished in February 1948 for guitarist and sometime Fender employee Speedy West. (I'll say more about Speedy later on.)

Merle Travis and Paul Bigsby. (photo: West) This and the previous photo were both taken in Merle's back yard, 1949.

Now it was thanks and good-bye to Paul Bigsby and Ray Massey, and then back to my vacation home base in Monrovia.

CHAPTER 6

THE SOLID-BODY ELECTRIC STANDARD GUITAR

For many years Merle Travis and Leo disagreed over which of them should be declared the "father" of the solid-body standard electric guitar. Leo didn't say too much about it. Merle was the one who seemed to think he should have received more credit. Merle and I had become good friends as time went by, and he told me his version of the story, but perhaps it would be better to let you read an excerpt from an article Merle wrote.

The show Merle talks about in the article was produced by Cliffie Stone every Saturday night through the years 1946 and 1947 in the small town of Placentia, near Fullerton. Many entertainers have credited their success to the television and personal appearance shows Cliffie promoted in southern California. In those years, Leo Fender still had his Radio Service, and he went to the Saturday night shows in Placentia to make sure the PA system was working properly.

Here are Merle's recollections as they appeared in the Fall 1979 issue of the *JEMF Quarterly*, published by the John Edwards Memorial Foundation:

RECOLLECTIONS OF MERLE TRAVIS: 1944–1955.
Part 2

In 1947 I wouldn't go twenty feet unless I was on my motorcycle. That's when I met a man who was the announcer at the motorcycle races out around Lincoln Park in Los Angeles County. His name was Paul A. Bigsby. We all called him, "P. A."

P. A. had built Joaquin Murphy a steel guitar that was a work of art. It had a beautiful sound. I kept wondering why steel guitars would sustain the sound so long, when a hollow body electric guitar like mine would fade out real quick. I came to the conclusion it was all because the steel guitar was solid.

Another pet peeve of mine was changing strings on a guitar. When I lay my guitar down in my lap to change strings, the ones that were on the bottom are on the wrong side. They're awkward to change. I wondered, why not put all the pegs on one side.

One day over at KXLA in Pasadena P. A. Bigsby came over to watch the broadcast. That's when I cornered my friend, Bigsby.

"Can you build a guitar like I'll draw the picture of?" I asked him point-blank.

"I can build anything!" the un-modest Paul A. Bigsby bellered, smiling, as he always did.

I grabbed a piece of script paper and started drawing. I drew a guitar with a peg-head showing all the pegs on one side. In the depth, I showed it to be a little over an inch thick. I drew a fancy curve at the end of the neck, the position dots were made up of a spade, a heart, a diamond and a club. I wanted them inlaid in mother-of-pearl. I drew an armrest and a fiddle-like tailpiece, both for decoration.

"Here's what I want." I told Bigsby as I handed him the drawing.

"Don't worry, I'll make it and it'll be perfect!" the man said.

In a few weeks, P. A. called.

"Travis, I've got that crazy looking guitar you wanted," he jarred through the receiver, "what's more it's perfect and it's beautiful. I've even built a case for the thing."

I headed out to Downey to see what he'd done. There it was. Exactly like I had in mind, except I really didn't expect him to build it out of birdseye maple, with a walnut pick-guard with my name inlaid in it, plus a tailpiece made of polished walnut and the playing card position dots were, in every way, flawless. At the end of the neck, inlaid in mother-of-pearl, he had got in his three cents worth. The name Bigsby, which was later to become a famous name among musicians, was inlaid in a scroll of mother-of-pearl.

The instrument sounded wonderful, for its time. It drew lots of attention every Saturday night when I'd play for a dance with Cliffie Stone out at a little place called Placentia. It was four miles from Fullerton, California. That's where my friend Leo Fender lived. Leo did some fine work too.

One night he came out to the dance. I suppose he dropped by to see the young man that was causing such a fuss, Tennessee Ernie, the boy who would dress in oversized overalls, a hat turned up in front...pinned with a huge safety pin, sporting a front tooth blacked out. But when he'd sing, down would come the rafters.

Leo Fender asked me how I liked that type of guitar. I explained all the good things about it, bragged a lot on myself and possibly mentioned that P. A. Bigsby had built it for me. Leo wanted to borrow it until the next Saturday night. He said he wanted to build one like it. Next Saturday night Leo Fender brought my guitar back. Along with him he brought one almost like it. I thought it was a fine instrument and told him so. He asked me to try it out, which I was pleased to do.

His instrument was true, sounded fine and played very easy. Of course, Leo hadn't taken the time to build one of birdseye maple with all the fancy stuff in just one week. But he had built one like my Bigsby. As more and more musicians saw my Bigsby, they went out to Downey to have Paul A. Bigsby build "one of them solid-body guitars that's real thin with all the pegs on one side."

Bigsby was always his own man. He built a few, then he balked. He told me about the people that kept coming to him.

"I'm a pattern-maker in a factory. I'm no guitar builder. I don't have time to build one of those silly things for you. Go out to Fullerton and look up Leo Fender. He'll build you one, but not me!"

One man went to Leo Fender. Two men went to Leo Fender. Two thousand men went to Fender. Leo Fender put up a factory. They built Fender guitars. They built Fender bass instruments (which he developed). They built Fender steel guitars, they built great Fender amplifiers. They sold Fender strings of all kinds.

Years later Fender sold out to CBS for something like thirteen million dollars, the papers said. Leo Fender retired.

It all started back in the forties. Many years later I was to see some young man with a beautiful Fender guitar.

"How do you like your Fender guitar?" I'd ask. "It's the greatest," says the young man.

"I designed that guitar," I'd say.

The young man would look at me a little strange and walk away. I can just hear him saying, "I saw this ol' dude. He questioned me about my Fender, then went off his rocker. Said he designed it...some nut!"

Once Chet Flippo with *Rolling Stone* magazine in New York interviewed me in California. I took a chance and told him the story. His piece came out that I was a little dingy, more or less. I imagined I'd designed the Fender guitar, that he'd gone to the factory and they told him I never used a solid-body guitar in my life.

Mr. Forrest White, who was with the Fender Company for years as a vice president, heard about Flippo's write-up, and sent me some pictures of P. A. Bigsby and me in my back yard where I hadn't lived since 1949. I put it with my collection of a few more hundred pictures of me playing my Bigsby before a Fender solid-body was built.

I'm happy to say that Leo Fender is still a very good friend. So is Forrest White, the man who built the Music Man amps before retiring. They're both ace high in my books.

Merle Travis

Merle wrote the article in 1979 after he had patched up his relationship with Leo. A little later I will tell you where and how he and Leo became friends again. Many people have asked me if I thought the solid-body guitar that Merle had designed and Paul Bigsby made for him had any influence on the solid-body prototype for the Broadcaster/Telecaster guitars which Leo would eventually mass-produce. My answer is, yes, most definitely. There is no doubt in my mind.

Many people may think Leo had all of the ideas for the design of all the Fender instruments and amplifiers. This is not true, but this does not mean that any of the credit for his accomplishments should be taken away from him. Leo listened to suggestions from musicians and was receptive to ideas regardless of where they came from. Remember, he did not play the guitar—never even learned to tune one, so the only way he had of knowing what was good or unacceptable for the musician was to ask. He had the ability to take those suggestions and ideas, and perfect them. His ability and his accomplishments were fantastic in my opinion. Leo Fender deserves any and all credit given to him. I can't tell you in words how much respect I had for this man.

Perhaps there is one idea that should be discussed now, which has to do with the design of the neck head (headstock, if you prefer). I asked Leo just where the idea came from to position the keys (Merle called them peg heads, and Leo called them patent heads) all on one side. He said that idea was as old as the hills. He said Croatian people, who he thought lived in Yugoslavia, made stringed instruments using that idea many years ago. He had seen pictures of those instruments in books while he was still in high school. Speedy West backs up Leo's story all the way. Speedy told me he had an old book that shows one instrument with a headstock that is almost a dead ringer for the one Merle Travis drew for Bigsby to make. Speedy was sure Merle had seen that picture. So what, and whom, do we believe? One thing we have found out: It was not Leo Fender's original idea—but he sure made it popular.

So, we can assume that Leo saw the custom solid-body guitar which Merle Travis was playing on Cliffie Stone's show in the little town of Placentia on Saturday nights during the latter part of 1947. There are a heck of a lot of words in that last sentence, and there is a lot of weight in what those words say about the mysterious origin of the solid-body electric.

Leo may have borrowed and promptly returned Merle's guitar, as Merle said. However, that was not to be the final prototype of the instrument Leo would eventually mass-produce. You see, the prototype Leo showed to Merle had three keys on each side of the head of the neck. Leo spent the balance of 1947, the entire year of 1948, and the first six months of 1949 perfecting a prototype that he would manufacture. This one had six keys on one side—but no truss rod yet. Hm! And so started the many years of controversy.

The next part of the story was told to me by Al Frost, a former executive of the Valco Manufacturing Co. (maker of National and Supro brand Guitars). Al paid a visit to my office at Fender after he had sold his interest at Valco in the latter 1950s. He said Don Randall brought two prototypes of the solid-body guitars to the National Association of Music Merchants trade show in New York City in the summer of 1949. Each had only one pickup. I asked Al what his first impressions were of the instrument. He said he thought it had a very unique appearance but that he would not want to produce the prototype he was shown. He said it was apparent that the neck did not have a truss rod, and he felt this would cause a lot of trouble down the line. Al said he told Don he thought it would be a mistake for him to sell the guitar as shown.

Charlie Hayes had been employed at Radio-Tel Sales (Radio & Television Equipment Co.) by this time, and he told me about Don's reaction to those comments. Don told Leo he was afraid to sell the guitars unless he installed truss rods in the necks, but Leo did not think they needed truss rods. Charlie said Don told Leo to just forget about making the guitars then, because he was not going to place orders for them without the rods. Needless to say, Leo told me the tooling had been completed to install the truss rods by the end of 1949. However, the first small production run was not completed until late spring of 1950 in order for the guitars to be ready for the Chicago NAMM show in June. But—something had been added. The 1950 Radio-Tel Sales catalog showed a picture of a single-pickup guitar. However, the guitar that made the show that year was a two-pickup version with truss rod. Leo and Don called it the Broadcaster.

I asked Charlie if there was much interest in the new guitar at the show, and he told me that the dealers and competitors didn't seem to think much of it. He said, in fact, some of the competitors called it a "canoe paddle" and "toilet seat with strings."

Leo and Don decided to call the single-pickup solid-body guitar the Esquire. However, the Broadcaster had the spotlight now and the Esquire would not be put into production until early 1951—with truss rod, of course. Production of the Broadcaster was limited until the latter part of 1950 (even though some would try to tell us that quite a few were made as early as 1948—this is pure fantasy!). Sales of the Broadcaster were gradually picking up through the end of 1950 and into 1951 due to the commendable effort of Don and his sales force to sell the dealers and musicians on Leo Fender's idea of a "plank with strings." Then came the explosion! Gretsch served notice that they had been marketing a drum set called the Broadkaster (with a *k*) and the name was legally protected. Fender was told to cease and desist use of their trade name. The Broadcaster was changed to Telecaster in February 1951.

I asked Leo how he and Don came up with the names for the guitars. He said the name Broadcaster was used because of the popular radio broadcasts in the 1940s. The name Telecaster was chosen because TV was just becoming popular in the beginning of the 1950s. For whatever reason, the name Telecaster meant success.

What about patent protection in those early days? The U.S. Government Patent and Trademark Office will grant two kinds of patents, on either an invention or a design. A patentable invention is summarized as "any new and useful process, machine, manufacture, or composition of matter, or any new and useful improvement thereof." A patentable design is "any new, original and ornamental design for an article of manufacture." The patent application is subject to "conditions and requirements" which are, in essence, that the idea must be yours and you must have proof that it's yours.

So let's examine the Esquire and Broadcaster/Telecaster. An Invention Patent was filed January 13, 1950, for the Combination Bridge and Pickup Assembly that was used on these guitars. The patent was granted October 30, 1951. Look at Patent #2,573,254 on page 43. This was a new idea. No one had come up with a "useful machine" like this before, so there was no problem obtaining a patent.

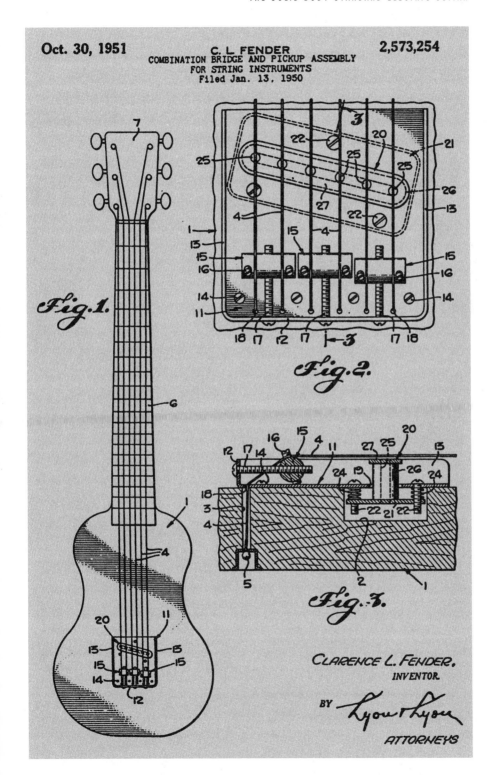

Now look on page 45 at the patent with "Des." before the patent #164,227. It was filed April 23, 1951, and granted August 14, 1951. In this one, Clarence L. Fender claims only to have invented "a new, original, and ornamental Design for a Guitar," illustrated by front, side, and back views. That was it! The drawings of the three different views were the only claim filed for the new Fender solid-body guitars.

L to R: Noel Boggs with a Fender Custom 3-neck steel guitar; Phill Gray, vocalist; Bill Carson with a Telecaster; unknown drummer; Eddie Kirk on upright bass; 1952. (photo: Fender)

You see, this was a Design Patent only. There was no claim to the head design (you know the story). There was no claim to the fact that it had a bolted-on neck; I found that this idea had been used by Rickenbacker and Dobro many years before. (This was told to me while I was employed for a short time at Rickenbacker.) Leo told me the scale and fret placement had been copied from a Gretsch archtop guitar. This is why it was 25½" from the nut to the bridge. There was no way Leo could have patented the pick-ups at that period of time because the Patent Office would have told him it was already being done. You must remember that they were faced with

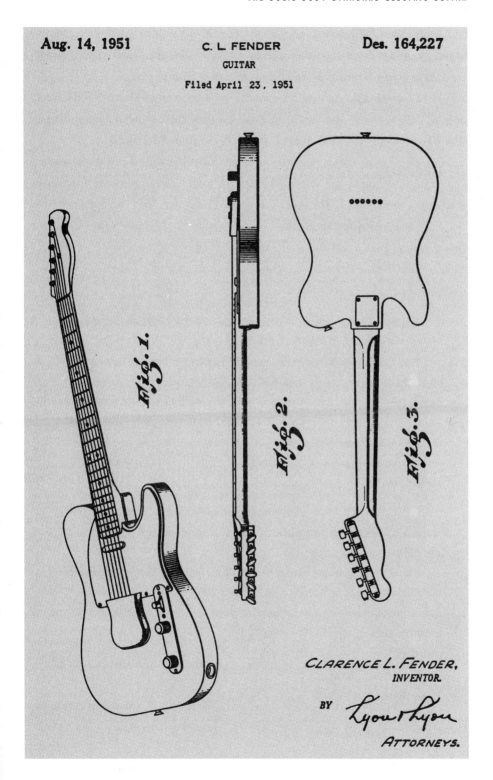

Aug. 14, 1951

C. L. FENDER

Des. 164,227

GUITAR

Filed April 23, 1951

Fig. 1.

Fig. 2.

Fig. 3.

CLARENCE L. FENDER,
INVENTOR.

BY

ATTORNEYS.

something they did not have much experience with, and they were cautious about granting patents on the unknown. So, really, this didn't leave much for Leo to claim—only that he had made a new kind of guitar.

Leo was able to obtain one more patent on the Telecaster. He filed July 31, 1953, for protection on a Tone Control for Stringed Instruments. The patent was granted March 12, 1957. (See Patent #2,784,631.)

Leo Fender's introduction of the Esquire and Telecaster was a great contribution to the music world—for many guitar players, for those who enjoy the sound of the guitar. It's true, however, that the guitars were not very well accepted by dealers or players in those early years because this idea was really "off the wall" from what they had been used to seeing. This is what Leo and Radio-Tel Sales came up with to get their foot in the doors of those cautious dealers:

TELECASTER GUITAR — The original of the solid-body guitars and the proven favorite of countless players.

The Telecaster guitar features a fine hardwood body in beautiful blond finish, white maple neck with adjustable truss rod, white pickguard, two adjustable pickups, tone and volume controls and a three-position tone switch. Two-way adjustable Fender bridge insures perfect intonation and fast, easy action. The Telecaster guitar is noted for its wide tone range and is equally adaptable for fast take-off playing as well as rhythm.

ESQUIRE GUITAR — Many outstanding Fender features are to be found in this economically priced modern instrument, and it is most outstanding in the low price field.

The Esquire guitar features a beautifully finished blond hardwood body, white maple neck with adjustable truss rod, white pickguard, two-way adjustable bridge, adjustable pickup, tone and volume controls, three-way tone change switch.

You guessed it. This pitch began to work and the rest is beautiful, successful history.

As important as the Broadcaster/Telecaster is, it was not the only thing Leo began working on that year. He started production on one of my

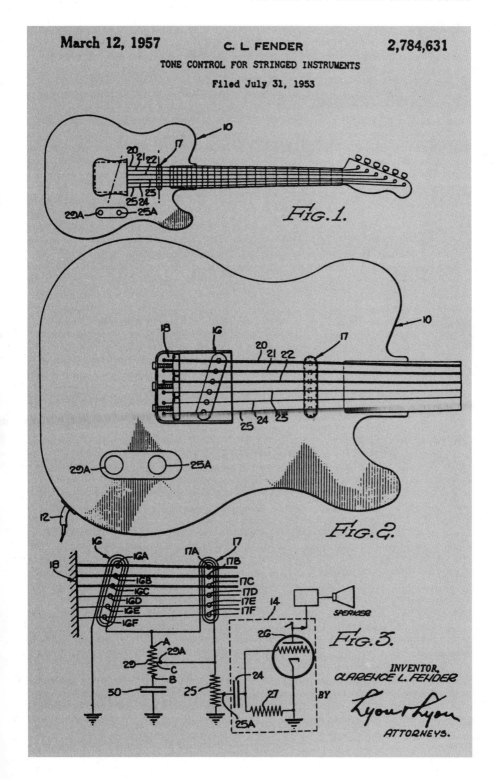

March 12, 1957

C. L. FENDER

2,784,631

TONE CONTROL FOR STRINGED INSTRUMENTS

Filed July 31, 1953

Fig.1.

Fig.2.

Fig.3.

SPEAKER

INVENTOR.
CLARENCE L. FENDER

BY

Lyon & Lyon
ATTORNEYS.

L to R in foreground: Noel Boggs, Leon McAuliff, Freddie Tavares. (photo: Fender)

L to R: Don Randall, Freddie Tavares, Alvino Rey. (photo: Fender)

all-time favorite Fender steel guitars—the Custom 3-Neck steel guitar. The sound was fantastic and it was built like an army tank. This is what Leo and Radio-Tel Sales had to say about it:

> Progress has demanded that this instrument be produced for the most discriminating performer. The Custom 3-Neck guitar is the ultimate in modern electric instruments and incorporates features found only in Fender Fine Electric Guitars, making it the favorite of many of today's top professional artists.
>
> This guitar is fashioned of the finest quality light or dark hardwoods, handsomely crafted and hand-rubbed to a mirror-like piano finish. It employs the new improved Fender direct string pickup units which are without compare on today's market.
>
> Each bank of strings is raised to give proper clearance and a silent lever-type switch is provided for selecting the desired bank of strings, a separate switch is also provided to enable the player to use all three banks of strings simultaneously.
>
> The Custom 3-Neck guitar is ruggedly constructed and so designed to maintain accurate tuning over a long period of time, and will continue to maintain its tuning under considerable changes of temperature and humidity which is extremely important in professional use.

At this point in time (1948), the small sales group had enough different models of musical instruments and amplifiers to get the attention of many new prospective dealers, and Leo's business began to grow. The two sheet metal buildings, which had looked so huge to him when they were first built, looked very small now. The property he purchased to build those buildings also included the adjacent empty lot on the corner of Pomona and Santa Fe, so he decided to build a new building there. He would then have a more suitable facility for the office and his research and development lab and would open up more room in the original two buildings for manufacturing.

Leo called his friend, Grady Neal, and they started plans for the new building. Grady was a darn good general building contractor whom Leo trusted to give him a quality job at a reasonable cost. Grady told me a story about Leo that will give you an idea of Leo's thinking about going the

The new Fender building at 122 S. Pomona St., Fullerton, 1950. (photo: Fender)

Doc Kauffman with one of the first Broadcaster guitars, 1950. (photo: Fender)

"extra mile" to do the best job (just the way he made his amplifier cabinets). Grady said he had completed the cement block shell of the building and was ready to place the roof joists. The building was approximately 36 ft. wide by 30 ft. deep, and had a center wall erected from the front to the rear. This meant there was only a span of 18 ft. for the roof joists. He had planned to use 2" x 8"s which would have been

plenty strong for that short span. Leo said, "Grady, do you think those 2" x 8"s are strong enough for the job?" Grady replied, "Yes I do, Leo, but if you are concerned about it, 2" x 10"s, of course, would be stronger." Leo said, "Good, use 2" x 12"s." Grady laughed, and told me that it had to be the strongest roof in the country on a building of that size.

The City of Fullerton tore the building down a few years ago to make room for a parking garage. They should have preserved it for historical reasons. I bet they were surprised at how strong it was when they tried to tear it down.

CHAPTER 7

THE FENDER
PRECISION
BASS

Leo Fender did not invent the electric bass. I saw one in the mid-1940s when Smiley Burnette (Gene Autry's old side-kick) played at a theater in Alliance, Ohio. His backing group had a Rickenbacker electric bass. It actually looked like a broomstick with a pickup. It had no frets and it was played just like the old "dog-house" in an upright position.

Leo Fender was the first one to make an electric bass with frets that was played like a conventional guitar. Again, he took an idea and perfected it.

I asked Leo why he came up with the electric bass in the first place. He said, quite simply, "There was a need for such an instrument. In the forties and fifties there were many guitar players who played in bands who would switch over and play the upright bass. The big 'dog-house' was a heck of a thing to try to haul around. It really caused a problem if the upright bass player had to get to a microphone to sing. The need was for a portable bass with frets that could be heard over the band. If the bass had frets, then the player would not have to listen to see if he was on pitch."

Leo started designing an electric bass to fill that need in 1950. The first production basses were not made until the latter part of 1951, and they looked like over-sized Telecasters. I asked Leo how he came up with the name Precision Bass. He said, "It was simple. If a player noted the right fret, the tone was right on—a precision result."

Strings for the prototype electric basses did not exist because there were no instruments to put them on. Simple enough? Leo had to take gut strings and wrap them with small gauge iron wire for his first units. He said this was a heck of a job. Of course, after the bass proved successful, he had V. C. Squire make the strings for him. He had been buying all of his guitar strings from them, and I also continued to buy our strings there after I was employed as manager in 1954. CBS acquired Fender and took over the management in January 1965. Soon after that they bought the V. C. Squire Co.

I asked Charlie Hayes how the Precision Bass was accepted at the 1951 NAMM trade show. He said, "Those who were not sure if Leo was crazy when he brought out the solid-body guitar were darn sure he was crazy now, since he came up with an electric bass. They were convinced that a person would have to be out of their mind to play that thing."

Leo, Charlie, and Don Randall were not discouraged about the first impressions of the bass because they were sure they had a winner. I know the competition had to be worried when they saw the following sales pitch:

PRECISION BASS — one of the greatest of modern instrument developments. Fast becoming the favorite of musicians in every field. Compact in size, but very large in performance. Requires only a fraction of the effort to play as compared to old style acoustic basses. Extremely well suited for that fast delicate playing technique. When used with proper amplifier, it will produce considerably more volume than old style basses. The tone leaves nothing to be desired and the portability is the answer to every bass player's dream.

Consider this. In the back pages of most musicians union directories they list almost any instrument you can think of, and under each heading, the musicians who play that particular instrument. I know for many

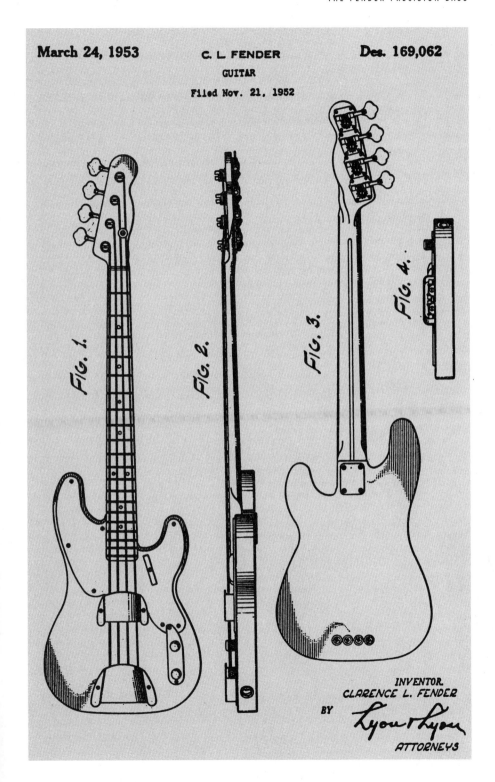

March 24, 1953

C. L. FENDER

GUITAR

Filed Nov. 21, 1952

Des. 169,062

FIG. 1.

FIG. 2.

FIG. 3.

FIG. 4.

INVENTOR.
CLARENCE L. FENDER

BY

ATTORNEYS

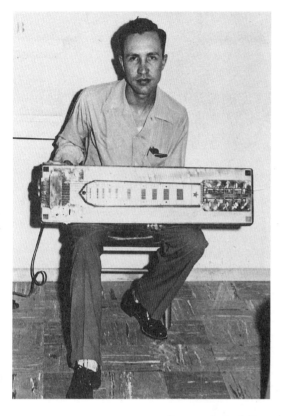

Forrest with his 10-string steel guitar in 1951. He made it in 1944, when he lived in Akron. It has the same preset rhythm and lead wiring, with switch, that was first commercially used on the Jazzmaster 13 years later.

years the directory for Union Local 47 in Los Angeles listed "Fender Bass" rather than "Electric Bass." I think it was a great honor for Leo because I do not know of any other instrument that was listed in that manner.

Today the Precision Bass is the most widely used electric bass throughout the world. I personally think this was Leo's greatest overall contribution to music, and I believe he, too, thought it was his greatest accomplishment. It is almost impossible now to find anyone who is still playing the old "doghouse" upright bass.

One of the best moves of my life was the move from Akron, Ohio, to California in 1951. We had over 13 inches of unexpected snowfall in the early part of that year and it caught my wife, Joan, and me without tire chains for our car. It was impossible to move the car without them, and I had to walk to many different stores before I was able to find a set. Joan and I decided right then that we would not spend another winter in Akron. Actually, I think we had been trying to find an excuse to move to California for a long time. We both had very good jobs at Goodyear Aircraft in 1951. Joan was secretary to one of the company executives, and I had a good position in the Management Control Department. We were both earning a darn good salary for that, and it was really a big decision to just leave without any employment lined up. Even so, we both quit our jobs and moved to Riverside, California.

I drove down to Fullerton to have lunch with Leo on May 25, 1951. It was only a 35-mile drive from Riverside. I told him we had moved to California. He asked me what I planned to do, and I told him I would probably find work in Riverside. I had brought along my 10-string steel guitar that I had made in 1944. Leo took a picture of me with the guitar in the reception room of his new cement block building on the corner of Pomona and Santa Fe. He asked me all kinds of questions about it. I knew he was very busy so I turned down his invitation to walk through the factory. Then it was back to Riverside.

Before long I was employed as an industrial engineer at Food Machinery Corporation in Riverside. I helped write the assembly procedure for building the LTV-5 Amphibious Tank for the Marines. I also developed a scheduling system for use in building the tank. The system was adopted by Commander Ayers, working out of the Pentagon, for use by five different companies that built the tank.

In 1952, Leo made a change in the appearance of his Twin Amp cabinet. The grill cloth was extended all the way across the front, from sideboard to sideboard, and the change made the cabinet look much wider than it actually was. It looked 100 percent better, and the whole line of amplifiers was updated with the new look. They were all covered with that now-famous diagonal brown-and-white striped, airplane luggage linen.

Nineteen fifty-two was also the first year of the Student Set—a lap model steel guitar and amplifier sold together. The guitar was the Champion, which featured a hardwood body covered with mother-of-pearl acetate plastic and a replaceable fretboard. The tone and volume controls were positioned for easier playing than those of earlier models. The jack was moved from the end of the body to the side, and it was recessed.

The small Student Set amplifier cabinet was a new version of the Champion 600, now called the Champ. It was built just like the large professional amplifier cabinets, with ¾" pine lock-jointed corners. Leo would not build anything unless it was as strong as a horse. And, of course, it was covered with the same high-quality diagonal brown-and-white striped airplane luggage linen. The little amp had two input jacks, volume control, jeweled panel-lite, an extractor-type panel-mount fuse holder, and a 6" speaker. Leo made all of his amplifiers—big or small, low or high priced—easy to service. Remember, he had been in the radio service business.

By the end of 1952, Leo had developed the Stringmaster line of steel guitars. These would be made in two-, three-, and four-neck models. Up to now, his Dual Professional and Custom 3-Neck steels were the best he had to offer the professional musician. And, of course, those steels featured his fantastic sounding direct string pickups. The Stringmaster line was equipped with the conventional-style look in pickups. In other words, the strings would pass over the magnetic wire coil rather than through the coil. He also designed the Stringmasters with two pickups on each neck. He called this the dual counter-balanced pickup. He mounted the pickups close together in order to eliminate hum and noise picked up from external sources—in other words, for a "hum-bucking" effect. The dual pickups, he claimed, provided a wide range of sound impossible to achieve in the single pickup type of guitar.

Leo incorporated a new system for switching and mixing pickups that enabled the player to obtain any tone from low bass to high staccato with one change of the tone control. He claimed the tone range of the new Stringmasters was far greater than anything he had yet developed. He also made the pickups fully adjustable to help ensure tone balance. Each neck had its own control which could be preset to balance the tone of the two pickups.

Each neck of the Stringmasters was elevated and the body was cut away along the side of the fretboards to provide ample playing clearance on all necks. The guitars were heavy and were equipped with four telescoping legs that provided a playing height ranging from a sitting to a full standing position. Leo designed those telescoping legs, and the clutch adjustment for the legs was great.

The Stringmaster necks were fitted with an adjustable bridge so that the intonation could be adjusted anytime to compensate for different string gauges, ensuring that the guitar would always be in perfect tune. Another really outstanding feature was an adjustable-spacing bridge, which allowed the player a choice of narrow, average, or wide string spacings.

Now here was a real exclusive that Leo offered the player on his Stringmaster steels: It was possible to string one of the necks with special bass strings, which allowed a tuning an octave lower than the ordinary steel guitar tuning. This was great for new sounds and effects that had not been possible before. Noel Boggs was the one who I feel really mastered the Stringmaster bass neck.

Noel Boggs with the Fender 4-neck Stringmaster steel guitar, 1956. Noel helped Leo design the instrument with his many ideas.

At first, the two-, three-, and four-neck Stringmasters were available with the 22½" scale only. (Scale is the distance from the bridge to the nut.) Then, in the middle of 1955, the two-, three-, and four-neck steels were available with a 24½" scale also. This really added to the musicians' choices of top-quality steel guitars.

Leo designed this guitar to make completely obsolete all other steel guitars. Sadly, the great Stringmasters have gone the way of the dinosaurs and become extinct in this age of pedal steel guitars.

In 1952, Leo realized he was going to need more room to work—a lot more room—in a location that would allow him to expand as needed. He bought several acres of land with a frontage of approximately 200' on South Raymond Avenue, one of the main streets in Fullerton. The lot extended back along a side street, East Valencia Drive, far enough for future expansion to a total of nine buildings.

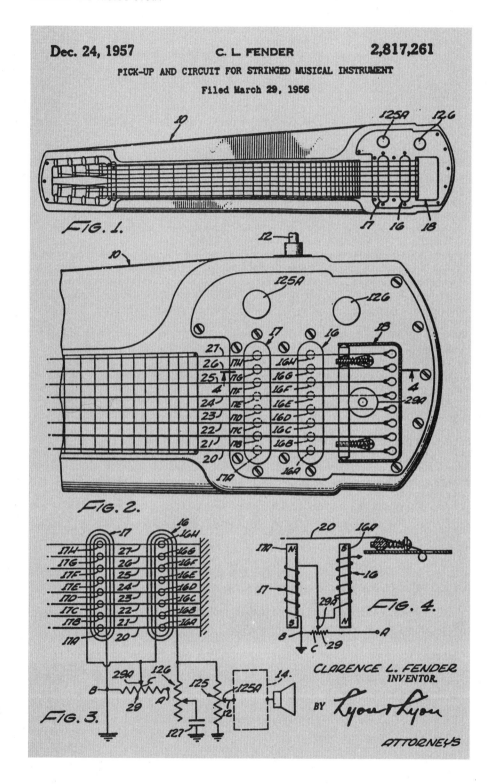

Dec. 24, 1957   C. L. FENDER   2,817,261

PICK-UP AND CIRCUIT FOR STRINGED MUSICAL INSTRUMENT

Filed March 29, 1956

FIG. 1.

FIG. 2.

FIG. 3.

FIG. 4.

CLARENCE L. FENDER
INVENTOR.

BY Lyon + Lyon

ATTORNEYS

He called his friend Grady Neal, the building contractor, and Grady went to work on four 40' x 120' concrete block buildings. The buildings were quite simple in structure, with an 8' sliding door and a 3' access door on each end. There was a 10' alleyway between the first and second, and between the second and third buildings. Leo thought he would put up several buildings this size, so that if the music business went "flat" (you will have to be "sharp" to catch that), he could rent them out separately. Grady promised that they would be ready for occupancy by the latter part of 1953.

You will remember that Leo liked Hawaiian music and had heard a lot of it in his early years because of a steamship company's promotion of its Royal Hawaiian Hotel. (With Hawaii's recent influx of population, I bet they wish they had kept quiet.) In 1934, a distinguished gentleman named Harry Owens formed The Royal Hawaiians orchestra, and they remained the principal entertainment attraction at the Royal Hawaiian Hotel until 1940. That year he took his large troupe of entertainers on a tour of the United States and Canada. Their return to the Royal Hawaiian was spoiled by the Japanese attack on Pearl Harbor on December 6, 1941. Harry brought many members of his group to California, where they became a featured attraction in motion pictures, recordings, and distinguished hotels. In the late 1940s, he became one of television's pioneers with his own program.

I've told you this story because the young man playing steel guitar for Harry Owens all those years was none other than Freddie Tavares. Freddie was a true Hawaiian, born on Maui in 1913, and he loved the islands. He told me he lived at the Royal Hawaiian Hotel during the years the orchestra played there. He said his life was surfing, swimming, and sunning on Waikiki beach during the day and playing music at night. His brother Ernie was also one of the original musicians in the orchestra.

Eventually Freddie Tavares wanted to leave the orchestra, so he trained another well-known musician (at least to us old-timers) named Eddie Bush to replace him. Not long after that, Freddie met Leo. Freddie was a godsend for Leo because he had experience in mechanical and electronic drawing, and he could also play the standard guitar and bass. He was just everything Leo needed to help him in research and development.

Freddie was on frequent calls from movie and recording studios in those days, and Leo could not afford to pay him hourly what he was making at the studios, so he went to work part-time for Leo, beginning in March 1953. Leo could get by with his part-time help at first, but before too long, Freddie was working full-time. He remained Leo's right-hand man in research and development until Leo sold the company to CBS.

In the meantime, there were some interesting things going on behind the scenes. You will recall that Leo had been dissatisfied with the performance of the Radio and Television Equipment Company as his distributor. Around the middle of 1953, he formed a new company, Fender Sales, Inc. There were four equal partners: Leo Fender, Don Randall, F. C. Hall, and Charlie Hayes. Each invested $25,000.00 in the new venture.

Donald D. Randall, circa 1967, president for many years of Fender Sales in Santa Ana, California. (photo: Elson-Alexandre)

The formation of Fender Sales, Inc., with Don as president, would turn out to be one of the smartest things Leo ever did at Fender. You can have the best product in the world, but if no one knows about it, what good does it do you? Don not only thought he had the best product, he made darn sure that everyone heard about it. I thought his ideas on marketing were outstanding. He made Fender Sales, Inc., into one of the best sales organizations in the history of the musical instrument business. This is not just my opinion; I heard the same comment from many others, including many of our competitors.

At the same time, something else was happening that Leo, Don, and Charlie did not know about. F. C. Hall was negotiating a deal with Adolph Rickenbacker to buy the Electro String Instrument Corporation. Think of the history of this company, with all of the "firsts" it had in the development of electric stringed instruments. F. C. Hall was conservative but he was a smart businessman. He bought Electro String in December 1953. Friend, this would cause some trouble.

Fender's first four manufacturing buildings in 1954, the year Forrest began working there. His Buick is parked at the left of the front side door and Leo's Lincoln is parked at right. (photo: Pacific Air)

And now, the big move. Before the end of 1953, the entire operation of the Fender Electric Instrument Co. was moved into the four new concrete block buildings at 500 South Raymond, Fullerton, California. This was truly a major event in the early history of Fender. This is where Fender would experience its greatest growth, where it became one of the greatest success stories in the history of the musical instrument business. This is where Leo would spend his last working days as head of the company that bore his name. This address would be no more after the company was sold to CBS, a move that almost destroyed the Fender name. But, thank God, the name was saved.

CHAPTER **8**

FENDER ELECTRIC INSTRUMENT CO. 1954

Freddie Tavares told me this story. He said that in the very early part of 1954, Leo and he were talking one evening after work and Leo seemed sort of worried. Leo told him that things were not so good as far as cash flow was concerned, and no matter how hard he worked, the situation didn't seem to improve any. He complained that there were not enough hours in the day for him to get everything done, that he just had time to hit the high spots and the rest was not taken care of. Freddie told Leo he thought he should get some help in management. Leo said he didn't have anyone working for him with any experience in management. Freddie told him he should look for someone to bring in before he killed himself with all the hours he was putting in. He said Leo didn't say anything but it looked like he was really thinking.

Call it perfect timing. At least that's what it seemed to me after Freddie told me about his conversation with Leo that evening. I will always be grateful to Freddie for that.

In the latter part of April 1954, I drove down from Riverside to have lunch with Leo. Our lunch was almost over, and I noticed that Leo had been rather quiet, like he was preoccupied in thought. He said, "I have

Leo in 1954 with his new 60-ton Multi-Max punch press, which was used to punch and form amplifier chassis.

been looking for someone for a long time with your background, someone that I can trust, to help me in management of the company. Would you be interested?"

I said, "I really don't know, Leo, I guess you know I have a pretty good job now [I was still an industrial engineer at Food Machinery in Riverside]. Would you mind if I would take a look at your present operation?" I had not seen the factory since he had moved into the new buildings.

He said, "Fine. Let's get on back and I'll show you through." He seemed real quiet on the way back to the plant, like he had a lot on his mind.

We arrived and started the walk through. I don't want to sound like I am too critical, but the place looked like a complete mess, and they had been in the new buildings for less than three months. I'm not talking about housekeeping; the place was not all that dirty. But it was obvious that no planning had been done before they moved in. There was absolutely no evidence of work flow. Amplifier and guitar assembly benches were all mixed together—no separation at all. When someone ran out of parts, he got up slowly and walked down to the stockroom in Building #4 and tried to find his own. It was obvious from the way they were working that they were not on an incentive plan.

We arrived at the stockroom and I was in for another shock. The parts bins were as mixed up as the assembly benches, only ten times worse. I absolutely could not believe that the parts bins were not separated by content and nomenclature. And all this time there were employees roaming around looking for parts and asking "Where's this?" and "Where's that?"

I asked, "Leo, what kind of material control do you have?"

He said, "What do you mean?"

And I said, "How do you know, for instance, when it's time for you to reorder parts?"

He said, "Oh! That's easy. We just look in the bins and if there are not very many left, we reorder."

Friend, I kid you not. That is exactly the conversation we had. It was most obvious to me now why he was looking for someone to help him. And again, please understand. I am not trying to find fault with my friend. This was not his bag, and by the same token, there was no way I could do the things in Research and Development he could.

We walked back to his office and sat down. He said, "Well, what do you think, are you interested?"

I replied, "Leo, there is only one way I could agree to come in. I would have to have a free hand to do what I know has to be done."

He said, "Like what?" It seemed like his thoughts were going a mile a minute now and I was sure he would be opposed.

I said, "One of the first things I would do is to put in a material control system. It's operating like a job shop now."

He said, "Look! I don't like a lot of red tape. Usually it causes more problems than its worth."‘

I replied, "I don't like red tape either. You will have to have a minimum of necessary controls, though, if you expect to have a successful operation." I asked him what my position would be and how much would it pay.

He said, "I would want to start you as the plant manager because that is where I need the help. If that works out all right, then I will be able to spend my time in the lab because I have a lot to do that I haven't been able to get to."

Then he told me the most he could afford to pay. It was $45 a month less than what I was making on my job at Food Machinery. That seemed like a lot of money back then. He said that I could expect a decent raise later on if the operation was running well enough to afford it.

I said that was satisfactory to me because I could see there was plenty of potential if a person was allowed to do what was necessary to correct some obvious problems.

I told him there was something else that I would want if I went to work for him. I would expect to be able to say what was on my mind at any time concerning any problem. That would be the only way I could do a decent job for him. He said that was the way it should be and he could understand why I would ask for that kind of an agreement. He said we should both feel free to say what was on our minds. And buddy, did we ever.

Leo and I had our agreement concerning employment and I left for Riverside where I would work out my notice at Food Machinery before I could start with Leo.

To confirm that Leo hired me to help him with management because of my work knowledge, I included this "Special Bulletin" to describe my job at Food Machinery before starting with him. Please understand: it is not meant to be boastful. He had no one else working for him in the early years with the kind of education and experience he needed.

SPECIAL BULLETIN

TO: A, B, C, D, & E.
No. 127
June 12, 1953

In line with Management's Cost Reduction Program throughout the Division, Mr. Forrest White, Industrial Engineer, has been assigned the project of analyzing our commercial operations from the point of view of reducing costs through work simplification, improved methods and procedures, and elimination of waste.

His first assignment will be in the Commercial Assembly and Crating Departments. In performing this work, Mr. White will need the assistance and cooperation, not only of the men and supervision directly involved in assembly operations, but also of every other department in the Riverside works. We know that our Departmental Supervisors and many of their key employees have a wealth of knowledge and ideas which, if properly analyzed and coordinated with those from other departments, will result in very substantial cost reductions. It will be Mr. White's function to review these suggestions with you and take the necessary steps to see that the best ones are put into effect. Improvements made from your suggestions will be credited to your good management and supervision.

It will be appreciated if everyone who received this bulletin will see that his department cooperates to the fullest extent in this cost reduction program. Mr. White will be concentrating on assembly and crating operations at first, but it is planned that similar studies will be made in other departments throughout the plant as soon as possible.

Mr. White will continue to report to George Bartlett.

Kenneth Dawson

Kenneth Dawson
Works Manager

RELEASED BY:

J. K. Dunbar

J. K. Dunbar
Industrial Relations Manager

At the time I started working for Leo Fender, Dale Hyatt, who had radio servicing and production experience while working at Fender's Radio Service, left Fender and went to work selling cars. George Fullerton, the production foreman, had been a delivery truck driver before going to work for Leo in production in 1948. By 1953 he had been promoted to Production Foreman. He reported directly to me from May 1954 until I left CBS Musical Instruments in December 1967. This may clarify any confusion about the early Fender years management structure that may have resulted from articles written during the later years. I know some of those stories really confused me. I told Leo I didn't recognize the company they were talking about in many cases. He told me that he was not the one who had given misleading information to the writers. He also told me he could understand why I was disturbed about the stories. This was one reason he thought it was a good idea for me to write a book telling the true inside story. Everything written here can be authenticated.

May 20, 1954. This was an important day for me since it would mean the beginning of the most enjoyable years of my work experience. It was 35 miles from Riverside to Fullerton, but it was a pleasant drive down through the Santa Ana canyon. I had driven it many times before but never with the unusually good feeling I had that morning.

I arrived at the plant at 7:30 a.m. The working hours were 8:00 a.m. to 4:30 p.m., so Leo had unlocked the front door because George Fullerton had not arrived yet. I went inside and walked over to a small sliding glass window with a ledge, built into the right wall as you entered the reception room. The bottom edge of the window was about 48" high and was the means of communicating between the reception room and the inner office. I noticed there were three desks in the small office and the combination receptionist/secretary/ bookkeeper was seated at the desk next to the glass opening.

I introduced myself and told the receptionist I was there to see Mr. Fender. She said she had been expecting me and that she was Ione Lambert. She said she would tell Mr. Fender I was waiting and for me to please be seated.

This left me alone with my thoughts. Leo had told me that he and Ione were the only ones working in the office. Since there were three desks in the office, I assumed one of them had to be mine. The center one facing the wall was probably the one because it was the only one that was cleaned off. There was no doubt in my mind...that was my desk...I would be seated in there in no time...I thought...and thought.

I had left Riverside at 6:45 in order to arrive at the plant by 7:30. This was, of course, after I had a good breakfast, with three big cups of coffee. I looked at my watch as it approached 9:00 a.m., and still no sign of Leo. I was seated facing the little glass door opening all this time and, like clockwork, almost every half-hour Ione would slowly peer over the top of the ledge from where she was seated at her desk to see if I was still there. After the fourth or fifth time, I was almost hypnotically entranced by staring at the ledge wondering when those two eyes would slowly raise above the ledge again with that curious, inquisitive look. But, soon I'll be in there beside her, seated at my desk, and she won't have to peer over the ledge anymore...I thought...and thought.

A little after 9:00, the door leading from the reception room into the factory area was quickly opened and Leo stuck his head around it to see if I was there. He smiled without saying a word and, just as quickly, the door was closed. I had opened my mouth to say good morning, but the door had been closed before the words came out. I was relieved that he finally knew I was there. Speaking of relieved...I wished I had not drunk three cups of coffee...maybe if the cups hadn't been so big...It won't be long now and I'll be in the office with all of this waiting behind me...I thought...and thought.

It would be another hour and three "eye peers" over the ledge before I would get a glimpse of Leo. Still the same as before. Door opens quickly...head stuck in and around door...smile...no words...door closed just as quickly...just as the eyes were sinking behind the ledge. Maybe it would have been better if I had just drunk two cups of coffee...small cups...I thought...and thought.

And then, the magic hour! At exactly twenty minutes before 11:00 a.m., Leo Fender quickly opened the door, came into the room, smiled, and uttered these most welcome words, "Well, I guess you would like to start to work." I noticed that the eyes had slowly appeared over the ledge

to see what was going on. I followed Leo eagerly through the door into the
factory area. He asked, "Do you have any questions?" It was then that I
uttered my first historical, and most urgent, words as the new Fender plant
manager, "Yes, I sure do. Where is the men's restroom?"

As God is my judge, this was the way it happened on that first
morning. You may feel that the lengthy dissertation of detail was exaggerat-
ed concerning the time it took for Leo to finally speak to me on my first day
of employment. This, however, will give you some idea of the pace he had
set for himself to get the overall job done at that time. He had no compe-
tent help in management. He had to try to keep all of the loose ends tied
together in his own way. I didn't say that I considered his way to be efficient, because it was most difficult for Leo to set proper priorities in plant
management. If he happened to think of a new idea he wanted to try in the
lab, then everything else took a back seat.

When I came out of the restroom, needless to say I felt much better. I was all prepared to go try out the chair at what I assumed was my
desk in the front office. But so often what we have rationalized in our
thought process is shot down in reality. Leo said, "Come with me. There is
a little job that I would like for you to help me with." He led me back to the
front of Building #3. This was the combination wood shop and amplifier
cabinet building. To the left, as we entered the front door, was obviously
where they covered the cabinets. Then Leo said, "The fellow that was covering the cabinets quit so I would like for you to help me here until I can
hire someone to do the covering."

This was definitely not what I had visualized as a function of the
plant manager. I had not done any kind of production work in years and
now here I was faced with doing a job that was really not the most desirable. The method and facilities for covering amplifier cabinets at Fender in
1954 were quite antiquated to say the least. I didn't want to seem stupid or
reluctant to learn this challenge in dexterity, but I am afraid I was not a
good enough actor to seem all that enthused about my unexpected assignment. I would like to think I can learn as fast as the average person, but
friend, you would have to be far above average to learn as fast as Leo was
instructing. He went through the briefing on cabinet covering like a dose of

salts through a tin horn—one time through and good-bye, Charlie Brown! Then he was off to put out another fire. Parts unknown.

I was expected to cover cabinets for the Deluxe amplifier, and this was much better than if I had to start on cabinets for the Twin Amp or other unknown monsters. Now, let's see...I use the ¼" plywood templates to cut the material to size...then I apply the glue with a brush (and try to get more on the material than myself) and hope I can apply the material to the right place on the cabinet. Hm! Wonder if I could get my old job back at Food Machinery. Well, to say the least, I am sure there were no records broken for the number of cabinets covered per hour. I wondered at the time what the production foreman must have thought about the new guy Leo brought in to cover the amplifier cabinets without introducing him or saying anything about it.

I was on that darn job for over a week and quite often Leo would zoom past me like a bat out of (somewhere); and I didn't seem to find the opportunity, or nerve, to ask him what was going on, to complain about my unfortunate circumstances. Then one day, out of the blue, he came up to me and said, "Well, you have been here almost two weeks; do you have any ideas about changes that should be made?"

I said, "Yes, why don't you get someone else to cover these cabinets?" He laughed and told me that he had hired someone to take care of it and that I should come into the front office the first thing in the morning, dressed the same as for production work.

There is one thing I forgot to tell you. You will remember my lunch with Leo in April. I had on a coat and tie because that is what I wore to work as an industrial engineer. Leo said, "If you decide to work for me, I do not want you to dress like that. You would be out in the factory much of the time and you should wear old clothes so that when you get your hands dirty you can just reach down, wipe them off on your pants, and keep on going." So help me, that is the truth. So, you see, when he asked me to cover the amplifier cabinets I was dressed for it, the same as I would have been if he had asked me to sit down at the cleaned-off desk in the front office. You didn't have to have a very large wardrobe to work for Leo.

I asked Leo if he had told George, the production foreman, why I was there. He said "No, I want you to tell him."

I could not believe what I was hearing. I said, "Leo, I should not be the one to tell him. You are the one who hired me."

He replied, "You should take care of the personnel problems, being the plant manager. That is one of the reasons you have the position." It was obvious that he had made up his mind and that the unpleasant duty had been passed to me.

I had plenty of time to think it over on the way home that night and while returning to the plant the next morning. I arrived early the next morning. Leo had given me a set of keys the night before, so I opened up the front door for the first time and also the door leading into the office. For the first time I sat down in the new chair in front of the new desk that was cleaned off. I say that with tongue in cheek. If you could have seen Leo's desk you would understand why. The top of it looked like a rat's nest, and this condition would not change no matter where the desk was moved

Forrest in his "Fender Fashion" clothes, in the office at 500 S. Raymond. (photo: Fender)

as we expanded our operation. When I would ask him why he didn't clean it off a little, he would tell me that he knew exactly where everything was and that the papers (and you name it) shouldn't be moved.

When Leo came in the office a little later, the first thing he asked was, "Have you told George yet?" I told him that I had not but that was one of the first things I planned to do. There were so many things to do that needed immediate attention, it was hard to decide which way to turn. However, I knew the problem of telling George was a priority.

I went over to George's office in the assembly building, and he seemed a little surprised to see me. He said, "I wondered where you were. I didn't see you in cabinet covering." Then I told him that I had not been hired to cover cabinets but to be the plant manager. He said, "I don't believe you." I told him I could understand that but if he didn't believe me he should ask Leo, and that I would appreciate it if he would get the problem straightened out as soon as possible.

I went back to the main office and by this time Ione had come in. I told her about my difficult task of telling George, and she said she wasn't surprised that Leo left it up to me to tell him, adding, "You will find that he doesn't like to get involved with things that are unpleasant. Anyhow, welcome aboard!" I would find that Ione's health was not all that good and that what I had interpreted to be unfriendliness was just a case of not feeling well. She would become a good "right arm" in explaining their procedures, since this did not seem to be of much importance to Leo.

I worked at my desk for about an hour, to give George plenty of time to talk to Leo. I did not want to go out in the factory to start taking notes without a clarification in George's mind as to what I was doing there.

George was in his office. He did not seem too happy and I could understand that. I told him there were many things I would want to change, and that the first thing would be to rearrange all of the workbenches and racks in the assembly building. He asked me why, and I explained that it was to separate the amplifier and guitar sections to help eliminate congestion and to establish a decent production flow for both areas. It was apparent that he did not understand what I meant by production flow. He asked, "What makes you think that you can come in here and after two weeks decide that everything is wrong and needs changing?" I told him that if I didn't know, then those who had taught me would be very disappointed in my ability and would assume that I hadn't learned much.

The move was reluctantly made in the assembly building, and those employees seemed pleased with the improved working conditions. George finally came around and admitted that he thought things were running much smoother and he could understand what I meant about an efficient production flow. I did not worry too much at that time about moving heavy machines in the cabinet department and metal shop, because they were all tied into 220-volt lines, and there were many other things that had much higher priority.

Speaking of the metal shop, I told you before that Leo liked tools and machinery. I also found out, the hard way, that he did not seem to mind how much noise was generated by heavy machinery. I mentioned that there had not appeared to be much planning done before they moved into these new buildings. For example, the first building, which included the main office, was turned into the metal shop. Now, there was one 60-ton punch press which was used to blank and form amplifier chassis and two 30-ton punch presses which were used for miscellaneous jobs. They were located just outside the uninsulated front office wall. There were other small presses and miscellaneous machines that made for a pretty complete metal shop. The large presses made a heck of a lot of noise and shook the floor when they were being used.

On May 20th, Leo gave me a copy of the sheet which showed the "Balance of Orders Unfilled" from Fender Sales.

Balance of Orders Unfilled 5-17-54

	#203	#195	#194	#188	#183	#174	#169	#144	Total
Pro Amps		50							50
Super Amps		50							50
Deluxe Amps		100	100	28					228
Princeton Amps		100		9					109
Student Amps			166						166
Twin 12 Amps		25	25			25			75
Bandmaster Amps			25						25
Bass Amps		25				25	25		75
TN B.			22						22
TN D.			5						5
8 DN B.		15	11						26
8 DN D.					1				1
6 DN B.									0
6 DN D.		10							10
8 SN B.			5						5
8 SN D.			10			3			13
6 SN B.									0
6 SN D.			6						6
Student Guitars			147						147
Telecasters		50		2					52
Esquires		25			5				30
Bass Guitars		15							15
4N B SM					7				7
4N D SM									0
3N B SM		10			3				13
3N D SM		10							10
2N B SM		15							15
2N D SM		15							15
Leg Sets (3)		50	16						66
Leg Sets (4)		25	18						43
Foot Pedals (Dlx)								200	200

The unfilled orders were shown to indicate which amplifiers and instruments were being made at the time I started to work for Leo. Perhaps it would be helpful to explain the abbreviations that were used on what we would call the Production Sheet because it told us what we had to build. TN B — Triple Neck Blond; 8 DN B — 8-String Double Neck Blond; 4N B SM — 4-Neck Blond Stringmaster, etc.

The production foreman would not tell me any more than he had to. This made my job even more difficult than it was already. I thought I would try to find out just how secretive he would be. I asked him what those numbers were at the top of each column of figures. Anyone should know they were purchase order numbers. But he replied, "Oh, they are just numbers we use. They are not important." As God is my judge, that was his answer and I will never be able to forget that as long as I live. Leo asked me several times to terminate him because he felt that he had not been productive. I told Leo I did not want to do that. I always liked to give a person a job, and I hated like the dickens to take a job away from anyone. But after his answer about the numbers, I was really tempted.

The next move was to try to get the stockroom in Building #4 in decent shape. I needed extra help to have the parts bins moved around, and the help was not given freely. George's disappointment of having to report to someone other than Leo was obvious, and he was not too friendly. I took this into consideration and tried to be as considerate as possible without being too demanding.

The stockroom was a complete shambles. I had them restack all of the bins so that alike parts were grouped together and in order by part number or by description (value). Nomenclature was updated for proper identification of the various parts. I wish you could have seen the difference in appearance after the move was made. The employees looking for parts to replenish their workbenches spent less than half the time they took before. And as soon as I could install my new system, they would not have to leave their workbenches. The stockroom would be off-limits.

Leo said he did not want a lot of red tape. I can relate to that. I have seen "hot shot" controls that were a pain in the posterior and proved to be a disaster rather than an aid in manufacturing. I knew we needed to have complete control over our purchasing and inventory records, and was hoping I could find a simple ready-made form that we could use to solve our problem. I checked with Moore Business Forms, a nearby company, and found it would take three separate forms to give us the complete simple control I wanted. So I designed my own material control card.

There is no way we could have operated very long the way Leo was maintaining his inventory. He did not have the time to personally keep track of how much inventory he had on hand and none of his employees knew what to look for to solve the problems in control. There were several simple but necessary factors needed to assure a balanced inventory, reasonable cost control, and a means for uninterrupted growth. We had to know how many separate parts were used per unit. What was the cost-break based on volume of purchase? Who were the best suppliers as far as cost and reliability? Were there specification tolerances to be considered? How many pieces were needed based on our latest production schedule, and should we have the parts delivered based on a monthly delivery schedule? And what about the all important lead-time, the time between purchase and delivery?

Those of you who have experienced the agony of waiting for parts when your assembly line is shut down will know exactly what I am talking about. The simple control system I set in took care of our problems. The front office prepared all new 5" x 8" "Parts and Material Record" cards showing the part name, description, how many were required on each amplifier or stringed instrument, requisition and purchase order numbers and dates, supplier name, invoice number, cost, and any back order information. The front office would also establish the minimum amount of parts remaining before reordering. The minimum amount was based on lead-time from the supplier. The stockroom supervisor assigned bin numbers for all parts, making sure the bins were in the proper location by part number, name, and value.

A perpetual daily inventory was simple to keep because the supervisor made sure that the new balance of parts was recorded after each withdrawal was made for production. The supervisor was responsible for seeing that the flip side of the parts and material record card was kept up to date. When the number of parts in the bin were down to the minimum amount shown, a parts order requisition was made and forwarded to the front office along with the parts and material record card. The purchase order was made, the data recorded, and the card was then returned to the stockroom along with a copy of the purchase order. The card size was increased to 8½" x 8½" as the company grew. Some readers may turn up their noses at this round-robin simple system, thinking it was not sophisticated enough. I can only say that we were always able to keep a balanced inventory and we were very seldom out of parts. And the bottom line was that Leo Fender liked the system very much because there was no unnecessary red tape.

Now the next step was taken in material control. I had small clipboards fastened at the end of each stringed instrument and amplifier workbench. The assembly workers wrote down the parts they would need, and the parts were delivered once in the morning and once in the afternoon. No more slow walking to the Stockroom and searching for parts. This was now declared off-limits for the assembly workers. A considerable cost saving.

The "Parts and Material Record" was printed on a 5"×8" flip side card when the system was installed. The card was increased to 8½"×8½" as the company grew. It controlled Fender inventory successfully from 1954 until CBS took over in 1965.

As time went by Leo seemed to understand why I had told him I thought he had been running the company like a job shop with his system of just looking in the bins to see how many parts he had left. He admitted that he would have had serious problems as the company grew.

It was difficult for Leo to let go of the management reins. He had been in the habit of doing everything himself, and he had a hard time accepting the fact that there was finally someone with ability who would take responsibility to get the job done. Let me give you an example:

In May 1954, when I started, there was no place in the office to hang your jacket. I told Ione we should have a couple of hooks on the wall. She agreed but she said, "You had better get Leo's permission first, because he has been taking care of problems like that." I thought if I didn't have enough sense to put up a 1" X 4" X 3' long board with three hooks, then why in the dickens did I have the title of Plant Manager.

You know, she was right. When I told Leo what I wanted to do, he acted real nervous and said he had better put it up because he would want it to be level. I explained to him that I had done cabinet work for my father and I had a level and knew how to use it. He finally agreed, and the job was taken care of to his satisfaction. In other words, it was obvious that I had to prove I had enough sense to come in out of the rain.

Now let me tell you how far he would go to stay out of a controversy, and about his idea of humor. I had been there for about two months. One afternoon the door to the office flew open and there was Leo, mad as a hornet, with some guy standing in back of him, in the doorway, leering over his shoulder. Leo yelled at me, "Look, if you expect to work for me, I don't want you to ever make a promise to someone and not keep it. I just don't operate that way."

The door was closed just as quickly before I had a chance to open my mouth. I asked Ione, "What do you think that was all about?"

Ione replied, "You got me." She didn't seem concerned in the least.

That evening, I was over in the lab and I said, "Leo, what were you talking about when you and that guy came to the office door this afternoon?"

He started laughing like crazy and said, "Oh! That was some guy I went to school with. He brought in a small appliance and asked me to replace the electric cord. I told him I would have it fixed and ready for him when he came in. You didn't want me to take the blame for it did you?" And I wish you could have heard him laugh. I was beginning to learn a little more about my friend and his unusual sense of humor. And you know, I couldn't get mad at him.

Musicians, and almost anyone else, could come and go, and had the run of Leo's radio service and the factory during the early years when

Jimmy Bryant with his early Telecaster. The photo was taken in the Capitol Records studio in 1952.

JIMMY BRYANT prefers a *Fender* GUITAR

the operation was very small. In 1954, we had over 40 employees, and I thought it was about time we had more control over who walked in any time they pleased.

Jimmy Bryant was a heck of a good guitar player, fast as greased lightning. He and Speedy West recorded some great instrumentals for Capitol Records. Anyhow, I had been in charge of the operation for about three months and Jimmy brought his Telecaster in for some service work and new strings. He drove his Cadillac in through the side gate, rather than the front where it was plainly marked for visitors. He walked into the final assembly building with a can of beer and was walking by the assembly benches drinking his beer and shooting the breeze with anyone who would listen. I had never met him and didn't know him from Adam. One thing I did know, however, was that we did not allow alcoholic beverages on the premises, and I didn't like to have the assembly workers bothered during working hours. I walked up to him and asked if I could help him.

Jimmy was extremely obnoxious in those days. I found out later that he didn't have very many friends because of his attitude during that period of time. He looked at me and said, "I don't need your help, I'm here to see Leo."

I told him that Leo had put me in charge as plant manager and I would be glad to help him in any way possible but that we did not allow alcoholic beverages on the property. He almost went through the ceiling. He said, "Look, I'm Jimmy Bryant and I have been playing your [expletive] Telecaster, but I don't have to play the [expletive] thing if I have to be told what I can or can't do when I come down here."

I said, "Look! I'm glad that you are playing our guitar but I still cannot allow you to drink that beer in here. You will have to take it out of the building and wait in the visitors room until I can get someone to help you. You will have to obey our rules whether you play our guitar or not."

A funny thing happened. He looked at me as if he could not believe his ears, that someone would tell him what he had to do. He apologized, threw the beer away, and I can say that Jimmy Bryant and I were the best of friends from that day on. He kept on playing the Fender Telecaster.

CHAPTER **9**

THE
FENDER
STRATOCASTER

Many musicians differ on whether Leo's greatest contribution in stringed instruments was the Precision Bass or the Stratocaster; but the Stratocaster is, without doubt, the most copied electric standard solid-body guitar in the world.

There are also differences of opinion on when the design work started and whose ideas were incorporated into the final production model. The Stratocaster was absolutely *not* designed and made for any one person. Its sole purpose was to expand the Fender line of musical instruments for additional sales.

Leo told me he had worked on the guitar as early as 1951, even to the point of designing the body and neck. I really doubt that the design work was done quite that early. Leo may have had some ideas on pickups, and perhaps went as far as designing the tremolo mechanism, but I would bet that was the extent of any Stratocaster design work in 1951.

Freddie Tavares told me the complete story of the concept and design of the Stratocaster. He said that when he went to work part-time with Leo in March 1953, no drawings had been made on the guitar, and he himself drew the shape of the body and neck according to Leo's exacting directions. I asked Freddie where the ideas came from for the guitar. He told me different musicians had offered their opinions, but he thought that Bill Carson gave Leo most of the ideas.

Hank Thompson and his Brazos Valley Boys, 1953. Billy Gray is at the right end, front. Bill Carson, to his left, has his Telecaster propped against a row of Fender amps.

Bill Carson was, and still is, a great guitar player. He played lead guitar for Hank Thompson from 1952 through 1954. He then went on to play lead guitar for Billy Gray, another member of Hank's group who had left to form his own band. I hired Bill in the middle of September 1957 as supervisor for guitar parts, assembly, and test. You can understand from his background as a musician why Leo would have paid a lot of attention to Bill's ideas.

Freddie told me it was Bill's idea to have six separate bridge sections for the Stratocaster, and he thought Bill should be given credit for the contouring of its body. Bill told Leo that the guitar should "fit like a shirt." (Bill wore western style shirts at that time, and those shirts fit like a glove around the waist.) Leo said that Rex Galion also told him it would be good to have the guitar contoured, but I have a hunch Rex said that after Leo had mentioned Bill Carson suggested the contour idea. It was probably a "me too" idea from Rex.

Leo should receive full credit for the shape of the body, the mechanical refinements of the six-section bridge assembly, and the tremolo unit. The tremolo was not an original idea. George Beauchamp filed for a patent on May 26, 1936, for a musical instrument with tremolo, and the patent (#2,152,783) was granted April 4, 1938. Paul Bigsby had also made his first tremolo unit before Leo designed his improved tremolo for the Stratocaster.

The neck head design is another matter. I think you would have to look at the solid-body guitar Paul Bigsby made for Merle Travis to form your own opinion. I personally don't think there is any doubt that it influenced the shape of the neck head on the Stratocaster.

George Fullerton said the 45-degree angle jack receptacle, located on the front of the guitar, was his idea.

Leo Fender applied for a patent on August 30, 1954, for the tremolo unit, which included the six-section adjustable bridge, and the 45-degree angle jack receptacle. Patent #2,741,146, was granted April 10, 1956. Surprisingly enough, there was no mention of the shape or contour of the body for the Stratocaster. Body contour was first mentioned, along with off-set waist, in Patent #2,960,900, which was for the Jazzmaster body. This patent was not filed until the late date of January 13, 1958, and it was granted November 22, 1960.

In crediting others with ideas for the Stratocaster, I do not mean to take any credit away from Leo. Even though he could not play or even tune a guitar, he was the one with the ability to accept those ideas offered to him, add his own innovations, and come up with a masterpiece like the Stratocaster.

There were a few Statocasters built in the spring and summer of 1954. These were considered to be prototypes and guinea pig models to test the performance and acceptance of the guitars.

Some writers would have you believe that the first production of Stratocasters was in the early part of 1954. One stated that there were 200

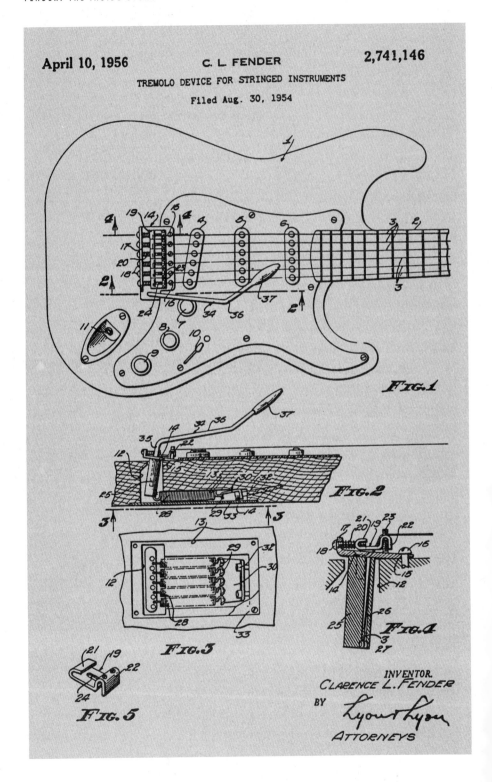

April 10, 1956

C. L. FENDER

2,741,146

TREMOLO DEVICE FOR STRINGED INSTRUMENTS

Filed Aug. 30, 1954

FIG.1

FIG.2

FIG.3

FIG.4

FIG.5

INVENTOR.
CLARENCE L. FENDER
BY
Lyon + Lyon
ATTORNEYS

unfinished bodies and 150 unfinished necks in stock to meet initial orders. That was right—to meet initial orders. But stocking up on unfinished necks and bodies in anticipation of orders is *not* a production run. It is "work in process inventory." A production run is a completed, tested, out-the-door fulfillment of a purchase order. The first production run of the Stratocaster (with tremolo) was in the month of October 1954, to fill Purchase Order #242 (for 100 units) from Fender Sales, dated October 13, 1954. The first production run for non-tremolo Stratocasters was in April 1955, to fill Purchase Order #314 (for 25 units), dated March 29.

I would never know how many or what kind of instruments or amplifiers were going to be ordered by Fender Sales until the day that order was received in the mail. Leo and Don were not getting along; and, as plant manager, I was in the middle. The first time I was allowed to have that all-important inventory information was January 1965, after CBS had acquired the company and Don Randall was in complete charge. I consider Don to be a good friend of mine but he will never know the amount of frustration I had to go through, peering into my crystal ball for the answers I needed to keep a balanced finished goods inventory at Fender Sales. Guess who the salesmen and dealers probably blamed? That stupid plant manager. This is the first time this information has ever been made public and one of the many reasons why I have called this book the true "inside story."

This is what Fender Sales had to say about the Stratocaster in 1954: "Perfection in a solid-body comfort contoured professional guitar providing all of the finest Fender features. Choice hardwood body finished with a golden sunburst shading, white maple neck, white pickguard, and lustrous chrome metal parts. Three advanced style adjustable pickups, one volume control, two tone controls and a three-position instant tone change switch. The adjustable Fender bridge ensures perfect intonation and softest action. The neck has the famous Fender truss rod. The Stratocaster is available with or without the great Fender built-in tremolo."

I told Leo when I first saw and tried the Stratocaster that there should have been a lock on the tremolo so you could change the strings in an easier manner. Other than that, I thought the guitar was great. You will notice on his next guitar, the Jazzmaster, he put a lock on the tremolo and trademark registered it as the "trem-lok."

Many great guitar players adopted the Stratocaster as their favorite instrument. There are too many to mention them all, but I am sure you will recognize the names of Dick Dale, Buddy Holly, Jeff Beck, Jimi Hendrix, Ry Cooder, Eric Clapton, Elden Shamblin, Stevie Ray Vaughan, Adrian Belew, Danny Gatton, Steve Howe, Yngwie Malmsteen, Robin Trower, Robert Cray, Eric Johnson, James Garver, Steve McClure, Richie Blackmore. There are so many more, including Bill Carson, whose ideas helped to make the Stratocaster the great instrument that it is.

Billy Gray's band, 1956. Billy Gray is second from the right and Bill Carson is fifth from the right, behind his Stratocaster.

Billy Gray

Billy Gray and His Western Swing Band
The Nation's No. 1 New Big Western Band

use *Fender* Fine Electric Instruments
Exclusively

I would like to tell you a story about Bill. On many weekends, Leo Fender and I were at the factory. One Saturday morning Bill came in "singing the blues," because the neck of his Cimarron Red Stratocaster was worn out and he needed a replacement. His "Strat" body was one of the first ones made. It could have been the very first, since he was the "suspected father" of the thing. Bill was playing in Billy Gray's band at that time, and he came crying to me that he needed a new neck. I told him that it should not be a problem and I started to look for a replacement. Any other time I could have found a dozen Stratocaster necks, but not that morning. I said, "Bill, I'm sorry, we don't have any Strat necks left in stock and there is only one that I know of and it's mine." He asked me if he could see the one I

Bill Carson in 1956, with one of the first Stratocasters. (This is the photo of Forrest's "one and only" bird's-eye maple neck!)

was talking about. I told him it was in my office and he could see it but it was absolutely not available. He saw the neck and immediately fell in love with it. I could understand why, because I had been in love with it ever since I first laid eyes on it. It was the most beautiful bird's-eye maple neck that any of us had seen at the factory, and I was saving it to put on my own guitar.

Well, he started in, and you have never heard such begging in your life. It is painful to hear a grown man cry, and Bill Carson could put on an act like you had never seen or heard before. I finally knew the only way to get rid of him was to give in. So I put my beautiful neck on his well-used Strat body. Friend, he was grinning like the cat that just ate the mouse. And how did he show his appreciation? He has his picture taken with the darn instrument and sends it to me to rub it in. The picture he sent me, of my "one and only" neck, is in this book. I told him that some day the whole world would find out how he took that neck from his friend. I will bet, if the truth is known, that he is still using that neck and that it has been transferred to a late Fender guitar body with the latest in pickups. I wonder if he will ever tell the true story—how it belonged to me and he finally conned me out of it.

Bill occasionally came by the factory over the next few years, and he must have liked what he saw a little bit, because in September 1957 I had the pleasure of hiring him. Bill did an outstanding job making sure that all instruments going out the door had been assembled and tested with loving care. You can give him a lot of credit for the reason so many musicians prefer pre-CBS instruments. He would later become Guitar Production Foreman when we incorporated in 1959.

Bill transferred to Fender Sales in Santa Ana in 1967 to train for the position of sales representative. He has been a great asset to Fender through the years, but contrary to what has been written in a special Stratocaster sales document, he never served as plant manager or director of marketing. Don Randall, as early years president of Fender Sales, told me that Bill Carson was never involved with Fender marketing decisions. Bill is still with Fender, as the district sales manager for the Nashville area. I believe they would have to look for a long time to find a better person for the job. He is a great musician, great personality, and a great friend of mine for many years. I am proud to say that I was the one who brought him on board with Fender.

Being able to offer employment to many wonderful people, who helped us through the years, offsets a lot of the frustration and heartaches that seem to be a part of management. I can understand why Leo wanted to divorce himself from the everyday problems. I will never forget this next story about Leo, because this was when I knew he had left those decisions up to me.

It was getting close to the holiday season in 1954, and I still had the feeling that I should brief him on any matters of importance so that I could get his reaction and input. I don't remember what the problem was, but I walked over to his lab room. I should have known by then that he did not like to be disturbed while he was deeply involved with his lab work. I said, "Leo." There was just a little grunt in reply. Again, I said, "Leo, there is something that I would like to tell you and I would like to have your opinion." There was no reply at all this time. I waited patiently for a couple of minutes and then for the third time I said, "Leo." That's as far as I got. And my mouth was still open. Leo slammed down his screwdriver, turned around with a disgusted look on his face, and said, "Look, you have your problems, and I have mine. Now, you take care of your problems, and I'll take care of mine."

From that time on I knew that he trusted me to use good judgment in taking care of the everyday management problems. I never made the mistake of bothering him again when he was deeply involved with his R&D lab work.

Actually, I did "bother" him another time in his lab, but it was out of desperation. There was a vacant room adjacent to the front office and Leo converted this area into his research and development lab during the latter part of 1954. There was a dual-room electric heater built into the center of the wall. It was about 4' high from its top to bottom with a heating element approximately the same length. Leo positioned his lab workbench in the corner of the room alongside the dividing wall between the lab and office. My desk was in the corner of the office in the same position as his lab workbench on the other side of the wall. Now, the dual-room heater was in back of his lab stool and my office chair. The heating element and protective guard on each side of the wall was made of very light gauge metal. Sound passed through that wall heater a lot better than heat did.

Now picture this. You have never heard a noise as loud as Leo Fender testing an amplifier. The amplifier would be positioned on his workbench with its open back facing him as he was seated on his stool. He would have an old guitar laying face up on a stool beside him. Now, he would turn the amp up to almost full output, and with great gusto, he would strum across the open strings constantly, constantly, and more constantly. And, in the meantime, I would be sitting at my desk just on the other side of the wall, trying to carry on telephone conversations with parts and material suppliers. The wall heater, not to be outdone, would be vibrating like crazy as the violent sound waves were gushing through its inner parts. You may wonder at times why some plant managers act a little strange after they have been exposed to the challenges of the average work-day. It was almost impossible to hear on the telephone. Especially if some gal was trying to imitate Marilyn Monroe's suppressed breathing technique while you were asking about the delay in shipment of your last purchase order. I do remember one day when I was talking to one of our suppliers in Chicago and Leo was testing his latest version of the mighty Twin Amp. Leo had that baby cranked up pretty good, and the guy on the phone asked, "What is that noise? Are you guys having an earthquake?" I replied, "No, that's just Leo Fender."

In absolute desperation one day, I asked Leo if it would be all right if I tuned the guitar so that he would be strumming an open chord rather than the standard open-string tuning. This met with his approval, and it helped a little—but not much.

How does a Trumpet Master sound to you? Or a Saxocaster? Maybe I shouldn't blow this around, but Fender almost got involved in the horn business in the latter part of 1954 and early 1955. The idea turned out to be almost as bad as those fictitious model names. Leo had not yet moved his desk out of the front room office, and Ione and I couldn't help but overhear some of the many conversations he had with Sales partners Don Randall, Charlie Hayes, and the fellow they were buying the horn company from. Since children may look at this book I will refrain from relating some of Leo's comments during those conversations. You would be correct in assuming that he was not too enthusiastic about instruments that had no strings attached. I think there were strings attached in the whole horn deal though, and that was why Leo was a little disturbed. It was decided that Charlie would be honored by having the brass section of Fender named the Hayes brand. They printed literature praising the new line of Hayes horns, but it was a waste of money. The horn business blew its last breath during the year 1955. It had no more chance of survival than the White student instrument line Leo was developing at the time.

I have fond memories of my first holiday season at Fender in 1954. It was still rough financially, but you would not have known it by Leo's actions as time for our Christmas party was drawing near. I think he was beginning to see the light of success at the end of our tunnel, so there was much to be thankful for. We had around 40 employees and Leo asked me to order a gift-wrapped ham and a box of chocolates for each one. It was good to see the smile on Leo's face during our little family-like party. I don't think the employees expected to receive the ham and candy. It was good that they did not know Leo had to scrape the bottom of the barrel so he could spread some Christmas cheer. Noel! Peace on earth—especially at the Fender Electric Instrument Co.

In early 1955, I was in the woodshop in Building #3, and an employee from the stockroom came in and asked me what I wanted him to do with the "White" nameplates that just came in. I said, "If they are white, send them back because our nameplates are brown and chrome."

He said, "No, you don't understand; they are 'White.'"

And, I guess I must have looked at him a little strange when I replied, "Look! I just told you if they are white to send them back."

Then he said, "Here, look at what I'm talking about." The name on the nameplate was White.

That was when and how I found out that Leo had used my name for the new line of "studio" guitars and amplifiers intended for music studios (not regular dealers), where students were taught to play instruments. The tube charts to be placed inside the amplifier cabinets said "White Instrument Co., Fullerton, California." Leo had not said anything to me about naming the line after me. I had been purchasing all of our manufacturing parts and material for a long time. Leo had ordered the nameplates and labels and must have told the supplier not to tell me because it was a surprise.

Season's Greetings

to our good friends everywhere

Fender ELECTRIC INSTRUMENT CO.
Fullerton, California

Even Santa plays a Fender at Christmas time. This card is from 1958.

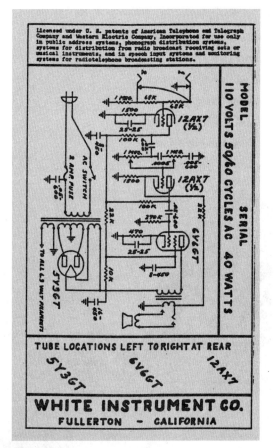

Licensed under U. S. patents of American Telephone and Telegraph Company and Western Electric Company, Incorporated for use only in public address systems, phonograph distribution systems, systems for distribution from radio broadcast receiving sets or musical instruments, and in speech input systems and monitoring systems for radiotelephone broadcasting stations.

MODEL
110 VOLTS 50/60 CYCLES AC 40 WATTS

SERIAL

TUBE LOCATIONS LEFT TO RIGHT AT REAR

WHITE INSTRUMENT CO.
FULLERTON — CALIFORNIA

This label was placed inside the amplifier cabinets made under the White Instrument Co. name to show the wiring schematic and tube layout. Leo ordered the labels and White amplifier name plates before Forrest knew Leo had named the new studio line after him.

I have the first White amplifier that was made in early 1955. It is still in the original carton and has never been opened. I also have a White steel guitar with legs. We received the first Fender Sales Purchase Order #402 for the new studio line, White Amp Model 80 and 6-String Steel, on September 13, 1955. We made those units in October/November.

F. C. Hall was busy promoting his newly acquired company, Electro String Instrument Corporation, during this early part of 1955. It was called just plain Rickenbacker by his partners, though. Leo, Don Randall, and Charlie Hayes, of course, did not like the idea that one of their partners was also a competitor. They did not want Rickenbacker to know how many guitars and amplifiers Fender was selling. Stay tuned for developments.

Leo had finished designing a new amplifier that I had the pleasure of naming the Tremolux. Fender Sales seemed to be pleased with it. They said, "The new great Fender amplifier incorporates the latest type of electronic tremolo circuit which provides a greater range of speed and depth than any previous type." The amp had a 12" heavy-duty Jensen speaker and 15 watts output. We received the first purchase order, #342, for the Tremolux Amp on June 1, 1955. The production run was completed by the end of the month.

One beautiful morning in June 1955, Charlie came over from Fender Sales to discuss some business with Leo. I'm sorry to say that Leo showed little respect for anyone whose presence would interfere with his beloved R&D lab work. You might think he was just plain rude, but he really didn't mean to be. I am sure that he honestly felt his lab work was far more important than anything else he could be doing, and that you as an intruder should understand that.

Anyhow, Charlie had been waiting to see Leo for some time. And no Leo. After a while I felt sorry for Charlie, and even though I had a lot to do, I decided I would spend as much time with him as I could until Leo showed up. Charlie really opened up regarding every aspect of his observations and opinions of the overall Fender operation. I learned much more about Leo, Don, and the Fender story during the short time I spent with Charlie that morning than I had during the past several months as plant manager. Charlie told me about Don's frustrations in his dealings with Leo. That was the first time I had heard Don's side of the story. I found out that there were two sides to the problems and that Don had reasons to gripe. Charlie and I both agreed that we had two friends who each seemed stubborn and did not want to give in to the other partner. It was hurting the company, and Charlie and I were in the middle of the conflict. We had become good friends, and he knew he could discuss things with me in confidence. I was someone he could talk to and get things off his chest. (There were things he told me that will not appear in this book because he had my word that I would not repeat them.)

Charlie was older than I was and for some reason he always called me "Kid." He knew that Leo had named the new studio line after me and he said, "Kid, we are going to make your name as well known as Leo's." Well, I knew that statement was ridiculous but Charlie had a way of saying things that made it sound good regardless. He was a top-notch salesman and he could have come as close to selling you the Brooklyn Bridge as anyone.

Leo finally showed up around noon and the three of us went to lunch. They kicked everything around—the horn business, F. C. Hall and Rickenbacker, problems relating to Don and Leo, new products needed, etc. It was the longest lunch period I had ever had with Leo. We finally went back to the plant. By this time, Charlie had Leo's attention, and he and Leo continued their conversation in the lab.

It was almost 5:00 p.m. when Charlie and Leo finished, and I was sitting at my desk. Charlie waved at me as he stuck his head through the reception desk window and said, "So long, Kid." As far as I know, those were the last words he ever said to anybody. My friend Charlie Hayes was killed in a head-on collision while he was driving back to the Fender Sales

The amplifier assembly line at Fender Electric Instrument Co. in 1955. (photo: Fender)

office in Santa Ana. They called our office right after it happened, and I went over as soon as possible to pick up his briefcase so that it wouldn't fall into the wrong hands. His death was a tremendous loss to his friends and to the Fender organization. He was one of the good guys.

Harold Rhodes decided to join Fender by fall 1955. He brought the prototype of an electric piano with him. Harold was very friendly and I was pleased that he was with us. There was no doubt the piano had great potential and I am sure Leo knew this, but it was evident that it needed much design work before it would be ready for production. It was difficult to figure out why Leo agreed to take on this added burden when he was occupied with many other projects. It was not long before Leo and Harold disagreed about the piano mechanism and the number of keys. You can be sure that this was going to be the pattern for a few years.

By the end of 1955, major changes had taken place within Fender Sales. Leo Fender and Don Randall had informed F. C. Hall that they felt his purchase of the Electro String Instrument Corporation was a conflict of interest, and they voted him out of the company. Leo and Don bought out the interests of Charlie Hayes's widow and F. C. Hall at the same time. Now Leo and Don each owned 50 percent of Fender Sales. It was agreed that Don would serve as president of the sales office and would devote his full time to the marketing of Fender products. Leo still owned 100 percent of the factory, Fender Electric Instrument Co.

It is really too bad that Leo and Don could not get along, because they were so capable. Remember the cartoon of the two donkeys on each end of a rope, pulling in opposite directions trying to get to some food? Picture me in the middle with the rope around my neck.

CHAPTER 10

THE
MIRACLE
MAN

Leo Fender should have been called the "miracle man of new products." He could come up with something entirely new in a little over three months time. And, don't forget, he was coming up with these new units mostly by himself, basing a lot on what musicians and Sales told him they needed. Freddie Tavares spent most of his time recording the information in drawings and specifications. Of course, Leo never limited himself to a certain amount of working hours. He would get up in the middle of the night to make notes or a drawing of a new idea or an improvement in a product already being produced. His wife, Esther, used to get mad at him while they were on vacation or a short weekend trip. She told Joan and me that Leo would always take his pencil and pad with him to make notes, and he didn't seem to be interested in much of anything else.

Leo came up with Fender's first ¾-size standard guitar in 1955. We received Purchase Order #402 from Fender Sales on September 26, 1955, before we knew the name of the model or whether it was for the one- or two-pickup model. We did not finish the first production run until around the first part of May 1956, because we had to order the decals for the

Musicmaster single-pickup guitar. The orders started to roll in for this popular little instrument, and I used to wonder where in the heck all of those guitars were going. By this time it was plain to see that Fender was going to become one of the greatest musical instrument and amplifier manufacturers in the world.

The two-pickup ¾-size model was named the Duo-Sonic, and we received the first purchase order August 15, 1956. Orders came rolling in again, but we were set for the production run and those guitars were built pronto.

In the meantime Leo had been busy. He came out with two new amplifiers in the spring of 1956. The Harvard Amp had an 8" Jensen speaker, with 10 watts output, and the Vibrolux had a 10" Jensen speaker, with 10 watts output and a tremolo circuit. We received a Fender Sales order for the Harvard and Vibrolux amplifiers, April 17, 1956. The amplifiers were made in July 1956.

During the winter of 1955 Leo had started designing an electric mandolin. We received the first sales order on July 13, 1956, and they were made in October 1956.

Leo had been working on a pedal steel guitar for quite some time, and we had a prototype made up for testing. Speedy West was the first one to check it out for tone, mechanical performance, and ease of playing, and he pointed out some things to Leo which were very important. The proto-type was a double-neck 8-string guitar, and the two necks were the same height. Speedy told Leo that the outside, second neck should be raised higher, like a stair step, for ease of playing. Speedy's three-neck pedal steel gui-tar, made by Paul Bigsby, had the second neck higher than the first and the third neck higher than the second. Speedy thought that the bridge of the guitar should have roll-ers to support the strings. A stationary bridge without rollers would break too many strings. He also suggested changes on the tone of the pickups. Leo made those changes and Speedy then said he was pleased with the guitar.

Speedy took delivery of his updated Fender prototype pedal steel guitar, Model 1000, in 1956. He played it on a Hawaiian album he recorded for Capitol Records that year. His daughter, Tauni, was born in 1956,

SPEEDY WEST and his new *Fender* 1000 Pedal Steel Guitar

Speedy West with his "1000" pedal steel guitar. He had the front panel custom made with his name on it.

and one of the songs on the album was named for her, with a slightly different spelling of her name. He also used his new Fender pedal guitar on the first songs Bobby Bare recorded for Capitol Records in 1956.

Leo designed the pulling mechanism for the pedal guitar so that you could pull the string sharp or flat with just slight changes in the hook-up. I thought his idea for the mechanism was absolutely ingenious but that his system of small steel cables between the mechanism and pedals looked like a rat's nest. I absolutely thought it stunk to high heaven and I told him so. (Leo wanted my honest opinion on everything, and we had our original agreement that I was to feel free to express my opinion at any time.) I thought he should use connecting rods to fasten the pulling mechanism to the pedals. Leo's idea was probably the best after all, because as Speedy

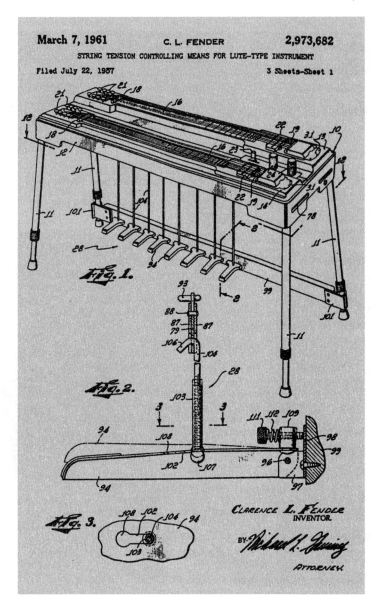

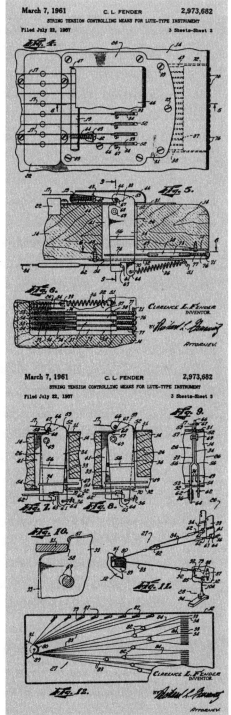

pointed out, "You could turn the Fender Pedal Guitar upside down and make fast tuning changes by moving the cable connections. You could not use rods on the kind of pulling mechanism that Leo had designed for the pedal guitar."

It should be pointed out that on prototype instruments or amplifiers, many of the parts are made by hand, and the permanent tooling is not made until the prototype has been thoroughly tested and approved. This was the case with the pedal steel guitar. We received the first purchase order for the Pedal 1000 Steel Guitar on July 13, 1956, followed by another on August 3, but we did not have the tooling ready. The first production run would not be completed until the first week of April 1957.

Alvino Rey also came into the plant in 1956 to try the prototype pedal steel guitar and to offer his opinion. I asked him how he would like to have his standard guitar fixed so that he could change his tone and volume setting from lead to rhythm by just flipping a switch. Alvino said, "That would be great. Can it be done?"

Alvino Rey with an early Stratocaster, 1955.

Alvino Rey trying out his custom "Fender 1000" pedal steel guitar in Leo's lab, 1957. (photo: White)

I said, "Sure it can be done. I had that system on a solid-body standard guitar that I made back in 1942." I told him I got the idea after I saw him at the Paramont Theater and noticed how much trouble he was having trying to adjust the controls on his Gibson guitar. You may remember I told you that I could not get Leo interested in that idea because he was not a guitar player. Then I said, "Leo, listen to what Alvino is saying. No one is using that idea on a commercial standard guitar and we should make one like that because it is needed." Alvino agreed. Leo didn't say anything as he slowly rubbed his chin. This was standard procedure when someone gave him an idea and he was thinking about it. You know the answer. Leo came up with the Jazzmaster using my idea on the presetting and switching arrangement for rhythm and lead.

In the 1950s, there was a very popular television show called *City at Night* that originated from Station KTLA-TV in Hollywood every Wednesday night. The announcer and engineers would take their mobile truck and visit different stores, factories, or any other place of interest in Southern California. The station called Fender asking permission to visit because they had received many requests for them to show our operation. I asked our employees if they would be interested, since they would be required to come back to the factory at night. Needless to say, they were excited over the possibility of their friends seeing them on TV. The program was scheduled for a live telecast on Wednesday, October 17, 1956, from 8:00 to 9:00 p.m.

The big night finally came and, would you believe it, most of the employees were dressed like they were going to their high school proms. Leo and I were dressed in our regular everyday work clothes, and I would imagine the viewers wondered if we were working for the assembly personnel. We had a big laugh over the impression we must have made.

The announcer, Ken Grauer, first introduced Eddie Cletro, a regular on a local TV show called *Western Varieties*. He was strumming a Stratocaster. The announcer then introduced Leo Fender as the "genius who made all of this possible." Leo started the tour by showing how the Stratocaster bodies were made through all of the operations prior to the finish department.

I had asked the production foreman, George Fullerton, to explain the operations through the neck department. The announcer had the opportunity to stand and jump on one of our guitar necks that had been suspended between two blocks, showing just how strong the necks were with the truss rod installed.

I conducted the tour through the assembly and final test operations of the Stratocaster guitar. We showed how the pickups and controls were mounted on the pickguard and then fastened to the body. We also showed how the neck was fastened to the body with four screws, the way the strings were put on, and then the actual testing of the instruments to ensure that there were no high frets and that intonation was correct.

We were now ready for the jam session to demonstrate the sound of Fender instruments. Noel Boggs, who had come down from Hollywood to help us out with music for the show, played the Four-Neck 8-String Stringmaster steel guitar. Eddie Cletro played the Stratocaster with tremolo. The next musicians were our own employees. Al Petty played a prototype Fender Pedal Steel Guitar. Al had been working on small parts assembly at the time, and I later made him the foreman over amplifier assembly. Gene Galion played a Stratocaster with tremolo. Gene was employed in final assembly and instrument testing. Freddie Tavares played the Precision Bass. Eddie Miller played a Telecaster. Eddie was employed in the woodshop at the time, which brings up a separate story:

Eddie was working in the woodshop one day and he stopped to go to the restroom. I was told that he was in there for an unusually long time. Now, in addition to working at Fender, Eddie had been writing songs. When he came out of the restroom, he had a few sheets of toilet paper in his hand. He told some of the employees, "I just wrote the lyrics for my new song." That wasn't just any ordinary song. It was that great country/pop crossover classic, "Release Me." Friend, that is the true story of a song that has been recorded by well over 400 different artists. Eddie later wrote a gospel version he called "Release Me (From My Sin)." It was sung by James Blackwood and was the title song of a Grammy Award–winning religious album.

Eddie was one of the founders of what would eventually become the Academy of Country Music (ACM) in Hollywood, along with Eddie Dean, one of the singing cowboys, and Johnny Bond, who was in the Jimmy Wakely Trio and appeared with Gene Autry on the CBS radio show *Melody Ranch* for many years. Eddie Dean and Johnny Bond were my and Leo's close friends, and their organization, the ACM, would involve Leo a little later in his life.

Eddie Miller left the Fender Electric Instrument Co. in the latter 1950s to become a representative for Fender Sales in Nashville. He would later write songs full-time, and his hits included "There She Goes" and "Thanks a Lot." His songs were recorded by Ernest Tubb, and many other country and pop artists. He died of a heart attack April 11, 1977, in his Nashville home. He was the co-founder of the Nashville Songwriters Association International (NSAI), a member of its Hall of Fame, and in his final years was a member of the NSAI board of directors.

I finally received my first raise. You will remember that I had taken a cut in pay when I joined Leo in 1954. The raise was a healthy one, because things were much better financially for the company. By the end of 1956 I had installed a plant-wide incentive program using individual piece-work and group bonus plans, tied directly to my quality-control plan. I believe it is a big mistake to install incentive programs unless they are tied hand-in-hand to quality control. Therefore, each one of our employees acted as an inspector, since faulty workmanship had to be corrected, and was charged either against individual piecework rates or the amount of the earned group bonus. Shares of the

Fender Electric Instrument Co. 1956 Christmas Party. The musicians, L to R: Gene Galion, Telecaster; Bill Carson, Strat; Al Petty, Stringmaster Steel; and Danny Michaels, Telecaster. (photo: Fender)

The Fender Electric Instrument Co. at 500 S. Raymond in 1955. (photo: Fender)

group bonus were based on the amount of man-hours worked during the week: 40 hours=100% share; 30 hours=75% share. The plan was successful because the employees were happy. They were making good money. I received a good raise. Leo Fender bought his first 40' yacht. Leo had Grady Neal build two new cement block 40' X 120' buildings. And last, but not least, in later years musicians would pay a premium to buy pre-CBS instruments that were made in those early years because of the good quality workmanship and sound. Any debates?

By the end of the year 1956, Leo had moved his research and development lab into the new Building #6. The metal shop, which Leo had to work so closely with for handmade prototype parts, was moved out of the front building and into the new Building #5. The stockroom was now in Building #4. This improved conditions a lot. We would not have to listen to those loud punch presses anymore in the front office, and Leo finally had enough room to do his job the way he wanted to. He could crank those new amps up to the explosive point and not drive us all up the wall.

In April 1957, we finally completed the first production run for the Pedal 1000, and Leo Fender presented the first one to Shot Jackson. Shot was playing steel with a group from Nashville at San Diego's Municipal Auditorium on March 30, 1957. The group included Ernest Tubb, Kitty Wells, Johnny and Jack, and Billy Byrd. Shot had been playing with Roy Acuff's band and had been using Fender steel guitars and amplifiers for

Leo and Forrest presented the first Fender pedal steel guitar to Shot Jackson in 1957 while he was appearing with Ernest Tubb in San Diego. L to R: (back row) Ernest Tubb, Kitty Wells, Johnny & Jack, Forrest White, Billy Byrd (front row) Leo Fender, Shot Jackson.

quite some time. He would soon be manufacturing the Sho-Bud pedal steel guitar with his friend Buddy Emmons.

Barbara Mandrell was also presented with one of the first production run Fender 1000 Pedal Steels. Barbara's father, Irby Mandrell, was a Fender dealer during that time.

One of the best-sounding amplifiers that Leo Fender ever designed was shown by Fender Sales at the 1957 National Association of Music Merchants (NAMM) show in Chicago at the Palmer House. It was the Fender Bassman Amp Model 5F6. The controls on the top-mounted chassis were: presence, middle, bass, treble, volume bright, and volume normal. Two inputs were provided for the bright channel and two for the normal channel. The secret of the sound was the four 10" Jensen heavy-duty speakers made to Leo's specifications. You could use that same chassis with other speakers and the sound would not compare with Leo's marvels. If you are a musician and have the opportunity to buy one of those old Bassman Amps, and the speakers are in good condition, grab it.

I attended the 1957 NAMM show in Chicago. Fender Sales had asked Speedy West to demonstrate the Pedal 1000 and Roy Lanham was there to back him up with the Stratocaster. We made some show model Blond Stratocasters with tremolo and gold hardware. We received the first Purchase Order for these on June 18, 1957. The first order for Blond Stratocasters with tremolo and chrome hardware was received September 8, 1957.

In my opinion, the NAMM shows were much better in the early years when they were held in hotels. The Palmer House in Chicago was my favorite. Companies had the same rooms assigned to them year after year, and you knew where to find your competitive friends. There were only a few companies that manufactured stringed instruments then: Fender, Gibson, Gretsch, Martin, Harmony, Kay, Guild, Valco (National), and Vega. It was like a family affair. The National Association of Music Merchants is the parent association that musical instrument manufacturers and dealers belong to. The manufacturers of guitars, other stringed instruments, and accessories, belong to a sub-association (within NAMM) called the Guitar and Accessory Manufacturers Association (GAMA). I represented the Fender Electric Instrument Co. and attended the annual GAMA meeting with the other members each year.

Earl Finley, Forrest, and Eldon Shamblin at the assembly department in 1957. Earl was stringing and adjusting Eldon's Stratocaster. (photo: Fender)

Buck Owens
and his band
play

Fender
MUSICAL INSTRUMENTS

Doyle Holly, bass; Don Rich
and Buck Owens, Telecasters;
1958. These were the first
Fender guitars with edge
binding.

The first three Fender guitars to have body edge binding were Telecasters with special mixed ground-glass finish. They were made in early 1958. Fred Martin, of the Martin Guitar Company, had been kind enough to show me through his factory. He showed me the special tool they made to cut binding strips, and what material and what adhesive to use. One Telecaster was for Buck Owens, one for his guitarist, Don Rich, and one was a spare. A matching Precision Bass was also made.

I attended the WSM Disc Jockey Convention in Nashville in November 1957. My reservations were at the old Andrew Jackson Hotel, the headquarters for the convention. Fender Sales had started to display Fender merchandise at the convention each year. This year was a little special because the Fender 1000 Pedal Steel Guitar was shown for the first time. "Deejay Week" later became the WSM Birthday Celebration and eventually CMA Week (named for the Country Music Association). The radio people moved their annual meeting to the springtime and now call it the Country Radio Seminar.

I attended all of the conventions during the time I was with Fender because I had so many friends in Nashville. One morning I went down

A rare photo of steel players assembled in the Fender Sales display room at the Andrew Jackson Hotel, 1958. L to R: (standing) Jimmy Day, Johnny Sibert, Jerry Byrd, Leon McAuliffe, [?], Speedy West, Buddy Emmons, Don Helms, Bud Isaacs, Bobby Foster; (front) Linda Riley, Don Davis, [?]

to the hotel coffee shop for breakfast, and there were no empty tables. I noticed that over to the side, an elderly, distinguished-looking gentleman was seated alone at a table for two. I walked over and said, "Pardon me sir, would you mind if I shared this table with you for breakfast since there are no other seats available at the present time?"

In a very courteous manner he replied, "You will be quite welcome, young man. Please sit down." I was surprised to learn that I had the pleasure of sharing the breakfast table with "Uncle Art" Satherley. He had started Gene Autry in the recording business and had recorded Gene's first big hit, "That Silver Haired Daddy of Mine." I found out that he was the first to record Bob Wills and His Texas Playboys, and he had named Bob's great song "San Antonio Rose." He had also recorded Leo Fender's favorite song "Faded Love," which Bob had written. By this time, Bob had been using Fender instruments and amplifiers exclusively, and he had also become Leo's and my good friend. Uncle Art Satherley had discovered and recorded many artists who had been inducted into the Country Music Hall of Fame, including: Roy Acuff—1962, Tex Ritter—1964, Red Foley—1967, Bob Wills—1968, Gene Autry—1969, Original Carter Family—1970, Bill

Bill Carson with Ray Whitley,
who wrote Gene Autry's theme
song "Back in the Saddle," and
Jazzmaster guitars, 1958.
(photo: White)

Monroe—1970, Original Sons of the Pioneers—1980, Lefty Frizzell—1982, Marty Robbins—1982, Little Jimmy Dickens—1983, Floyd Tillman—1984, Lester Flatt and Earl Scruggs—1985, and Roy Rogers—1988. Uncle Art was inducted into the Country Music Hall of Fame in 1971.

That morning at breakfast I had no idea this retired former vice president of Columbia Records would become my close friend in later years. In 1978, he asked me to take care of all his personal business in music, and I did so until his death at the age of 96 in 1986.

During that time I was successful in re-uniting him with Gene Autry. Due to a misunder-standing, they had not seen each other for over 15 years. The Nashville Network (TNN) called me for permission to fly to California to tape some inter-views with Uncle Art Satherley. I told them that would be fine and asked if they would like to have Gene Autry included in one of the interviews. They said that would be ter-rific. I called Gene's secretary, Maxine, and told her the story. She got back to me: Gene said okay. And the interviews were taped in May 1983. I took Uncle Art to Gene's private box at Anaheim Sta-dium, the California Angels' home field, and the interview with those old friends was videotaped there. I wish I had taken my tape recorder and had taped the stories they told before the video interview about their early years. The interview with Uncle Art alone was taped later that day at his home in Fountain Valley, California.

Jack Lameier, Director of Promotion, CBS Records, Nashville, was Uncle Art's good friend and also a good friend of mine. Through his exhaus-tive efforts, we were able to complete a memorial album for Uncle Art in 1991 entitled *Uncle Art Satherley, Country Music's Founding Father*, released on CBS's American Originals series. It was the last recording pro-duced by Uncle Art. I had the pleasure of being an executive producer of

the album, along with Jack Lameier and Steve Buckingham. Here is a copy
of my letter, which appears on the album explaining how it was produced:

Uncle Art Satherley was one of the most impressive men I
have ever met and I am honored to say he was a dear friend. His
comments on this album were recorded during a three-month
period in the summer of 1982 nearing his 93rd Birthday. He did not
want his wife, Harriet, to know he was working on his memorial
album, so we would drive to a park near his home in Fountain Valley,
California, using my inexpensive portable tape recorder. Uncle Art did
not seem to be concerned that my car was being used as a studio and
the sound quality would be questionable. He was recording again after
many years and to him this was the only thing of importance. We have
presented the voiced comments of "Mr. Country Music" and perhaps
all else is of no consequence. Mr. A. E. "Uncle Art" Satherley was called
by his Creator on February 10, 1986. Country Music has lost one of its
greatest contributors. He was the first recipient of the Academy of Country
Music's Pioneer Award and was the oldest living member of Country
Music's Hall of Fame.

Forrest White

Forrest White and "Uncle"
Art Satherly in 1978. (photo:
H. Satherly)

"Uncle" Art Satherley and
Gene Autry at Anaheim Sta-
dium in 1983. They had not
seen each other in over
15 years.

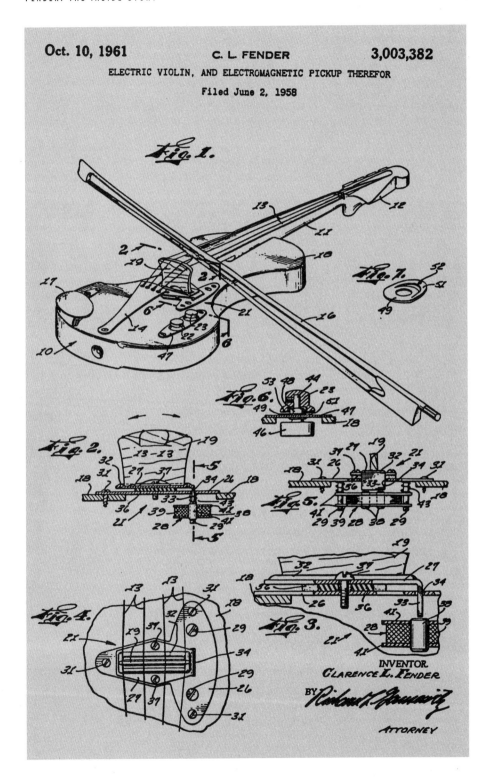

Leo Fender was pleased that I had helped Uncle Art Satherley, and I was surprised at the extent of his interest. Leo knew he had been a secretary to Thomas Edison in the early years. Leo had worked on a record changer; Edison invented the phonograph...fellow inventor?

I had taken the first production prototype of Leo's new electric violin with me on the plane to the Disc Jockey Convention. You will observe that in this case I call it "production prototype." We had made a few test prototypes which we knew would not become our final production model. This was the first unit made which we thought would be ready for a regular production run, but Leo was not sure all of the bugs had been worked out. So he had me take the violin with me so that some of the "fiddle" players in Nashville could try it out and give us their opinions before we went any further. It had not been completely assembled before I left the factory, and I had to work on it in the hotel room in Nashville.

Many well-known musicians tried the violin backstage before the Friday and Saturday night *Grand Ole Opry* shows at the Ryman Auditorium. Roy Acuff, Howdy Forrester, Tommy Jackson, and some others whose names I do not remember tried the "fiddle," as they called it. They all liked the sound and the way it played, but their only objection was to the weight. This was the reason the Fender Electric Violin died almost before it became alive. Wade Ray and Harold Hensley, two excellent "fiddle" players, are the only musicians I know of who played these instruments for any length of time.

We received the first Fender Sales purchase order for 100 of the Electric Violins on August 12, 1958. We did not make those violins until November. We received another purchase order for 100 December 5, 1958. Then no more were made until 1970.

Bob Wills was one of our most loyal and dedicated Fender equipment boosters. He had a steel player named Billy Bowman working in his band in the spring of 1958 on a tour of Southern California. Billy, for some reason not known to Bob, had gone to Rickenbacker and made a deal to use their equipment. The first Bob knew about it was when he saw the equipment on stage. He fired Billy for making changes in the Texas Playboys' equipment without clearing it with him.

Bob Wills's bus, a common sight in Fender's parking lot, 1958. L to R: Billy Bowman, [?], Forrest White, [?], Freddie Tavares. (photo: Fender)

Many people do not know Bob Wills had one of the largest of the "big bands." He had a horn section that could compete with Benny Goodman, Glenn Miller, or any of the other big pop bands of the forties. However, horns did not make the money for him that his fiddle did. People went to hear Bob Wills and His Texas Playboys for western swing. He started it, and he was the undisputed King.

There are many other stories about Bob Wills. Bob had some problems with the bottle over a period of time and he went through more than one fortune. He and the Texas Playboys were playing a show one night, and one of the sponsors had been using mannequins to model suits and other clothing. It so happened that one of the mannequins had its arms in the same position that a musician would while playing a Fender bass. Bob's brother, Luke, was his bass player and a natural-born prankster. While Bob was backstage on a break, Luke stood the mannequin in his normal position on stage. He then put his western hat and jacket on the mannequin and hung his Fender Precision Bass around its neck. Jesse Ashlock and Bob were playing twin fiddles with the band, and when the break was over Bob came out swiftly on stage and up beside Jesse, and then it was "Take it away, Playboys." In just a few bars of the first fiddle tune, Bob glanced back toward his new bass player, and with a slight frown on his face, he leaned over to Jesse, while still playing, and said, "Who is that fellow back there playing bass?" Luke had tipped Jesse off, and Jesse said, "Oh, that's just one of the local good old boys who wanted to play a song with the band." Bob said, "Oh!" He played a little longer and leaned over to Jesse again and said, "Who did you say that was?" Jesse again said, "Bob, that's just one of the local good old boys." Again, Bob just said, "Oh!" Then for the third time he leaned over to Jesse and said, "I don't care who that [expletive] is, you tell him if he wants to play bass with Bob Wills to turn the [expletive] bass up so I can hear it."

I had the pleasure of spending quite a bit of time with Bob and the boys when they occasionally appeared at the Golden Nugget in Las Vegas. Here is a copy of one of the letters we received from him. The original in my file has almost faded out.

BOB WILLS

America's Most Versatile Dance Band

May 12, 1958

Fender Electric Instrument Co.
500 South Raymond
Fullerton, California

Dear Mr. Fender:

I am writing in regard to a steel guitar which I would like you to make up for me. I would like a four neck steel ready to pick up and go on my next trip to California which will be the last of this month and the first of June.

The Fender guitar I had was sold without my knowledge by Billy Bowman, who made some sort of informal commitments to Rickenbacker, whereupon they let him use one of their guitars which I am still using.

I prefer Fender equipment, and as I have Fender speakers, I would like a Fender steel guitar instead of the Rickenbacker. I will definitely keep the new Fender guitar if you would make it up for me.

We can discuss this matter further when I am out there.

Yours truly,
Bob Wills

We had been making the Fender 1000 Pedal Steel Guitar, which was an 8-string double-neck instrument, and now we had received our first Fender Sales purchase order for the Fender 400 Pedal Steel Guitar on January 7, 1958. This was an 8-string single-neck instrument. It must be pointed out that there was a lot of work involved in building pedal steel guitars, and only a few at a time were sent to Fender Sales.

I have mentioned how much I tried to interest Leo in making a guitar with preset switching for rhythm and lead. I told you that he was rubbing his chin in thought when Alvino Rey agreed with me that circuitry like I had used in 1942 was needed on commercial guitars. The chin-rubbing had paid off. Leo had designed a new guitar which he called the Jazzmas-

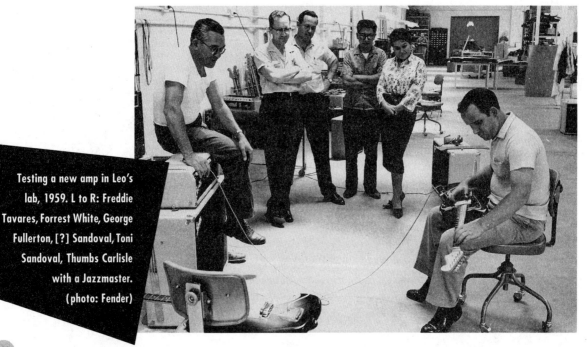

Testing a new amp in Leo's lab, 1959. L to R: Freddie Tavares, Forrest White, George Fullerton, [?] Sandoval, Toni Sandoval, Thumbs Carlisle with a Jazzmaster.
(photo: Fender)

ter. It incorporated my preset tone and volume, rhythm and lead idea along with the idea I had given him about a tremolo locking system.

Leo used body contouring on the new guitar, but he also came up with a new idea of the offset waist. I really didn't know if I liked the looks of the new Jazzmaster or not. I told him that I thought it looked like a pregnant duck when I first saw it, but I finally got used to it and liked the idea. Leo filed for patent protection on the new ideas January 13, 1958, and Patent #2,960,900 was granted on November 22, 1960.

We received the first Fender Sales purchase order for the Jazz-master on August 1, 1958. Production was later that year.

Leo had asked Grady Neal to put up three more cement block buildings, 40' x 120', just like the six we were now using. Construction was started in 1958 and completed in 1959. We had now used up all of the acreage Leo had purchased in early 1953. The company was growing by leaps and bounds. And we were making a nice profit with our incentive and quality program.

Those new cement block buildings were not the only building work Grady Neal did in 1958. He built a new home in Fullerton for Mr. and Mrs. Leo Fender. Joan and I had bought a lot on a cul-de-sac in Fullerton and our home was built in 1957. Then, Leo and Esther bought the lot right across the street from us to build the following year. We were very close friends with Leo and Esther. Leo and Esther told me what they wanted in a home, and I had the pleasure of designing and drawing the floor plans.

During that time, I had been scheduling production meetings in my office every Wednesday at 10:00 a.m. There was much frustration with the results of those meetings because I still had the same problem that Leo had complained to me about when I agreed to help him in management: I could not get the production foreman to accept the responsibility of making decisions to help solve manufacturing problems. Every time I brought up a problem which he should have taken care of, I would get the same answer: "Something should be done about it." That usually was as far as he handled it, and I would have to take time off from my many responsibilities to take care of it. He would say later on (during the G & L period), that he didn't like to be treated "like a puppet on a string." If that were the case, then the

C. L. FENDER

GUITAR

Filed Jan. 13, 1958

2,960,900

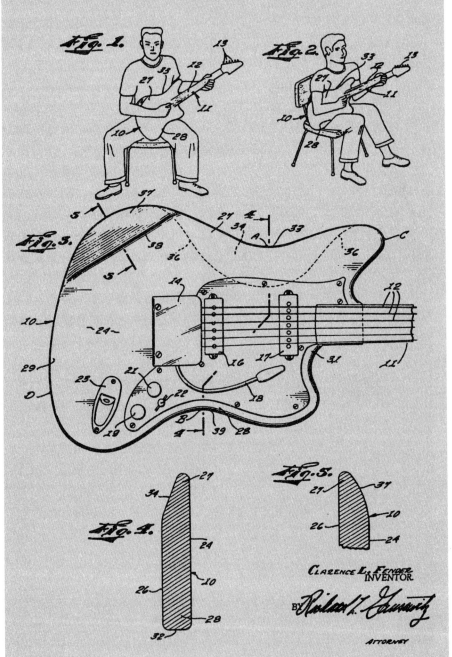

string must have been broken. (I was told that this reluctance to accept responsibility was an issue again in later years at other companies.)

I'll tell you a story about Freddie Tavares that ties in with the same problem. Freddie was usually very mild in nature, gushing with enthusiasm and telling clean, funny stories. Occasionally though, he would become upset about something; and, if he was really upset, he would jump, flat-footed, up and down. At my request, he always attended the weekly production meetings in case we had a question about how he and Leo were coming along with new projects, or if we had a problem with manufacturing something they had designed. One day after our meeting, it was very obvious that Freddie was upset. He waited until everyone else had left my office, and then I found out in a hurry what was bothering him. He said, "Forrest, you make me so mad. Why do you always insist on repeating the same problem over and over?"

It was not quite that bad. I said, "Freddie, there is a very good reason why I always open the meeting by discussing any manufacturing problem we may have, bring up the subject again around the middle of the meeting, then close the meeting by reminding our key people about the problem." I asked him if he remembered some of the meetings we had a few weeks prior to the one held today. I had asked what had been done about the manufacturing problems we had discussed in our last meetings. A few said they had not even heard about them. I said, "Now, Freddie, you know the reason why I repeat the problem. Perhaps everyone will hear about them at least one time during each meeting." From that time on Freddie never complained about the repetition. He told me he understood and thought I was right. The jumping was taken care of, temporarily.

I am so thankful I had the opportunity to have lunch with Freddie a few months before he passed away. I am not sure if he knew then that he had the health problem that called him away. If he knew, he certainly did not say anything about it. He had had an interesting life, and I thought he had told me most of the unusual things he had done. During that lunch he told me a couple of things I hadn't heard before. He said he was the one who had played the ukulele in Elvis Presley's movie *Blue Hawaii*. He also said he was the one who played the steel guitar opening for the Looney

Toons cartoons. Words cannot tell you how much I thought of Freddie Tavares. He was my dear friend, and Leo Fender was so fortunate to have his help in research and development.

Design Patent 186,826: Electric Guitar; Clarence L. Fender, Fullerton, CA; Application December 18, 1958, Patented December 8, 1959.

Design Patent 187,001: Bass Guitar; Clarence L. Fender, Fullerton, CA; Application January 6, 1959, Patented January 5, 1960.

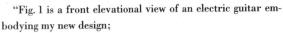

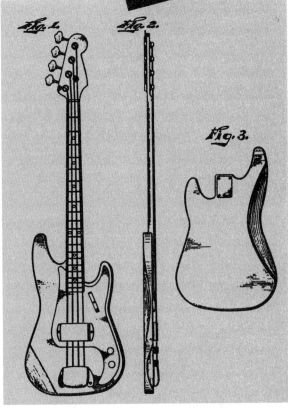

"Fig. 1 is a front elevational view of an electric guitar embodying my new design;

"Fig. 2 is a left side elevational view thereof, portions of the tuning screw means being omitted for convenience of illustration;

"Fig. 3 is a rear elevational view thereof, the tuning screw means being omitted for convenience of illustration; and

"Fig. 4 is an end elevation of the guitar....

"I claim: The ornamental design for an electric guitar, substantially as shown and described."

"Fig. 1 is a front elevational view of a bass guitar showing my new design;

"Fig. 2 is a left side elevational view thereof; and

"Fig. 3 is a rear elevational view showing only the body of the guitar.

"I claim: The ornamental design for a bass guitar, substantially as shown."

FENDER ELECTRIC INSTRUMENT CO., INC.—1959

Many companies become corporations for the tax advantages. Professional people, such as doctors and lawyers, as well as individual entrepreneurs, incorporate for the same reason. You must have officers in a corporation, although their titles do not necessarily mean that their duties or responsibilities must or will change from the way they have been serving the business in the past. In the case of an individual incorporating, a wife, husband, son, or daughter could serve as an officer. Leo Fender knew this when the Fender Electric Instrument Co. filed for incorporation in 1959.

The incorporation was announced in the following article, which appeared in the May 1959 issue of *The Music Trades*.

Leo Fender, President, Fender Inc., 1959.

FORREST WHITE ELECTED V. P.
& GENERAL MANAGER OF FENDER

C. L. Fender, president of the Fender Electric Instrument Co., Fullerton, California, recently revealed the election of the firm's officers and reviewed the company's progress since its founding in 1945 and its plans for the future. Forrest White, plant manager for the past four years, is now vice president and general manager. George Fullerton was elected vice president in charge of production, and Peggy Howland, secretary.

The Fender Electric Instrument Co. has experienced a rapid growth during the past fourteen years under the leadership of C. L. Fender. He pointed out that the number of personnel has increased to more than one hundred since 1945 at which time the company commenced production of Fender Electric Guitars and Amplifiers with four employees.

In keeping with the necessary expansion to meet the needs of Fender dealers throughout the world, the company recently completed four additional modern buildings specially designed for electric guitar and amplifier manufacture. The Fender Electric Instrument Co. now utilizes nine buildings with a total production area of approximately fifty-four thousand square feet.

The company will continue its extensive research activities in electric guitar and amplifier design and construction in order to provide Fender dealers and their customers with the finest electric musical instruments and amplifiers.

Don Randall deserves a lot of credit for keeping his word on a deal he made with his salesmen. He told them what their commission percentage would be when they started with Fender Sales. The sales volume was low in the early years because there was not that much to sell. The different territories had to be built up with new dealers who were not all that anxious to tie in with a new oddball manufacturer who had the gall to attach strings to a toilet seat. Many of those same dealers today are on easy street because they were lucky enough to climb onto the bandwagon of that genius with the gall. They found that the name Fender seemed to have a little magic, and profit, attached to it.

As the years went by and the company grew, the pay of the salesmen was greatly increased. But, take your hat off to Don Randall; he did not cut their commission percentage. They were allowed to grow with the company.

Fender Sales must have liked the looks of the Telecasters with binding around the edges that we made for Buck Owens. We received an order for what they were going to call the Telecaster Custom and Esquire Custom. The purchase order was dated July 23, 1959.

We were anxious to try our new Fred Martin–trained expertise in producing those guitars with edge binding. I have always been grateful to Fred for being so helpful to me in those early years. He seemed to take a liking to me for some reason because he said he had shown me many things in their factory which he had not shown to any other competitor. In my opinion, Fred Martin was one of the giants in the musical instrument business. I am proud to say that he was my friend.

We first started to use the brown Tolex covering material on the amplifiers during the latter part of 1959. The material was made by the General Tire & Rubber Co. from my old home town of Akron. That material was tough as the dickens and could take a lot of abuse, and it was much easier to work with than the tweed material we had been using.

I mentioned that Leo used to cause me a lot of manufacturing problems, even though he didn't do it intentionally. Here is an example: Leo had hired some of our employees as soon as they were barely old enough to work. Two of those exceptionally good employees, Lupe Duarte and Lily Jaimes, had been with him from the day he had formed the company. Remember that Leo Fender, above all, was a perfectionist, and Lupe and Lily both thought he was the next thing to a deity. He had almost spoiled them rotten because, hey, these were his kids; he had practically raised them. (In all seriousness, it gave me a great feeling to know that employees and their employer can show such loyalty to each other.)

United States Patent Office

Des. 192,859
Patented May 22, 1962

192,859

**AMPLIFIER AND LOUDSPEAKER UNIT FOR
ELECTRICAL MUSICAL INSTRUMENTS**

Clarence L. Fender, 221 N. Lincoln, Fullerton, Calif.

Filed June 1, 1959, Ser. No. 56,146

Term of patent 14 years

(Cl. D26—14)

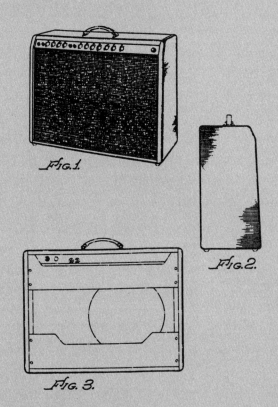

Fig. 1.

Fig. 2.

Fig. 3.

FIGURE 1 is a front perspective view of an amplifier and loudspeaker unit for electrical musical instruments, embodying by new design;

FIGURE 2 is a side elevation of the unit, illustrating the side not shown in FIGURE 1; and

FIGURE 3 is a rear elevation.

The dominant features of the design reside in the portions shown in full lines.

I claim:

The ornamental design for an amplifier and loudspeaker unit for electrical musical instruments, substantially as shown and described.

References Cited in the file of this patent

Radio-Electronic Master, 20th edition, 1956, page B–39: Cabinet DBR–2 illustrated at A; page B–39: 3-in-1 cabinet UC–3 illustrated at D; page M–36: Power supply 12RS6D; page U–107: Pointer knob 1000SS.

Lupe and Lily had been wiring guitar small parts assemblies and amplifier chassis from day one. Their work was outstanding. When Leo had a new project he was working on, he would have them do the wiring for him. There were many production runs of the larger professional amplifiers that had electronic design changes made right in the middle of the run. Leo would get an idea that he thought would improve the performance of the amplifier, and he would go direct to Lupe or Lily and have them make the wiring change.

Now, you must remember, Lupe or Lily would be the only ones to know about the change. Let's say you are the one who checks a final-wired amplifier chassis to see if the performance is okay before it is mounted into the cabinet. One of the important test checks is to make sure the voltage is at a certain level at the various predetermined checkpoints. Now you have been cruising along just fine and the voltage on every chassis has been checking out on the nose. Then, it happens. You receive a chassis that will not check out—voltages are different. You are on an incentive plan that pays well for the number of perfect chassis you check. You know you cannot pass it on to the next operation for cabinet mounting, because you have to put your numbered stamp of approval on it. If it is found to be defective after it has been purchased, guess who they come back to asking why?

This was a problem that had been happening often. Final-checking the wired chassis was one thing, but there were other problems when these "Leo, on-the-spot changes" were made. I had to keep a balanced parts inventory at all times. Some of his changes threw my "parts required per chassis" figures out the window.

Dick Stout was my amplifier department supervisor. One day one of those quickie changes had been made and he had not been told about it. My office door flew open and in he came, absolutely unglued. He said, "Forrest, I have had it. I have been trying to final-check a Bassman chassis for over two hours, and then I find out that Leo had Lupe make another change without me knowing about it. I cannot work like this anymore."

Dick was ready to walk out the door. He was a heck of a good electronics man and he was doing a darn good job of running his department in an efficient manner. I could not afford to lose him. I said, "Dick, I don't blame you for being upset, I don't like it either and I promise you I will take care of the problem immediately." I asked him to sit down and take it easy for a few minutes, and I started a conversation with him that had nothing to do with workday problems. Before long he had settled down and was ready to go back to the amplifier department. Thank God, I had been able to keep a good employee for the time being. Now I had to make sure the same thing did not happen again, or he would not have confidence in what I told him in the future. I knew that he would expect swift action to be taken and he deserved that kind of support. This is how I took care of his problem and created one of my own.

NOTICE

ANY EMPLOYEE WHO MAKES CHANGES IN GUITAR OR AMPLIFIER ASSEMBLY WITHOUT CLEARING IT THROUGH HIS OR HER IMMEDI-ATE SUPERVISOR IS SUBJECT TO IMMEDIATE TERMINATION.

Forrest White

I took the notice out personally and tacked it on the bulletin board in the amplifier department, and called Dick over to look at it. He read it and asked if it would be all right if he took his vacation early—like immediately. I said not to worry, it would be okay. I didn't tell him that I was thinking about taking my own vacation early—like immediately—also.

Friend, it didn't take any longer than a dose of salts takes to go through a tin horn before my office door flew open again, and this time it wasn't Dick. It was Leo. If you think Dick had been unglued, you ain't seen unglued like Leo was unglued. It was one of the few times I saw him when he couldn't think of what to say. I can tell you it wasn't "Hello, how are you?" It was more like this…in fact exactly like this: "[Expletive], you would think that since this is my company I should be able to do as I [expletive] well please!"

I innocently asked, "Is there something wrong, Leo?" Now my innocent-sounding question didn't help the situation at all. He seemed even more unglued as he replied, "You know very well what's wrong. It's that [expletive] notice on the bulletin board."

I said, "Okay, I'll take it down if you want to lose our amplifier department supervisor. Then, too, you will have to assume the responsibility of running the company because I can't do my job effectively either, if you have no respect for organization."

He looked at me sort of funny and was real quiet for a minute or two. He sat down and said, "I guess you are right." The notice stayed on the bulletin board. Dick was happy. The assembly workers were happy. I was relieved. Leo was…I really don't know how he was. But it solved the problem.

I had to fight my friend at times to help him. It reached the point where, if there was a loud noise, Freddie would say, "That's just Leo explaining something to Forrest." You must remember that Leo and I would never get mad at each other personally. Our disagreements were always over how to get the job done. He didn't like anything whatsoever to interfere with his pet project of R&D. I knew him well enough, though, to know that he would be looking with interest at the bottom line of our financial report each month, and that I had to fight like the dickens to protect my management priorities.

The 1950s proved to be an outstanding period in Fender history. Our growth rate was phenomenal. It was quite obvious that our employees felt proud to be associated with a company which had virtually turned the music world upside down with innovations in sound. By now almost everyone interested in music knew that a Fender was not necessarily an extremity on the side of a car. Leo had been elevated from our competitors' "oddball" classification to the "where does that guy get all those ideas" status. You must know that I personally was very proud of the association with my sparring partner–friend Leo. What wonderful years those were for me.

Nineteen-sixty ushered in the newly designed Fender Jazz Bass. Some may wonder, why the Jazz Bass? Leo Fender, the everlasting perfectionist, learned to listen to musicians' comments in the early years, and that trait led to his personal obsession with "how can I make it better and more widely accepted?" Don Randall deserves much more credit than he has been given for feeding to Leo musicians' ideas that he had received through the Fender dealers and worldwide distributors. The Jazz Bass is a good example. Even though the Precision Bass was acclaimed worldwide, the Jazz Bass offered that little bit extra for those musicians who desired it: the more elaborate tone control system, offering a mellow jazz tone mix; the two 8-magnet pickups, redesigned for this instrument; individual string mutes; a neck that was more narrow at the nut; and the popular offset waist design that had been introduced with the Jazzmaster guitar.

Our first purchase order from Fender Sales for the Jazz Bass was dated March 3, 1960.

They say that gentlemen prefer blonds (I personally prefer my brunette), and it would seem that many musicians in particular preferred blonds in the early 1960s, based on the amount of orders we received for blond instruments. They were more expensive though. We had to charge 5% more for a blond model. (The "makeup" on our blonds was not Revlon, however. It was DuPont Duco lacquer.)

I have mentioned that Speedy West has been a dear friend of mine for many years. Speedy had a style of playing the pedal steel guitar that I have never heard anyone successfully imitate. The guy was just plain great. How good was he? Well, he played the pedal steel guitar on Bing Crosby's big hit on Decca (Personality Series) of "Y'all Come." Bing liked the job Speedy did so well that he asked Speedy to guest on his very first national television show. They were on stage in the spotlight when Speedy played and Bing sang "Y'all Come" just like they had recorded it.

Speedy was signed to Capitol Records, but he was in such great demand that he backed up artists on all of the major record labels. Coming out of Capitol one day, he ran into singing cowboy Tex Ritter. Tex had a little habit of making a snorting sound at times before he spoke, and he gave out a little snort and said, "Ha! You little curly haired [expletive], I finally heard a record today that you weren't on." (More about Tex and his relationship with Leo and me later on.)

Speedy had a slight stroke a few years ago and he still has so much pain in his right arm that he is unable to play his steel guitar anymore. Other than his right arm, he is in great health. He played a significant part in a period of very important growth for Fender in 1960. Here are his own words to tell you about it:

I was hired in 1960 to come back to Tulsa, Oklahoma. Fender Sales was building a big warehouse here, an outlet for better distribution, to serve the dealers in 37 states more efficiently.

I was hired to become the manager of that warehouse distribution point. It proved to be a great opportunity for me. I had never done anything like that before but I worked hard at it. Personnel at Fender Sales helped me to get my feet on the ground and it all worked out successfully.

Roy Lanham and Speedy West demonstrating Fender instruments, with Charley and Joan Anderson (Fender dealers) in the Palmer House display room at the 1961 Chicago NAMM show.

There were times when I would go back out to California and I recall that Leo, Forrest, and I would go out for lunch and they would inform me about any new products they were working on, and would ask me if I had any ideas that would help on their development. After lunch we would go back to the factory and they would show me the new products they were working on. They would hook one up so that I could hear the sound of it and then ask for my input. It made me feel real good that they wanted my opinion.

I had a great relationship with Leo Fender, Forrest White and Don Randall. Fender was a great company to work for. I feel, most definitely, that my life was enriched by knowing that ingenious man Leo Fender, and we were friends for over 40 years, from the very start of the Company, in his little Radio Shop, until the end of his life. He will be missed forever but never forgotten.

Speedy West

I am grateful to Speedy for his kind remarks and for the commendable job he did for Fender when he managed the warehouse in Tulsa. He said Don used to visit Tulsa quite often. He expected Don to tell him what he wanted done and if there were any changes to be made. However, Don never asked for any changes. He would always tell Speedy to keep on running it the way he had been, and that he wished the sales office in Santa Ana were running as smoothly. Speedy has a great deal of respect for Don; knowing Don as well as I do, I can understand why.

When a company is small, it is not too susceptible to the scrutiny of outside interests such as union organizers and various government departments. If that company shows continued growth and profitability, then it seems that many on the outside want to offer, and sometimes insist on, helping management make day-to-day decisions. As I mentioned, by the middle of 1956 I had installed the first incentive plan throughout the company and it was quite successful. The employees were happy with it because they were making more money than they would be able to at other companies in the area. And because their productivity had increased considerably with the incentive plan, Fender had started to show a decent profit margin. This became known to some of those outside interests, and they wanted to be cut in on the action.

The first unions grew out of the sweatshops operated by many companies during the industrial revolution. Their employees were poorly paid and mistreated. Working conditions were abominable, compared with what is acceptable today. The only alternative was for the employees to unite in trying to improve those improprieties. And so employee unions were born in self-defense.

I find no fault with employees belonging to a union if they feel it is necessary to protect their rights and improve conditions. I believe, though, that the original intent of organized labor has been tainted by the influx of undesirable beings who are interested in their own monetary gains, rather than the welfare of the employees they are supposed to represent. Sadly enough, the employee would be better off not to become involved with that kind of a sham.

This is exactly how our employees felt about outside union representation in 1956 when we were beginning to be bombarded with union organizers. The employees knew they were making more money by working with our incentive system than we would be able to afford paying them on a straight hourly basis, as would be demanded by a union. Unions are usually very much opposed to incentive systems.

I was working at my desk in the office one afternoon in 1956, and suddenly a piece of paper was stuck under my nose. A rough voice said, "Here, sign this. I'm going to be to be representing your employees."

I looked up, and here before me stood a rough-looking character, about 6' 4" tall, weighing around 225 pounds. I said, "Who are you and how did you get in here?"

He answered, "My name is [expletive] and I represent the [expletive] union. I walked in through the side gate and through the door at the end of the building."

I told him I would not sign anything without first discussing it with our attorney. I then told him that he was trespassing and for him to get his posterior out of my office before I called the police.

I meant what I said about calling the police. I didn't mean what I said about not signing anything until I discussed it with our attorney, because we didn't have one. We hadn't been able to afford an attorney before the middle of 1956. I had been making all the decisions until then— legal and otherwise. But we could afford one now. Especially after that big goon had walked into my office unannounced. So I looked for one and I found a good one. Expensive though. His name was Bill Walsh from Los Angeles. He had been an attorney for the Metro-Goldwyn-Mayer movie studio, and he had known Clark Gable and many other big stars in the heyday years of Hollywood. The thing of importance, though, was that he was the one who had written the guidelines for the installation of the United States National Labor Relations Board for the Los Angeles area.

Things were rough back in the fifties if you were an employer and strayed from the straight and narrow guidelines of the Labor Board. If you said "Boo" the wrong way to an employee it could be interpreted as being an infringement of his rights. I honestly got called before the Labor Board for telling a Cuban employee to quit singing Castro's praises because I was afraid the guys in the woodshop were going to kick his teeth in if he didn't stop.

I asked the older, long-service employees if they wanted me to recognize that union guy as their representative. They hit the ceiling. They hired an attorney and formed their own union which they called the United Industrial Employees of California (UIEC). They felt a lot better about their protection from outside union interference with their own union, and it had been sanctioned by the Labor Board. But the organizers did not let up. They kept trying to get their foot in the door, and it really became hot again in 1961. I was accused of many things, yet I had to be very careful of what I said, because the Labor Board seemed to let union organizers get away with murder while the employer was supposed to keep his mouth shut. Infringement of "rights," you know.

By 1961 we had quite a few employees. We were working out of eleven buildings by now—the nine that Leo had Grady Neal build and two more across the street. One was used for a service center and the other for parts storage.

I certainly did not want the new employees to think that what was being said by the outside union organizers was true. We had our company reputation to think of and I didn't want to contend with a morale problem. And the thing that really bugged me was that I felt our government was turning into a Gestapo operation against employers.

Now you must understand that I could not expect any comfort or advice from Leo. He absolutely refused to become involved with our management problems. And regardless of any stories you may have read or heard about, I was the one who was under the gun and had to make all of the management decisions during those years before CBS.

I was not allowed, under Labor Board guidelines, to discuss the harassment from the organizers with our employees. I would be accused of infringing on their rights to hear what the union organizers had to say. I didn't give a darn what they heard. The thing that burned me up was that I wasn't supposed to say anything in our defense. I decided to say something in the form of a bulletin. The association mentioned was our employees union UIEC. They had asked me to do something, and the outside union heard about it and filed charges. Here is a copy of my bulletin:

November 8, 1961

NOTICE TO ALL EMPLOYEES

We have issued this notice with the assumption that we are still permitted our constitutional right of free speech in America.

We believe that it is only fair to you employees that we are permitted to express our opinion and to be able to give you the true facts on the action we have taken toward certain controversial issues.

1. We have not been encouraging membership in any association. We took certain action that we were requested to take on a particular issue. We found that this was a mistake and we corrected that mistake.

2. We have not been rendering unlawful support to any associations or organization.

3. We never threatened to close our plant for any reason. We believe that the employee should choose what he may feel is to his best interest.

Please consider the fact that there is no law that compels a man to take the risks, and to work the long hours, that are necessary to establish a successful business, which in turn creates a means of living for those who accept his offer of employment. Understand, that during the early days, when the going is rough, there is no one who is willing to offer a helping hand, financially or otherwise. The irony of this story is that when he has become successful, then various outside interests are waiting to tie him up with red tape and to dictate his every move.

Reference: Webster's New Collegiate Dictionary:

"FREE ENTERPRISE — Freedom of private business to organize and operate for profit in a competitive system without interference by government beyond regulation necessary for keeping the national economy in balance."

(No comment)

We have the greatest country on earth. May God grant that we are able to hang on to the freedom that we all love so dearly, a freedom that is, seemingly, slowly slipping away from us day-by-day.

Forrest White

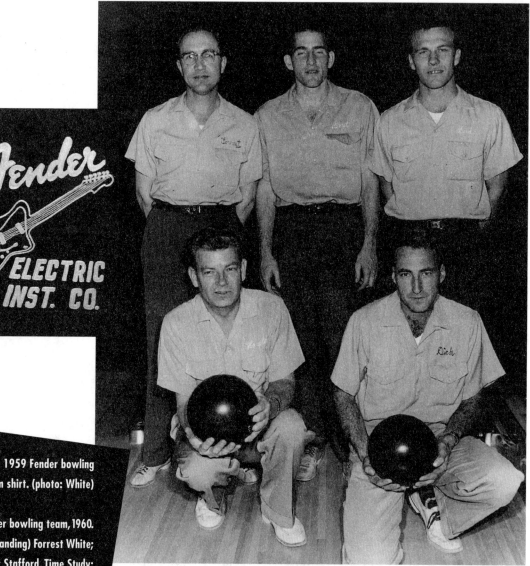

Back of a 1959 Fender bowling team shirt. (photo: White)

The Fender bowling team, 1960. L to R: (standing) Forrest White; Bert Stafford, Time Study; Bud Morgan, Stockroom Supervisor; (front) Harold Rhodes; Dick Stout.

I was honestly surprised that the Labor Board didn't raise the devil over the bulletin. Things seemed to smooth out after that and the outside interference died away. There were five major unions that tried to organize the Fender Electric Instrument Co. during the period of my management. None was successful.

During the time I was busy with my problems, Leo came up with the Fender Bass VI. This was a 6-string bass guitar, produced because of the popularity of the "Nashville Sound." My friend Harold Bradley told me that the new sound they were talking about was coming from a 6-string bass guitar made by the Danelectro Corporation. He had been playing that instrument on recordings made at Bradley's Barn, a studio owned by his brother Owen.

Leo introduced another product in 1961: the "piggyback" amplifier, with speaker and chassis in separate cabinets. The weight was now distributed between two cabinets, and it was a tremendous help to the musician moving his amplifier from one job to another.

I believe it is good policy for a company to support outside interests for their employees. In 1959, Fender sponsored its first bowling teams. I was allowed to bowl on one of the teams, and my teammates were kind enough to help me struggle through the first bowling season. Our piano man Harold Rhodes and I attended a bowling clinic for those interested in the fall 1961 bowling leagues. A person named Ray Winchell was instructing, and I was impressed with the ease with which he taught the basic fundamentals of the game. He was soft-spoken, with a pleasing personality, and Harold and I both thought he would be a good prospect for an employee. I was constantly looking for good employees because of our rapid growth. I asked Ray if he would be interested in discussing the possibility of employment with us, and to make a long story short, he joined Fender in September 1961.

Ray started in production at Fender but, like all of us, he wanted to improve himself. He left Fender in 1984 for a position in the Credit Department at Rolandcorp US. Ray was proficient in his new vocation and before long his peers elected him President of the Music Group's National Credit Managers Association. Ray returned to Fender a little later, and I will tell you how and when. At that time, you will learn why I am proud to be the one who brought him on board.

In 1962, Fender Sales was able to show my all-time favorite Fender guitar, the Jaguar, at the summer trade show in Chicago. The reason I like it so well is because it has a 24" scale and I have a small hand. It was just a lot easier for me to play than the Telecaster and the Stratocaster, which had the Fender standard 25½" scale length. This was Roy Lanham's favorite gui-

Roy Lanham with his Jaguar, 1962. Roy and Speedy teamed up to demonstrate Fender guitars and amplifiers at many Chicago music shows through the years.

tar also because it had the shorter scale neck. I am proud to own a 1964 pre-CBS Fender Jaguar guitar and I intend to keep it.

Harold Rhodes had reason to feel proud at that 1962 show. You will remember he joined Fender in the fall of 1955 with his electric piano prototype. He and Leo still hadn't perfected it, but they had come up with a new instrument—the Fender-Rhodes Piano Bass. This keyboard bass instrument would allow a piano player to play "bass" with his left hand, and it would become popular with small combos. Dealers got to see the Fender-Rhodes Piano Bass for the first time at the summer trade show. Harold's electric piano was soon to come.

You may wonder why it took from the fall of 1955 until the summer of 1962 to show the first Fender-Rhodes keyboard product when Leo had normally been knocking out a new product in around three months' time. Leo was dividing his R&D time between the demand for new stringed instruments and amplifiers and the demand for keyboard products. He would have had a keyboard product ready for production in a much shorter time if he had been making all of the decisions. Leo was the boss and could have made those decisions, but he had consideration for Harold. Harold is a great guy but he is also a dreamer. No matter what the design problem was, big or small, he thought a better answer (than the one we had) was just over the hill and we would probably find it tomorrow. He was conscientious and had good intentions of getting the job done. But his constant procrastination caused much frustration for Leo, Don Randall, the salesmen, the Fender dealers—and let's not forget the general manager.

CHAPTER 12

THE FENDER ACOUSTIC GUITAR

An unusual development occurred within our company in 1962. Would you believe the Fender Electric Instrument Co. name would not seem entirely appropriate from now on? Leo decided to venture into "non-electric" acoustic guitar manufacturing. He hired Roger Rossmeisl to help develop a new line of acoustic instruments. Roger had been employed by Rickenbacker for several years and had designed many instruments. He had been trained in the art of musical instrument making in his native Germany and was an excellent craftsman. You will note that I said Roger would "help" develop. Leo would personally become very much involved with the research and development of the new line.

Another unusual development happened in 1962. It was the most embarrassing thing that happened to me during my employment at Fender. At the trade show in Chicago in June 1961: I was elected to serve on the Board of Directors of an association which was then known as the National Association of Musical Merchandise Manufacturers, Inc. (It is now known as the Guitar and Accessories Marketing Association [GAMA].) Now this happened with Leo's blessing. I had told him they had asked me to serve on the Board and Leo seemed to like the idea and I had, in turn, told them I would be honored to serve if elected. The vote, I was told, was unanimous.

It so happened that I was the first person west of the Mississippi to have the honor of being elected to the Board. That honor would prove to be short-lived. I have no idea what happened, but shortly after I had been elected, Leo asked me to resign, with no real explanation as to why. I did not press him for an answer because, quite honestly, I was so darn hurt that I didn't care for an explanation. I have given it much thought since then. I still do not know the real reason, but it could have been one of three possibilities:

1. All of the major guitar manufacturers had been asked to periodically turn in their total amount of manufactured units to an accounting firm. From those figures they would come up with a grand total. The name of the company, with the figures they turned in, was to be kept confidential. Now, knowing the grand total of guitar units produced, each company could then learn how they were doing compared to that total. Fender was the only major manufacturer that had refused to give its production figures. Perhaps Leo and Don were afraid I would reveal those figures. If so, they should have trusted me more in knowing I would never do that without their permission.

2. I heard Don was disturbed that I had been elected to the board and had complained to Leo that he thought he should have been the one to represent Fender. I give Don credit for being a bigger man than that and discount that reason.

3. I also had the feeling that Leo thought I might be away from our operation too much attending board meetings.

I still do not know what Leo's reason was to this day. It was difficult for me to inform the Association that I could not accept the directorship after having told them I would be honored to serve. Especially after knowing I was the first one to be elected from the West. I was so embarrassed, I did not attend the 1962 show.

Fender Sales was able to show the first Fender prototype acoustic flat-top guitar at the national music show in Chicago in 1963. They didn't call it a prototype at the show, you understand, but that's really all it was.

The Fender acoustic factory was not ready for any serious manufacturing at this early date. Leo was curious to see what the reaction would be to his idea of how a flat-top acoustic guitar should be
made. Why? Because it was different. What did you expect from
Leo Fender? This probably came as a shock to the "purist" classical
and flat-top acoustic guitar players. The Fender flat-top had a detach-
able screw-on neck with no conventional heel. Horrors! This is the
way he builds his electric "toilet seats" and "canoe paddles" with strings.
And, heavens! this flat-top has an adjustable tube between the neck
block and tail block on the inside of the instrument.

Tex Ritter, one of the singing
cowboys, often visted Fender
in the early years. The guitar in
this photo is a Kingman flat-
top given to him by Forrest.
(photo: White)

Contrary to what you may have read, the main purpose of the
adjustable tube was to give the guitar "backbone" so that the neck would
not pull up with age, making the instrument difficult to play around the
12th fret. This has been a problem with many older flat-top guitars—
expensive or not.

It may be interesting to know that the large Fender flat-top was at
first called King. Dies were made and neckplates were produced using that
name. Later the name was changed to Kingman,
and the engraving was changed on the tooling
accordingly.

I have the original handmade show model
Fender King flat-top acoustic guitar. No serial
number was used. The sides and back are made
of rosewood. The neck has a rosewood cap (fretboard). The top is made of very close-grained
spruce. The closer the grain is, the better the
tone will be on guitars using spruce tops; the
wide-grained spruce tops are used on less expensive instruments.

I can tell you personally that the adjustable tube Leo put in those Fender flat-tops was
effective. The neck on my King has a fantastic
feel. The strings are as close on the full length of
the neck as any expensive Fender electric stan-

Tex Ritter
plays

dard guitar you ever played. The only objection we found to the adjustable tube was that it made the Fender heavier than conventional high-quality flat-top acoustic guitars.

There was one distinct difference between the sound of the Fender and the Martin flat-top acoustic guitars. The Martin sound seemed to surround you up close. The Fender sound projected more than the Martin. You could hear it much farther away. Both instruments had that full, deep bass sound.

I had a good feeling when I went to the music show in 1963 because I thought we had produced enough merchandise to make the salesmen happy. Almost every year, I had been faced with the same problem: We need more merchandise, we are losing sales because we don't have enough to satisfy the dealers. Well, this time I was sure I wouldn't have that problem. We had the new line of flat-top acoustic guitars at the 1963 music show in Chicago, and Fender Sales also displayed the first Fender-Rhodes pianos and celeste.

When I arrived at the 1963 show, though, I found I was in more hot water than ever. I have mentioned that I had never received any back order or inventory figures from Fender Sales, and because of that I had to guess what amplifiers and guitars to make on a day-to-day basis. Almost every salesman or dealer I ran into at the show was singing the blues louder than I had ever heard before. We needed a lot—a heck of a lot—more merchandise. I didn't have the heart to tell them that there was no more room at the factory to increase production. And I sure didn't want to tell them that we had no plans to increase the room at the factory. We hadn't known it was needed at that time. But, now—it was obvious—something had to be done—like immediately.

One week after the show, we had 26,000 additional square feet of production space and, believe it or not, we were up and running in that new space. Proper planning is so important in manufacturing management. Take a close look at what happened in the week after the summer 1963 show:

MONDAY — I left Chicago early in the morning and returned to California. I went to the factory in the afternoon to break the news to Leo.

We were in trouble with the salesmen and dealers and, somehow, I had to have a lot more room to increase production. My poor crystal ball, which I used to guess how much to build, needed a good polishing. Anyhow, I told Leo what we were faced with and here is exactly what he said: "Do whatever you think is necessary to get the job done. It's up to you."

TUESDAY — The Fender Electric Instrument Co. was located in Fullerton, within a mile of Anaheim, where Leo had leased a building for the new acoustic guitar operation. I went over to the Anaheim industrial area looking for additional floor space. There were two 13,000-square-foot buildings available almost next to the acoustic operation and on the same street. I signed the lease for those two buildings, obtained the floor-plan blueprints, and hurried back to my office to try to get caught up on the paperwork which had stacked up while I was attending the music show. I went down to Leo's lab that evening and told him what I had done and he seemed pleased. I took the blueprints home with me and started to work. I planned to move the entire amplifier cabinet and covering department. I drew to ¼-scale where to place every piece of equipment in those two buildings. I gave exact locations for all 120/220 electric outlets, electric dropcords for machine hook-ups, air lines, and everything else that was required for our manufacturing operations. Those drawings were completed before I went to bed that night.

WEDNESDAY — I had called Tuesday and made arrangements to have electricians, plumbers, and carpenters on the job at the new buildings at 8:00 a.m. Wednesday. They were on time, they received the drawings, began to work...everything on schedule. I told Roger Rossmeisl I planned to be in full production in those new buildings next Monday morning. He said I was crazy. It helps to be at times.

THURSDAY — All electricians, plumbers, and carpenters at work and on schedule. Roger still thought I was crazy.

FRIDAY — Full steam and on schedule at the new buildings. Our working hours at the Fullerton factory were from 8:00 a.m. to 4:30 p.m., with a ten-minute break at 10:00 a.m., lunch at 12:00 to 12:30 p.m., and another ten-minute break at 3:00 p.m. We sent all of the amplifier cabinet and covering department production employees home at the 3:00 p.m.

break. The department supervisors and I unhooked all of the heavy equipment, routers, disc sanders, dove-tail machine, band saws, glue machines, etc.

SATURDAY — The department supervisors were at the factory early. Anaheim Truck and Transfer arrived with large flat-bed trucks to pick up our heavy equipment, cabinet lumber, etc. Everything was hauled to the new buildings and all machinery was placed in its proper location. Electricians and plumbers were there to hook everything up. The cabinet lumber was stacked in place.

SUNDAY — Any loose ends were taken care of by noon, and the supervisors and I had the afternoon to rest—and celebrate.

MONDAY MORNING — We were in full production in the new buildings as planned, with only 1½ hours production time lost the previous Friday afternoon. Roger told me he had to take his hat off to me. I thought maybe he would tell me that he didn't think I was crazy after all. But he didn't mention it. In case you are interested, Leo said, "I'm not surprised," as he kept working on an amplifiier chassis. Just what did you expect? Remember, my friend told me that he would take care of his problems and I was to take care of mine. He did break down that evening, though. He laughed, and told me he thought it was a fine job. One thing about Leo, he didn't want you to become satisfied with yourself to the point of letting down on performance. He never did himself.

Eddie Miller on right, demonstrating the Fender Kingman backstage at Grand Ole Opry, 1963. (photo: White)

I attended the "bash" in Nashville again that fall. The Fender Sales display room had been moved down to a large room off of the lobby at the Andrew Jackson Hotel. This was the first time that room had been available and it was quite an improvement.

The Andrew Jackson Hotel, 1963. (photo: White)

On Saturday afternoon a young man came in and told me he would like to try our Fender Stratocaster guitar. He played up a storm on a couple of tunes. I asked him where he was from and he said the Los Angeles area and that he was a staff musician at Capitol Records. He told me he was interested in playing Fender equipment. I walked over and told Don about

L to R: Billy Byrd, Don Randall, Harold Bradley at the Andrew Jackson in 1963. (photo: White)

Buddy Emmons in the Fender display room with the "2000" 10-string doubleneck, 1963. (photo: White)

the young man, that he was a great musician, great personality, staff musician at Capitol Records, interested in promoting Fender equipment. Don said, "No, I don't think so. Guys like that are a dime a dozen." I went back over to the young man and, after asking him his name, told Glenn Campbell that I was sorry but Fender Sales had enough promotion musicians at the present time. I believe Glenn has earned quite a few dimes since then—with a competitor's equipment.

I don't mean to sound as though I am picking on Don, because he did a heck of a good job promoting Fender merchandise through the years. I still think he was the best thing that ever happened to Leo Fender (other than his first wife Esther).

Harold Bradley with the Fender Bass VI and Twin Amp, Nashville, 1963. (photo: White)

Leo Fender and Freddie Tavares on Freddie's 10th aniversary at Fender, 1963. (photo: White)

I mentioned that we began sponsoring bowling teams in 1959; we later started an employee bowling tournament and continued it for several years. The tournament lasted four weeks in the spring and four in the fall. We bowled three games each Saturday morning and the tournament was set on a handicap basis so that the women and men employees had an equal opportunity to win. We gave out trophies for High Individual Game, High Team Game, High Individual Series, and High Team Series. We had a very good employee/management relationship in those early years.

Fred Fullerton and Leo Fender in Leo's lab, 1963. (photo: White)

I also made arrangements with a local theater to honor a pass, providing admission for two persons, which was enclosed with a birthday greeting we mailed to each employee every year.

The year 1964 meant a lot for the Fender Electric Instrument Co. It was the year the popular, moderately low-cost Mustang Guitar was introduced at the national music show. The Mustang was available with a 22" or 24" scale. The 24" scale was the same length that had been used on the Jaguar in 1962. Leo had already been working on a companion Mustang Bass, which would be introduced a little later.

One of the main reasons I wrote this book was to set the record straight as to what really happened in the early years at Fender and to give you a better insight into Leo Fender, the man. There were many sides to Leo, depending on the occasion and his mood at the time. Did he have a sadistic side? No! Not as far as personally causing pain or discomfort to another. How about a sadistic nature in becoming amused when a person accidentally caused pain or discomfort to themselves? Let's see what Speedy West can personally tell you about that:

Leo on his latest "Aquafen" boat in 1965. (photo: White)

Leo Fender wasn't sports minded. For years after he could afford to play golf, or whatever, he just didn't care for that sort of thing. However, he finally became interested in boating. He bought a yacht...a big yacht... and he loved it.

Sometimes on weekends he would go over to Catalina Island. I was fortunate enough that he occasionally invited my family and me to go with him and his wife Esther.

I remember one trip in particular. It seems funny now...but it was not at the time...at least to me...but it sure was to Leo. We went over to Catalina and he had a tie down rope (buoy) to the bottom of the ocean. The yacht was so big he couldn't get any closer to the shore. He always pulled a dingy (small boat) behind his yacht, maybe it was 8' or 10' long, I don't know, and it had a small outboard motor. That was how we got to the shore if we needed groceries, or whatever.

This one time we decided to go to shore for something. We started back to the yacht, walked out on the dock, and Leo got into the dingy. The dock was wet from the waves. I stepped down off the dock to get into the dingy and I fell. I'm telling you it took the hide off of my leg from my knee to my ankle. Just skinned my leg something terrible. The blood was flying and I was in terrible pain. Leo started laughing, he thought that was the funniest thing he had ever seen. Through the years, he mentioned many times how amused he was over that incident.

Speedy West

Christmas Eve at the Fender residence. L to R: Leo, Esther, Joan, Forrest, Curtis. (photo: Fender)

Speedy knew that Leo Fender was one of his best friends, and that he would have laughed at that little accident (big to Speedy) no matter who it was. One time, Joan and I went with Leo and Esther to Catalina. We went ashore, and while we were walking, poor Esther's feet slipped out from under her and she took a hard fall. Leo thought that was funny too, but Esther didn't. She really told him off. And he thought that was funny also. My good friend Leo, with his many facets of temperament.

The year 1964 found us busy as the dickens at the factory, and I was still trying to guess what they were out of at Fender Sales so we would be producing the right mix of amplifiers and guitars to ensure a balanced finished goods inventory. I wished Don could have understood the problem he was causing me.

The only custom guitar we made from scratch to a musician's specifications in those early years at Fender was in 1964, for Jerry Byrd, whom I had written to about my 10-string in 1949. I had met Jerry at the Palmer House Hotel in Chicago at one of the music shows when he was demonstrating Rickenbacker steel guitars. F. C. Hall was gracious enough to let me spend as much time as I wanted to in his display room so that I could hear Jerry play. During the many years we had been friends I never asked Jerry to play a Fender steel guitar, out of respect for him and F. C. Finally, in early 1964, Jerry asked me if I would have a Fender guitar made for him according to his specifications. I told him I would consider it an honor, and all he had to do was tell me exactly how he wanted it made. I then explained why I had never asked him to play Fender, but I am sure he had known all along. A picture of the steel guitar we made for Jerry Byrd is on the cover of his excellent album *Satin Strings of Steel* (Monument SLP18033 Stereo).

I would like to again state that I consider F. C. Hall to be a good personal friend. In all the years I have known him he has been very courteous to me. Much has been said about F. C. in this book, and I hope you understand the things I have written about in those early years were the way things actually happened and not just my opinion.

In the fall of 1964 Leo seemed more quiet than usual. In fact, after I got to thinking about it, this quiet side of Leo had first become noticeable around the middle part of the year, and it became more evident as time went by. He didn't have much to say before I left for Nashville in October for the annual WSM bash, and he was even more quiet after I returned. He seemed to be leaving the factory more than he normally did, and the pace in the lab had slowed down considerably. I asked Freddie if he had noticed that Leo seemed awfully quiet for some reason. Freddie said that

Jerry Byrd with his Fender Custom steel guitar, 1965. This is the only instrument Forrest ever had custom made for anyone while he was at Fender.

Group on set of "Bonanza" in Hollywood, 1964. L to R: Marty Robbins, Charlie Aldridge, Dan "Hoss" Blocker, Forrest White, Lorne "Pa Cartright" Greene. Hoss owned and played a Fender Stratocaster.

he had noticed it and that he didn't think Leo had quite the drive in research and development that he once had. It was quite puzzling to some of us, to say the least.

One evening in late December, I went down to the lab and there was Leo seated at his workbench with his head close to the small electric heater he always had on the bench. He was holding his jacket up close to his neck trying to get relief from his sinus condition. This condition seemed to bother him more during the rainy cold days in fall and winter. (At least I can say it was cold compared with average California weather.) It was obvious that he should have been home in bed rather than at his workbench. He forced himself to continue working many times when he should have been resting. Leo would not give up. He seemed possessed with the idea that he had to be there at his post regardless of how he felt physically. I guess it must have been hard for him to forget those earlier days when he could hardly keep his head above water financially.

He said, "Sit down, I have something to tell you. You know I haven't been able to shake this sinus condition, and I think it's time for me to get out. Don and I have been talking to CBS Records about them buying the company." This explained a lot of things in a hurry. I told him I could understand why he would feel that way because of his health, even though it was hard for me to get the words out of my mouth.

He explained the whole deal to me and the fact that Don Randall would be in charge of the operation for CBS. They would take over on January 5, 1965. I first thought of what he had told me after the company had incorporated in 1959 and we had become officers. He said, "You shouldn't be too concerned about long hours now because someday you will be running the place." I didn't know why he should have said anything to me about the long hours because I had always been there early to open the doors in the morning, and made sure the doors were all locked before I went home at night. I had put in many 12-hour and some 18-hour days. I was usually there every Saturday and many times on Sunday. The only time I wasn't was if I was on a trip for the company.

There were a few working days left in December, and on one of them a new man showed up at the lab. Don had hired Paul Spranger, an electronics engineer. He was to be in charge of research and development for the new CBS/Fender. He had started before the actual CBS takeover because Don wanted him to spend a few days with Leo before he left at the end of the month. Paul had been employed in the aerospace industry. He was supposed to be well versed in audio engineering; however, he had absolutely no experience in mechanical aspects of designing and producing the sound musicians wanted in their amplifiers. This would prove to be what I consider Don Randall's worst mistake in all his years with Fender.

Monday evening, January 4, 1965, I went down to see Leo in his lab for the last time. We both found it difficult to act nonchalant. I helped him carry his personal belongings out to his car, pretended not to notice the tears in his eyes, hoped he hadn't noticed mine. He got into his car and I walked to the side gate. He stopped briefly on his way out, paused and said, "I don't know what I would have done without you." I wish I could tell you what those words meant to me. He stepped on the gas and was out the gate before I could answer. That was the last time I would let him out the gate as I had done so many times before. I watched until his car was out of sight.

And so, the curtain closed, ending the most wonderful years of my life.

CHAPTER 13

CBS/FENDER
MUSICAL
INSTRUMENTS—
1965

FENDER GUITAR COMPANY ACQUIRED BY COLUMBIA RECORDS
DISTRIBUTION CORP.— December 22, 1964

News from Columbia Records Distribution Corp.

For release January 5

The Fender Guitar Company has been purchased by Columbia
Records Distribution Corp., it was announced today. The purchase price
was $13,000,000.

Fender, a leading manufacturer of electric guitars and amplifiers,
developed the solid-body guitar in 1948. Since then it has continued as a
leader in the musical instruments field and has introduced significant
innovations and striking designs which have been widely adopted by the
industry. The Fender guitar is considered the outstanding instrument of
its type by both professional musicians and amateurs.

The two former principal owners and officers of Fender will continue
their functions with the company. Donald D. Randall will be Vice

President and General Manager of the new Fender Musical Instruments division of Columbia Records Distribution Corp. and C. Leo Fender will continue as special consultant in research and development.

Columbia Records Distribution Corp.
Seventh Ave. New York, N.Y.

The official release from CBS about the acquisition of Fender Sales and Fender Electric Instrument Co., Inc. was quite a surprise to our employees as well as many of our friends in the musical instrument business. Reporters from the local newspaper called early in the day of the release and here is the front-page headline that appeared the following day:

For $13 million
FULLERTON FIRM BOUGHT BY CBS
DAILY NEWS TRIBUNE
Fullerton, California, Wednesday, January 6, 1965

Like the Fender Electric Instrument Co., Inc., the Fullerton *Daily News Tribune* is no longer in business.

We received many telephone calls with questions concerning any contemplated changes in the company organization and policy. Quite honestly, I did not know the answers in the first few days after the change and did not learn what my fate would be until Don Randall called me and invited me to have lunch with him. It was then that I found out some of the disappointing facts of our new way of life.

Don, in my opinion, was always first class in his appearance and in the way he conducted himself. He just plain looked like a successful businessman. He was very gracious at lunch but he seemed a little unsure, even though trying to act optimistic, about what would happen to Fender, and to us personally, since we had been consumed by the CBS behemoth.

I knew that my title of Vice President and General Manager had gone down the drain because Don had that title now. Sure enough, I had been demoted to plant manager again, but that wasn't the worst part. I would be paid less than one-third of what I had been earning before. Don tried to console me by telling me I would still be earning a good salary.

Leo, Esther, Joan, and Forrest, 1968, in front of the Fender home, just across the street from the White home. (photo: Curtis White)

At this point, I would still be in charge of all the duties I had before—just with less pay. My responsibilities would soon be trimmed though, almost as much as my salary had been.

I have told you that Leo and Esther lived across the street from us in Fullerton. One evening, around the middle of January, the doorbell rang and there stood Leo with a big grin on his face. I asked him to come in and he handed me a package. He asked me to open it and his grin grew bigger as I carefully removed the wrapping paper and opened the box. Inside was a beautiful Seth Thomas combination clock and weather barometer. Leo said, "I thought you might like to have it." There was a small brass plaque on the front with these words:

TO: FORREST WHITE

IN APPRECIATION OF MANY THINGS

FROM LEO FENDER

I found it difficult to think of the proper words to express my appreciation to Leo for the beautiful gift. The wording on the plaque was not something I would have expected to come from Leo. Those of us who knew him well will tell you that he was not one to hand out compliments. He seemed so pleased to have given me the gift, and friend, it touched me deeply.

Make no mistake about it, the finance department at CBS carries a big stick. Mr. S. Gartenberg was Vice President of the Columbia Records finance department in 1965, and he reported to Goddard Lieberson, President of Columbia Records. S. Gartenberg was on a higher level in the company than Don Randall was at that time. Even though Don was a vice president, he reported to Executive Vice President Norman A. Adler. S. Gartenberg and Norman Adler were on the same level and they reported to Goddard Lieberson.

S. Gartenberg was responsible for CBS/Fender finance and he appointed a fellow by the name of Harold Travis to manage the finance department at CBS/Fender. It would have been so much better if Harold Travis had been more knowledgeable about problems involving the musical instrument business. Even so, it wasn't long before material control, which included purchasing, was under his direction. It is safe to say that Harold Travis and I had a few disagreements concerning procedures as time went by.

Stan Compton had been Don's right-hand man at Fender Sales, the same position I had as Leo's right-hand man at Fender Electric Instrument Co. Stan now had the title of Assistant General Manager under the new CBS regime.

We had not received very many purchase orders for guitars and amplifiers from Fender Sales the latter part of 1964, but in the first part of 1965 the orders poured in. Perhaps it was because Don was so busy working on the sale to CBS that he did not have the time he ordinarily would have taken to analyze their needs for merchandise. In all fairness to Don, I am sure that working on the sale would have required a lot of study and time. It proved to be worth it, of course, as evidenced by the sale price he negotiated for the company. I know Leo came out a lot better off due to Don's efforts.

I forgot to mention that right after CBS bought our company, some of the New York executives came to California to take their first look at the

Fender operation. Goddard Lieberson was with them and I was pleased to meet him for the first time. Our visitors seemed quite impressed with the factory and the fact that we had been operating out of 29 buildings in Fullerton and Anaheim. I told them that I had to run the factory without back order and finished goods inventory information from Fender Sales all those years prior to their acquisition. They looked at each other with their mouths open and told me they would have considered it impossible to operate like that. I answered that it might have been impossible but that I had no choice in the matter. They were not told about disagreements between Leo and Don.

I finally received figures for the finished goods inventory and back orders from Fender Sales. This was the first time in over ten years that this important information had been given to me. Now I could throw away my crystal ball. I wouldn't have to guess what to build anymore to maintain a balanced inventory. Just try to imagine how much petty disagreements cost the company in dealer and salesman dissatisfaction. It all seems so futile in retrospect. And yet, I am sure each of those two most capable individuals, Leo Fender and Don Randall, thought he had valid reasons for his actions. But it was hard on my digestive system.

Frank Martin, the son of the late Fred Martin of the Martin Guitar Company, visited the plant in early April 1965. I am so fortunate to have had such good friends.

C. F. MARTIN & CO. INC. *manufacturers of guitars, mandolins, ukuleles*

NAZARETH, PENNSYLVANIA • 18064 • PHONE: 215-759-2837 • EST. 1833

April 20, 1965

Mr. Forrest F. White
Fender Electric Instrument Co.
500 South Raymond
Fullerton, California

Dear Forrest:

Frank is back, and to say that he is enthusiastic about what he saw in Southern California, and especially at your plant, is an understatement. He was deeply impressed not only with the facilities you showed him but with your cordial hospitality in all respects. I want you to know that I am grateful to you personally for this evidence of your courtesy and friendly spirit.

We here take pride in the cordial relations we have had with you, and other members of your firm, from the beginning; and we are delighted to know that your business has grown and prospered far beyond expectations 20 years ago.

With best wishes for the future, we remain --

Yours cordially,

C. Frederick Martin

CFM/jb

Along the way to success, we had much help from many good suppliers and from those who offered specialty services. I really don't know what we would have done without one of those most special companies: Race and Olmsted, Tool & Die. Lyman Race and Karl Olmsted made all of our special power tooling and dies through the early years at Fender. When we needed something in a hurry, which was for every new product Leo designed, he would quickly call for Lyman or Karl and they were usually there within the hour to find out what the latest rush job was all about. It didn't require much effort on their part to get to Leo's lab in a hurry. They had built their tool and die shop across the alley from the back door of Leo's Lab building. I can't begin to tell you how important they were in helping with the development of our new products. No matter what we had to make, they came up with good ideas on how to tool for producing the parts.

Lyman for many years always called me "The man behind the man," referring, of course, to Leo. Lyman and Karl were our good friends, as well as offering us the best in tool and die service.

For many years we had used Kluson Patent Heads (keys) on the guitars, and we had to trim the ends off of the metal cover so they would fit on the six-in-row head of the neck. We left one end on the cover that we used for the first and sixth string keys. The ends of the covers were trimmed with the use of dies that were mounted on one of our small punch presses. Our metal shop was complete, and we made all of our own steel parts.

When CBS bought Fender, one of the first things Don wanted to do, and I thought was a great idea, was for us to make our own keys. I told Don I had an idea for a design that would eliminate the problem we had in mounting the Kluson keys. I made a drawing showing the case with the ends cut on an angle. The keys could then be mounted with the use of two screws and, of course, no end clipping was required. I gave the drawing to Lyman, and the new Fender Key cases were made to the design with the big Fender *F* stamped on the top. As far as I know, Fender Musical Instruments is still making keys that way. I know that Schaller, the German company, copied my design in making some of their keys.

There is an interesting side story to the making of the new CBS/ Fender keys. Jack Lorenz was the vice president of Columbia Records Development at that time. We had to have gear-hobbing machines to make the gears for the keys we wanted to make. The machines we wanted to buy were made in West Germany. Those machines were heavy as the dickens, but Jack Lorenz had those suckers flown to California by air freight. Isn't it nice what you can do when you have the money?

The gear-hobbing machines were set up in Race and Olmsted's Tool & Die shop and they made the parts for us because the machines had to be operated by trained machinists, and we did not have employees with that particular skill. The tolerance quality of our new keys was far superior to the Kluson keys made with ancient tooling.

Lyman Race passed away a few years ago but Karl Olmsted is alive and well, and he can verify that what I have told you in this book is true because the two of them worked so close to our operation on a day-to-day basis.

CBS moved very fast under Don's guidance in the design and plans for a new 120,000-square-foot building to be built on property adjacent to Building #9. The building was to have a completely dust-free environment and all of the up-to-date facilities, including a conveyor-fed finish department. This would be quite a departure from what we had been used to. It was to be ready for occupancy by the summer of 1966.

We had a lot to look forward to as far as a new facility was concerned; but, otherwise, disaster had struck. We had been invaded by a horde of "know-it-all CBS experts" at both Fender Sales and the factory. Leo Fender would have gone through the ceiling with all of the red tape they had in mind for us. These guys from the Big Apple were going to show us country bumpkins how the big boys operated. Too bad we had to find out.

Before long, they had the Sales Office so screwed up with their misguided approach to computers that our personnel didn't know what was on order—shipped or canceled. I was told the situation was chaotic.

By now I was really confused because I was being told that what I had been doing all this time was wrong and what we really needed was the new CBS approach to procedure perfection. You would think that any company that has the financial capability to acquire a proven successful operation would be prudent enough to let well enough alone and not make waves with wholesale changes.

My purpose in writing this book is not to find fault with others. I am doing my best to tell you exactly what happened. If I told it differently, then it would be the same as any other story told by those who were not there when it happened. Rest assured, I am not perfect. I have my share of faults. (I will tell you near the end of this book why some people did not like to work under my direction.) But also rest assured that I have told this story exactly as it happened.

It should be pointed out that Leo and Don were not the only ones who worked hard and helped to make Fender successful. There were a few more of us who, for reasons apparent, believe we also had a lot to do with that success.

It should also be pointed out that Don was not responsible for many of the problems that faced us at CBS/Fender Musical Instruments.

I will agree that CBS was a proud company in those early Fender years, and that they wanted to produce high-quality products. I do not fault the corporate officers of CBS for the many problems we faced. Most of the frustration was caused by the personnel they sent to Fender Sales and the factory to tell us how our job should be done. Many of their sophisticated, misguided procedures didn't work.

You will remember that Fender employees had formed their own union, United Industrial Employees of California, to protect themselves from outside union organizers. They were working under a contract which was with the Fender Electric Instrument Co. when CBS bought the company. A new contract now had to be signed with CBS, so they had one of their corporate vice presidents, K. Raine, fly from New York to assist me in the negotiations during the latter part of March 1965.

Bob Standen was president of the union at the time. One morning we had stopped for a brief break, and because the negotiations were progressing very well, Bob, Mr. Raine, and I were having a friendly visit. Bob said, "Mr. Raine, I'd like to tell you something that really has nothing to do with our negotiations. Our union has been keeping records for several years

and at no time do we show that Forrest made an unfair decision after he
had the facts." That statement really
meant a lot to me. Negotiations were
soon completed. The union contract
between Fender Musical Instruments,
a Division of Columbia Records Distribution Corp., and United Industrial
Employees of California was effective
April 13, 1965.

The new CBS/Fender building,
under construction, 1966.
(photo: White)

The first phase of construction
was progressing well on the new CBS
building toward the end of the summer of 1965. I received a phone
call from Don around that time telling me he wanted me to step up
production on the Musicmaster and Duo-Sonic ¾-size guitars. He said
he heard that CMI (Gibson) was coming out with a new line of ¾-size
guitars, and he wanted to beat them to the punch. Within ten working days
after the call I had ordered, installed, and had in operation nine new
spray booths that were used to finish the overnight increase in our ¾-size
guitar production. We were successful in heading Gibson off at the pass,
but we were now working in very close quarters as far as floor space was
concerned.

The new spray booths were among the last items bought while purchasing was still under my direction. Maybe that was one of the reasons
that function was taken away from me.

By now research and development, under Paul Spranger's direction, was off-limits to manufacturing. I am not sure if this was Paul's idea or
who actually was responsible for it. At this time, I really didn't much care.

In 1965 Tex Ritter was President of the Country Music Association
(CMA) in Nashville. In August of that year, I called him and said, "Tex,
you know that Leo Fender has sold his company to CBS, and don't you
think he should receive some kind of recognition for all he has done for
country music?"

Tex Ritter with Kingman
guitar, 1964.

I told you that Tex had the habit of snorting a little before he spoke. Tex let out a little snort and said, "Forrest, I think you are right. You know, I have the privilege of presenting the President's Award at the CMA meeting this fall, and maybe we could have a plaque made up for him for presentation. If so, what do you think it should say?" I told Tex that I thought it should mention something about what Leo had done for the sound of country music, and he answered, "I think that sounds like a good idea. Why don't you figure out what should be said and call me back." I thanked him and told him I would call him back within the hour.

I wrote something I thought would be appropriate and called Tex again. I said, "Tex, listen to this and see what you think." I read what I thought the plaque should say and he said, "Forrest, I think that is good. [CMA Executive Director] Jo Walker and I will have to rush to get the plaque made in time for the CMA meeting, but I think we can do it. Why don't you and Leo make arrangements to come back to Nashville at that time, and we will see that he receives the plaque."

I thanked Tex again and told him that Leo and I would be there. You must understand that I really stuck my neck out when I said that we would both be there. Leo was unpredictable, and what he would agree to do depended on his mood. It didn't matter what the situation involved or how important it seemed to you. What you thought was important, and what Leo Fender thought was important, could seem miles apart. The only thing I had in my favor was that Leo might be rested now that he had not been driving himself so hard by working at the factory lab.

That night, with fingers crossed, I walked across the street to see Leo at his home. We exchanged pleasantries. He asked me how things were going at the factory but I was evasive. Finally I said, "Leo, I'm going back to Nashville again this fall; why don't you plan to go with me?"

I was surprised when he was hesitant in replying and even more surprised when he finally said, "You know, that might not be such a bad idea, since I have never been to one of those shows you have been telling me about."

I was very much relieved, because I didn't want to tell him I wanted him to go back to receive an award. Tex and I both hoped that it could be presented as a surprise to him. I said, "Fine Leo, I will make all of the reservations and let's plan to go back to Nashville on October 20." He was grinning from ear to ear and told me it sounded like a good idea.

So, the big day came and we were on our way to Nashville. We checked in at the Andrew Jackson Hotel (it has since been demolished). Roger Miller, who later would become the "King of the Road," was working as a bellhop then, and he checked us into our rooms. I kidded Roger about it later after he became a showbiz biggie.

I unpacked before Leo and went down to the hotel lobby to see if there were any musician friends around. Just as I got off the elevator I heard loud sirens out in front of the hotel. I went outside and around to the side street to see what was going on. I saw people pointing and I looked up to see smoke coming out of a window two floors under the rooms Leo and I had just checked into.

Just then, who should walk up but Tex. He had been down at the Convention Hall, just a couple of blocks from the hotel, making arrangements for the Friday night banquet. He said, "Hi Forrest, what's going on?"

I thought it was pretty obvious, especially when he was looking up at the smoking window the same as everyone else. Anyhow, I answered, "Well, Tex, it looks like someone in the hotel is getting a hot reception for the WSM weekend party." Neither Tex nor I had the slightest idea at the time that the fire was in the room assigned to him and his lovely wife, Dorothy. They suffered quite a loss in damaged clothing, including Dorothy's expensive fur coat.

In the meantime Leo had smelled the smoke and could see it curling up past his window. Now, the old Andrew Jackson Hotel was ten stories high. When he smelled the smoke and saw those little curls rising, he started the famous "Leo Fender ten-story down the backstairs to the lobby run." It has been said that he broke all existing records and that no other notable person had received a hotter reception in Nashville. Many marveled that a man who had sold his company because of ill health could move so fast. Leo and I had a good laugh over what had happened, and he received a lot of good-natured kidding from his friends. I told him I was going to enter him as a runner in the next California open marathon. He held up well over all this.

Tex had a late night disc jockey program on Radio Station WSM in 1965. He asked me to come over to the station after Leo had gone to bed so that I could give him some ideas for his presentation speech of the plaque the following morning. I went over, as requested, and told him a few personal things about Leo during the time the records were playing.

Somehow I talked Leo into going with me to the annual CMA meeting the following morning, even though he didn't think much of the idea. I finally got him to agree after I told him our good friend Tex was going to conduct the meeting as president, and that out of respect for him, we should attend.

Thursday morning, October 21, Leo and I went down to the hotel coffee shop for breakfast. We had problems trying to eat because many musicians recognized Leo. You must remember this was the first time Leo had gone to Nashville during the WSM celebration. The musicians who had never met Leo insisted on an introduction to "the Man." I thought we would never get out of that coffee shop.

It would be difficult to accurately describe the friendly atmosphere which existed during those fantastic early-year WSM celebrations. Perhaps the same feeling exists today during that special time of the year. I would not know personally, because it has been many years since the last time one of my good country musician friends greeted me, "Hi Hoss!" (Maybe you didn't know that everyone in the inner circle at Nashville was called "Hoss." That may be the same greeting they use now or terribly outdated and replaced with another expression.)

We saw our good friend Chet Atkins as we were walking out of the hotel and accepted his invitation for lunch the following day. Chet is one of the greatest musicians I have ever known.

We arrived at the CMA meeting room and the meeting was already in progress. Before long Tex was ready to make the presentation to Leo and said the following:

The President's Award is optional, depending upon the decision of the President. Last year one was not given. This year I decided to present it to a man with two hands and a dream…started 20 years ago with a radio repair shop…made repairs on musical instruments…started making a few with his own design as more or less a sideline…later devoted full time to the building of musical instruments.

The road was rocky at first. Dealer acceptance was spotty. His partner would load a few instruments in his secondhand car, and start out from California demonstrating and selling.

He never participated in any protest marches…didn't tell our State Department how to run its foreign affairs…never wrote or sang any social protest songs…but to some of those modern young men and women, he did a strange thing. He worked…with his hands…his heart…his mind.

To those of us who know him, one thing stands out. On a visit to his factory in later years, a stranger would be at a loss to distinguish him from his employees, because his idea of work is not sitting behind an executive desk, but going down to the floor of the factory and making his ideas work by using his hands.

His inventiveness and genius in the field of design has revolutionized the musical instrument industry worldwide.

They say that no matter where he goes or how he is dressed… whether at church or in his work clothes…there are two things that are always with him. Somewhere on his person, he will have a pair of pliers and a screwdriver, just in case he may run across a guitar, bass, or amplifier that needs repair. I wonder if he has them this morning.

His firm was sold in January to Columbia Special Products Corporation, a subsidiary of Columbia records. Now he says he might find time to do what he always wanted to do, and never had too much time… go fishing. He certainly can afford it.

What a Horatio Alger story…what an inspiration his life could be to young men and women of our country…if they would quit marching… stop…look…and listen.

Members of CMA, the 1965 President's Award is presented to Leo Fender for his outstanding contribution to the sound of Country Music.

I wish you could have seen the expression on Leo's face when Tex began his speech. It came as a complete surprise. He now knew why he had been talked into coming to Nashville and asked to attend the CMA meeting.

Tex invited Leo to come up to the podium and then he gave him the plaque. My friend was at a loss for words; he just said, "Thank you very much," and he seemed to have a hard time saying that much. This is what was written on the plaque:

Tex Ritter presents Leo with the CMA "President's Award," 1965.

PRESIDENT'S AWARD

PRESENTED TO
C. L. FENDER
FOR OUTSTANDING CONTRIBUTION TO
THE SOUND OF COUNTRY AND WESTERN MUSIC
IN THE DESIGN OF STRINGED MUSICAL
INSTRUMENTS AND AMPLIFIERS

COUNTRY MUSIC ASSOCIATION
TEX RITTER, PRESIDENT

NASHVILLE, TENNESSEE
OCTOBER 21, 1965

It was obvious the presentation meant a lot to Leo, even though he did not have too much to say about it. You would have thought the plaque was made of gold the way he carried it back to the hotel. This was indeed a day to be remembered.

Earlier I told you that I would let you know where and how Leo Fender and Merle Travis became friends. Leo received his award Thursday morning. We had lunch with our friend Chet Atkins on Friday, and that evening we attended the CMA banquet at the convention hall. Bob Wills and His Texas Playboys furnished the entertainment.

I happened to see my old friend Merle, and he was a long way from where Leo and I were standing. It was obvious Leo hadn't seen him, as Leo was busy visiting with one of the musicians. I excused myself and told Leo I would see him in a couple of minutes because we

Leo, Pete "Brother Oswald" Kirby, and Forrest on the Opry stage, Nashville, 1965.

Leo Fender, Buck Owens, and Joe Maphis at the Nashville Municipal Auditorium, 1965. (photo: White)

were supposed to be seated for the banquet dinner right away. I quickly walked over to Merle, and after the usual "Howdy," I said I wanted to ask a favor of him. Merle and I were close enough friends that he said, "Sure, name it."

I said, "Merle, you and I have been good friends for many years and you know how much Leo Fender means to me. Leo is with me tonight and I would like to see my good friends become friends to one another. How about coming over to see Leo and sit with us during dinner?"

Merle said, "Forrest, I think that is a good idea, and if Leo is willing, I would like for us to be friends." So Merle and I walked back over to

Leo and those two acted like they had been bosom buddies for ages. Merle sat between Leo and me during dinner and from that day on solid-body guitars and their origin were no longer a problem subject between my two close friends. And that's the way it was Friday evening, October 22, 1965, in Nashville, Tennessee.

Leo and I attended the Grand Ole Opry on Saturday night, and it was back to California for us on Sunday.

CHAPTER **14**

CBS/FENDER
AT 1300
EAST VALENCIA

I received a very nice letter from Don Randall just before the Christmas holidays in 1965. He told me he was pleased with the factory's large increase in production while we were still maintaining our good quality standards. Quality standards, however, would soon start to nosedive. No fault of the factory.

(See Don Randall's letter on page 164.)

I will now give you the first example of how CBS underlings started to destroy the good name of Fender. You will remember purchasing was taken away from me as a part of material control. It had been placed under the direction of S. Gartenberg's new appointee, who worked in accounting at Fender Sales. Harold Travis had hired a new purchasing agent with an office at the factory. Now this guy was sure we had been paying too much for the material we were using to build the good Fender amplifiers and guitars, and he was going to save CBS a lot of money by shrewd selective purchasing.

One day a salesman stopped by his office with an unusual bargain in a close-out on magnet wire. The new man bought it at a bargain base-

Fender SALES, INC. / 1402 EAST CHESTNUT, SANTA ANA, CALIF. / Kimberly 7-0631 / GUITARS • AMPS • COVERS • CASES

December 15, 1965

Mr. Forrest White
FENDER MUSICAL INSTRUMENTS
500 South Raymond
Fullerton, California

Dear Forrest:

I think it is appropriate that as we near the end of the year we evaluate that which has happened over the past 12 months.

In doing so, I cannot help but be impressed with the remarkable job you have done in expanding production to an approximate 80% increase above last year. This is a remarkable feat by any measure and only serves to point up what a fine crew you have been able to assemble.

I want to extend my thanks to you and each and every one of those who have been instrumental in this effort. I hope you all have a Merry Christmas and a happy, bright and prosperous New Year.

Sincerely,

FENDER SALES, INC.

Donald D. Randall
Vice-President and
General Manager

DDR/cmy

ment price. There was a problem. It happened to be odds and ends of the wrong gauge and coating. I found out about it and said that we could not use that wire to wind our instrument pickups. I was told by one of the CBS marvels that I didn't have to tell him how to run the company. Those pickups with the oddball wire would have been used on instruments that were made starting around the end of 1967. I was certain Don did not know of this problem, nor did CBS executives.

Don came up with a good idea in the spring of 1966. He said there was a company located in Oregon, Illinois, that made darn good banjos. He bought the company for CBS, and he asked me to go check it out and to make arrangements for all usable tooling and equipment to be shipped to Fender. I flew back to Chicago, rented a car at the airport, and drove to this little banjo operation in Oregon, Illinois.

What a pleasant surprise. The banjos were more than great. They were fantastic. Dave Markel was the young man who designed the banjos and he owned the manufacturing operation. He was a friendly person and one of the most outstanding craftsmen I have ever met. His detail work, including beautiful mother-of-pearl inlays, was just the best you could find. The banjos had a sound that was second to none. When you hear a bell ringing, you know that the sound has a great sustaining quality, and it can be heard for a relatively long distance. This was the kind of steel Dave was using to make his banjos' tone-rings. Bell-quality steel is expensive compared to your ordinary mill-run steel.

Dave and I reviewed the complete inventory list of banjo tooling and fixtures that was worth saving and shipping to the new CBS/Fender building which would be ready for occupancy within the next 60 days.

The banjo operation was successfully moved to the new facility in Fullerton, and Dave was on board with Fender to make the best-sounding banjos many professional musicians have ever heard. Three styles were available: the short- and long-scale tenor 4-string and the country-style 5-string. Earl Scruggs, the acknowledged king of the 5-string banjo, said our Fender banjos were the best he ever heard. Remember, he said this about the banjos Dave made after moving to Fender when we were still using his material.

Then it happened. It was time to order more tone-rings. The purchasing agent hired by and reporting to Harold Travis must have thought it was ridiculous to pay such a premium cost to have those tone-rings made from bell steel. After all, steel is steel, right? Wrong! Anyhow, the guy ordered the tone-rings made out of ordinary steel. The cost was moderately cut. The tone of the banjos was drastically cut. Dave was almost in tears when he told me what happened.

Now, can you still believe the quality of Fender products was assured with this kind of lower-staff actions? Again, I am sure that Don Randall was not aware of this and I'll bet he would have blown his stack if he had known. A good communication line is a must if you expect to have a successful operation. When that line is cut, you can expect to have many problems.

After CBS acquired Fender, Roger Rossmeisl designed some new model guitars, acoustic and acoustic/electric, but they were not too well accepted. Roger probably was more successful with the quality of his instruments than CBS was with the quality of their solid-body electric standard guitars. Musicians still expected the same quality workmanship and sound that they were accustomed to with the early year models of Telecasters and Stratocasters, and Roger did not have to live up to such a precedent in standards. I had great respect for Roger's craftsmanship.

Roger produced the beautiful Fender hand-carved LTD. This baby was expensive and very few were made. He also produced the Montego I & II, the Wildwood Coronado series, the Wildwood acoustic guitar, the Coronado I & II and 12-String, the Coronado Bass I & II, Kingman and Concert acoustic guitars, Shenandoah 12-String, Palomino, Malibu, Villager 12-String, and the Newporter. Much effort. And, sadly, limited acceptance.

I told you the banjo operation had been moved into the new CBS/Fender building. It was ready for occupancy in the middle of 1966, and we were in the process of moving many of our departments into the improved facility. It seemed strange to have so much additional floor space to move around in. It was obvious: CBS wanted the best. Let me give you an example.

I was sitting at my desk in the old building office during the latter part of 1965. A gentleman came in and introduced himself as being in charge of CBS sound systems, and he was here from New York because he heard that I wanted a certain type of sound system in the new building. At first I thought he was kidding, and I asked, "Do you mean to tell me you came all the way from New York to discuss sound systems with me?" The answer was affirmative, and from now on I would not be surprised at anything our new parent CBS would come up with. I told him I had only slightly mentioned that I hoped we would be able to have a decent sound system in the new facility and that I hadn't asked for anything exotic. He

Nine early Fender buildings and the large new CBS/Fender building under construction down the street, 1966.

assured me I would be able to hear it no matter where you were in the new building.

He was right. He put in a line-level system. The louder the noise was in any department, the louder the sound system. I was afraid to ask how much it cost for the installation.

Another example: My office in the new building, and the adjoining conference room, had walnut-paneled walls. The ceiling was 10' high, and it cost more than $2,000 extra for the paneling just because the ceiling was higher than normal.

Architects William L. Pereira & Associates of Los Angeles did practically all of the building for CBS in New York and all points west. They took care of all of the interior designing for the new offices, carpet, drapes, colors of walls, etc. They also selected the new furniture. Now, I detest the ultra-modern look in furniture of any kind. The large table and chairs for the conference room were beautiful, but the desk and chairs they selected for the offices stunk to high heaven as far as I was concerned. By now the CBS plant engineer from New York had become a good friend of mine. I said, "Bill, there is no way that I will work off of that stupid-looking modernistic desk, I am going to move my old Steelcase desk over to my new office." He told me I couldn't do that because CBS had strict ideas about office furniture and they always went along with what their architect William Pereira picked out for them. I told Bill, "That may be true up 'til now, but you wait and see what I will be working off of in that new office." I did what I told him I would do. I moved the modern junk out and put my old standby Steelcase desk and chairs in.

When Bill came back he saw what I had done and he laughed. He said, "Okay, what kind of a desk do you want? We will have one made for you." I told him. They made a desk for my office and a picture of it is in this book. You can see that the date is July 20, 1966. It was beautiful. Bill told me I was the only one in CBS who had a custom-made desk.

This is the story I think is funny. The Fullerton Building Department called to ask me what address I wanted to use for the new CBS/Fender building, and they gave me some numbers to choose from. I selected a number. It was 1300 East Valencia. What I didn't know was that some of

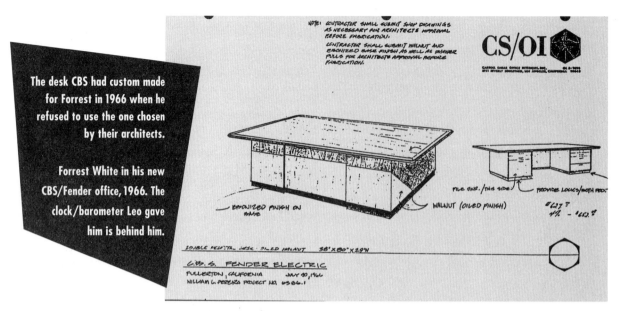

NOTE: CONTRACTOR SHALL SUBMIT SHOP DRAWINGS AS NECESSARY FOR ARCHITECTS APPROVAL BEFORE FABRICATION.

CONTRACTOR SHALL SUBMIT WALNUT AND BRONZIZED BASE FINISH AS WELL AS DRAWER PULLS FOR ARCHITECTS APPROVAL BEFORE FABRICATION.

CS/OI

BRONZIZED FINISH ON BASE

FILE ONE /THIS SIDE

PROVIDE LOCKS/BOTH PED.

WALNUT (OILED FINISH)

627
$42 - 652$

DOUBLE PEDSTL. DESK - OILED WALNUT   38" X 80" X 29¾

C.B.S. FENDER ELECTRIC
FULLERTON, CALIFORNIA   JULY 10, 1966
WILLIAM L. PEREIRA PROJECT NO. 6586.1

The desk CBS had custom made for Forrest in 1966 when he refused to use the one chosen by their architects.

Forrest White in his new CBS/Fender office, 1966. The clock/barometer Leo gave him is behind him.

the executives at CBS were superstitious. When Bill, the CBS plant engineer, heard what I had done he laughed even louder than he did about my desk. He said that CBS had built a new large office building on a corner lot in New York. They had preferred the address to show that the building faced the main bordering street. However, it would have been number 13.

Rather than use that number, they picked an address on the other bordering street. And to think I picked 1300 for the Fullerton address. Maybe they had a reason to be superstitious, the way things worked out for them in the musical instrument business.

Within a few days after I had moved into my new office, I had a visit from a very interesting person. He was a psychologist from CBS in New York and he reported direct to William Paley, the top man at CBS at that time. I cannot recall his name, but I remember so well what happened. I thought maybe he was there because of my custom-made desk. He told me his job at CBS was to check each person who had been promoted to, or whom they were considering promoting to, an executive position.

Please do not get a psychologist confused with a psychiatrist. A psychologist checks on actions, traits, attitudes, thoughts, mental states, etc., of a person or group. A psychiatrist deals with the branch of medicine concerned with the study, treatment, and prevention of disorders of the mind. So, you see, a psychologist doesn't think you have lost your marbles—yet. It was a relief to know he was the more desirable of the two kinds of analysts. In all seriousness, I'll tell you what was behind all of this.

The psychologist told me the reason he was supposed to check all executives was to make sure the person was qualified for the position they held in a particular CBS division. He said his report was confidential to everyone except William Paley. I told him I had nothing to hide and to feel free to ask me any questions, in detail, about any phase of the Fender operation.

Now picture this. He sat down in an easy chair with his pencil and pad. He looked down through his glasses when he wrote. He raised his eyes only, without moving his head, peering over the top of his glasses, when he looked at me to ask each question. Friend, I was receiving the third degree. He asked me everything you could think of. Questions about the Fender operation, what I thought was good or bad. What were our problems and what should be done to solve them. He asked me all kinds of personal questions, except maybe how many times I went to the restroom daily.

The questioning went on, hot and heavy, for a little over 30 minutes, without a single smile. Then, he stopped abruptly, laid down his pad and pencil and looked at me intently for over a minute. He must have been trying to figure out how I was reacting to his crossfire questioning. I asked him if there was anything else he wanted to know and to feel free to ask.

It was like the sun had just appeared over the horizon. There was the biggest smile you would ever want to see. He leaned back in his chair and completely relaxed. He said, "I was just over at the Sales office and talked to a few people. You are the first one I've questioned who seems to know what he is doing." (Don Randall was in New York at the time, and he was not talking about him, because Don was exceptionally well qualified for his position). Then I was surprised when he said, "Let me give you a tip. Be careful of some accountants. They will stick a knife in your back if they get the chance." He put his pad in his briefcase, got up and before going out the door of my office he said, "Let me know if there is anything I can help you with, and good luck."

It seemed plain now what had happened. The person I had been having problems with in accounting must have sent the psychologist over to cross-examine me and probably hoped he would find that I was not qualified for my job. If so, his little plan backfired. I will tell you something additional that I heard in a subsequent conversation with the psychologist which will not be to the benefit of the person in question.

Don Randall had not let any grass grow under his feet in doing a good job for CBS. The Fender Musical Instruments Division was growing by leaps and bounds. By now Don had acquired many new companies, including V.C. Squire Strings, which had previously made strings for us. He also acquired Rogers Drums, which manufactured a quality line of drums and drum accessories. And last, but not least, he acquired Electro Music, a company that manufactured speaker systems for electronic organs. Organs were very popular during that time.

Perhaps you wonder why I did not inform Don of some of the things that were going on which I thought were detrimental to the quality and productivity of the Fender factory. What would you do if you repeatedly asked to talk to him and you were told "Mr. Randall is not available"? He used to be available to me before he became a CBS executive. Friend, I am sure that Don did not know I had been trying to talk to him. We had been friends a long time and I know he would have talked to me if he had known. I believe he had respect for my opinions. There are some things that must be considered, though. Don was out of his office much of the time now because of his new position with CBS. Trips to New York were frequent in addition to music shows and visiting distributors and dealers all over the world. The factory was in Fullerton and the sales office was in Santa Ana approximately ten miles away. Then we have to assume that, with the new change in management, there were some who may have overstepped their authority by deciding just whom they thought Don should or shouldn't talk to. You can bet Don Randall made those decisions himself when he knew who was calling.

CHAPTER 15

CBS MUSICAL INSTRUMENTS— JUNE 1966

June 1966 was a dark period in time for those of us who had such great respect for the name Fender, because that was the time it was removed from the CBS Company name. As of June 10, 1966, I no longer worked for Fender. I worked for the CBS Musical Instrument Division.

CBS must have approved of the job Don Randall was doing because one of the top executives, Frank Stanton, released a memo on June 10, stating that Don would be heading up the newly formed division. Don Randall would now be reporting directly to the president of the CBS/Columbia Group, Goddard Lieberson. (You will recall Don had reported to Norman Adler, the executive vice president.)

I was now no longer just the plant manager. I had been given the title of Director of Manufacturing. I received a job description for that position that had been prepared by the CBS Organization Planning & Management Development Department. The title of that group seemed a little more impressive than the title I received. Understand, I was not to receive any more pay, nor any more authority—just a longer title. In all seriousness, it was a nice gesture—like taking a final bow before the curtain closed.

L to R: Harry Dotson, CBS/Fender Personnel Manager; Roger Rossmeisl; Forrest White; Babe Simoni, Production Foreman, 1966, at the acoustic guitar building.

I did not like some of the rumors I had been hearing concerning certain personnel in research and development. I was told they had been making fun of Leo Fender and had been knocking any new ideas he had to offer CBS as a consultant. Leo heard about the things they were saying, and I can tell you now that it curtailed his enthusiasm. CBS was the loser in this case, and those who were guilty of the disparaging remarks were not worthy of shining Leo Fender's shoes. Leo was a very proud man and his feelings were easily hurt, even though he would never complain or mention that what he had heard bothered him. Freddie Tavares was still working in research and development after the acquisition by CBS, and I will bet that Freddie told off that person, or persons, when he found out what was being said. Freddie never used profanity to express himself. His vocabulary was not that limited. When Freddie told you off it was with style — Hawaiian that is.

It was the latter part of September 1966, and up to now there had been no significant contributions from research and development since CBS had taken over management of Fender. Then it happened. A new amplifier was placed on my desk, and I was told that this was a new solid-state prototype amplifier that we were going to be producing. There were 14 different models in the new solid-state series, and I was asked to sign them off for production because they were anxious to get started. I told them to leave the amplifier and give me a little time to look it over, in case I had any questions. Well, the more I looked at that thing the worse I felt. You cannot believe what they were asking me to build. It was not designed for production and there was no practical way to service it.

I called Paul Spranger in research and development and told him about my concern, and what I had to say was not accepted very well. I can understand why he was not too receptive, because a lot of pressure had been put on him to come up with something for production. Nothing new in amplifiers had come out of R & D since Leo left in January 1965, and almost two years had passed since then.

I cannot find fault with Paul personally because of what was unacceptable to me in the amplifier design. Paul was a darn good electronics engineer, but in all fairness to him, he was brought in from the aerospace industry and asked to design products that were absolutely foreign to him. He could not have known how important it was to design amplifiers that were easy to service because he was not familiar with the many problems

The CMA membership certificate, 1966.

musicians had hauling them around from job to job. I think Paul Spranger was a victim of circumstances.

A small combo organ prototype was shown to me within a few days after I first saw the amplifier. They wanted it signed off for production also. After I looked at it I didn't feel much better than I did after I had seen the amplifier prototype.

It was imperative that I tell Don what my objections were on the new item they wanted me to release for production. I tried to call Don and…the same answer: "Mr. Randall is not available." I didn't know what to do at this point, other than to refuse to sign the new items off for production.

I had been asked at least five or six times over a period of time to sign the new prototypes off for production, and I refused to do so until I had the opportunity to talk to Don. But I was always told he was not available.

On December 6, 1966, Stan Compton, Don's right-hand man, came over to my office from Sales in Santa Ana. After a few minutes, he said, "Forrest, are you going to sign the new solid-state amplifiers and combo organ off for production?"

I replied, "I can't, because they are not worthy of Leo Fender's name and I want to tell Don Randall why I think so."

Stan said, "Don is not available. If you don't sign those items off for production, then we will bring someone in that will sign them off and you will have to report to him."

I said, "There is no way I will agree to that, so that means I will have to leave."

Stan said, "I am sorry to hear that, but it is exactly what I thought you would say."

Tuesday, December 6, 1966, was my last working day at Fender. I asked all of my key personnel to come to the conference room. I told them that I had too much respect for Leo to have any part in building something that was not worthy of having his name associated with it. I told them how much I appreciated the fact that he had given me the opportunity to become involved in the musical instrument business. Building guitars had been my hobby and he had given me the opportunity to earn my living at it for a relatively short period of time. I thanked them all for the help they

The new CBS/Fender building at 1300 Valencia, 1966. Forrest's office was in front at the far right. (photo: White)

Fender business cards from 1954 to 1967.

had given me, and I can tell you, there were a few tears shed in that meeting. Most of us had come a long way together. The last thing I said to them as a group was, "Please protect and hold the name Fender as high as you possibly can."

I collected all of my personal belongings, and when I walked out of my office door that day, I felt as if I had lost my last friend in this world. There had been no doubt in my mind through all those years of hard work—mixed with frustration—that I would be working at Fender until

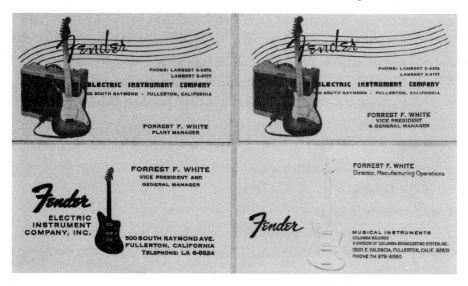

my dying day. Friend, we never know what tomorrow brings. We have to do the best we can today.

I would like to make one thing clear, and that is to give the real reason why I resigned from Fender. I have read several stories saying I left because I had a disagreement with CBS management over production methods. That is not true. It had nothing to do with production methods.

I resigned from CBS Musical Instruments because management wanted me to manufacture the newly designed solid-state amplifier line and the combo organ, and I refused because they were not worthy of the name of Leo Fender.

You may ask if I was that close to Leo. Can you tell me the name of anyone else who was a close enough friend to Leo to resign before they would build anything that was not worthy of his name? Did it hurt me financially? You bet it did. It has hurt Joan and me a lot over the years. Remember though, Leo and Esther were like family to us and there is a thing called conscience that would have haunted me the rest of my life if I had turned my back on the name Fender. I am darn sure not a hypocrite.

I walked across the street that evening to tell Leo that I was no longer with the company. Esther answered the door and she told me Leo was in his den and for me to go on back. Leo seemed to be feeling well and in a good mood, but that didn't last very long. I said, "Leo, I'm no longer with the company."

His smile disappeared immediately and he asked, "What did you say?" I told him again and explained to him just what had happened. I had not told him before that I had seen the new prototype solid-state amplifier at least two months ago, because I did not want to worry him about the design.

Leo was real quiet after I told him what had happened and I noticed something that I had never seen before. There were tears coming down his cheeks. He said, "What you need is your own company and if CBS didn't have me tied up in a contract we would start tomorrow." I didn't stay long after that because it was obvious that Leo was really disturbed about what had happened. At least I had something to think about.

I left Fender on Tuesday, December 6, and the next day the purchasing agent wrote a letter to the accountant telling him about the large surplus of inventory they had on hand. His recommendation was to reduce it at discounted prices but make no mention of the company name. We had operated with a balanced inventory for years, until material control and purchasing had been taken from me after the sale to CBS. Even though I had nothing to do with the large inventory surplus, I was told I was to be blamed.

The following Monday, December 12, I received a telephone call from Marc Carlucci at Chicago Musical Instruments (CMI). Marc was the Sales Manager for Gibson, Inc., which was owned by CMI at that time. Marc said they had heard that I was longer with Fender and asked me what I was doing. I told him that I had resigned and was just taking it easy at the present time. He said Mr. M. H. Berlin, CMI's Chairman of the Board, wanted to talk to me, and they wanted me to fly to Chicago as soon as possible with all expenses paid. I told Marc that I was not looking for a job at that time and it was too close to Christmas to go anywhere. He told me that Mr. Berlin would be very disappointed if I didn't come in the next day or so. I finally told him I would, and I flew to Chicago on Tuesday, December 13th.

To make a long story short, I met on Wednesday morning with Mr. Berlin and Stan Rendell, an executive in charge of CMI manufacturing. I was told that CMI was going to build a large 123,000-square-foot plant just outside of Asheville, North Carolina, to build cabinets for the Lowrey organs and the complete Lowrey pianos. Mr. Berlin said he wanted me to supervise the building of the plant in Asheville; to phase out the CMI facility in Grand Rapids, Michigan, where they were presently making the Lowrey pianos; and to move what I could salvage to the Asheville plant when it was completed.

I thanked them and told them I was not interested because I had no experience in building pianos. However, after more discussion, I agreed and became an employee of the Chicago Musical Instrument Co. on January 16, 1967. I was made Vice President of Lowrey Pianos and Vice President and General Manager of Asheville Industries, the name of the new facility. Mr. Berlin told me if he had known I would be leaving Fender six months ago he would have waited and made me President of Gibson. He had previously assigned another person to that position.

Joan and I would not move to North Carolina until the new plant was almost ready for occupancy, and this would take some time. In the meantime, I flew to CMI in Chicago and met with Stan Rendell. Stan and I left the next day for the Lowrey Piano factory in Grand Rapids. I was put in charge there and Stan flew back to Chicago. Grand Rapids would be my second home on and off during the next year until I moved the piano operation to Asheville Industries.

I had barely gotten my office in shape at Lowrey when I received a conference telephone call from CBS in New York. S. Gartenberg, from the finance department, and the psychologist who had put me through the third degree at Fender were both on the phone. S. Gartenberg said, "What's this I hear that you are no longer at Fender?" I explained what had happened, and I wish you could have heard some of their comments. Both S. Gartenberg and the psychologist believed that the accountant at the Fender Sales office had a lot to do with my problem. They were very much disturbed that I had left Fender. I told them about the overstocked inventory and the reason why. They both wished me the best of luck and said they were sorry things worked out this way, because they both felt I had done an outstanding job at Fender. The accountant was then terminated.

During 1967 and early 1968 I had been commuting between Fullerton, Chicago, Grand Rapids, and Asheville. During the long winter evenings in Grand Rapids, I wrote an employee handbook to be used in Asheville. Without my knowledge, the manager of the Manufacturers Association in Asheville entered the book in a three-state contest to determine the best recently written employee handbook. I was surprised to learn that my book won first place. The three states involved were Georgia, North and South Carolina.

The new building was completed in Asheville in March, 1968. The Lowrey Piano operation had been phased out from Grand Rapids, and all salvaged tooling, fixtures, and material had been shipped to the new facility. During this period of time Joan, our son Curtis, and I moved from Fullerton to Asheville.

The grand opening of the new Asheville Industries facility was September 12, 1968. Those attending included United States Congressman

Roy Taylor; John Majeski, Editor of *Music Trades*; and many city and county officials; Mr. M. H. Berlin, Chairman of the Board (CMI); Stan Rendell, President of Gibson (as of early 1968); and other executive and sales personnel from CMI. This was the first time anyone from CMI had seen the Asheville facility since the land had been purchased. Mr. Berlin would not allow anyone to come near it. This was how much trust he had placed in me. I had the full responsibility of putting it together.

Gibson

GUITARS AND AMPLIFIERS

September 16, 1968

Mr. Forrest F. White
Vice President-General Manager
Asheville Industries, Inc.
1000 Craigmont Road
Black Mountain, N. C. 28711

Dear Forrest:

Just a short note to thank you for the wonderful hospitality, and to congratulate you on the excellent job you have done in readying the Asheville Industries for production. All of your organization can be proud of the job they have done, and my special thanks to your secretary for her efforts. Keep up the good work.

Give my regards to Joanne, and to everyone for me.

Yours very truly,

Stan R.

Stanley E. Rendell
President

SER:bg

GIBSON INC. 225 PARSONS ST. • KALAMAZOO, MICHIGAN 49007 • (616) 381-7050
SUBSIDIARY OF CHICAGO MUSICAL INSTRUMENT CO.

Don Randall finally decided that he could no longer agree with the CBS/Group policies and he resigned in early April 1969. This was a darn shame, because Don had done such a good job in helping to make Fender so successful through the years. I wondered if he felt as bad as I did when I left the company.

The 1969 National Music Show was held in Atlanta, Georgia. Stan Compton, Don's old right-hand man, and Dick Sievert, who was in charge of the CBS-acquired Squire String Co., were attending, and I happened to run into them. Stan said, "Forrest, we have been looking for you. I wanted to tell you that we should have listened to you. We got most of those solid-state amplifiers back in our lap."

Then he said, "I want to take my hat off to you for the job you did in managing the Fender manufacturing facility. I didn't realize how much was involved and we should have never let you get away."

You have no idea how good that made me feel. I thanked Stan for his kind words and had to bite my tongue to keep from saying, "I tried to tell you about the amplifiers, and why didn't you let me talk to Don Randall?" I was told Don fired the aerospace engineer after he had to replace an amplifier pilot light while in Europe at a music show. He finally found out there was no easy way to service those solid-state amplifiers. I could have told him.

By this time George Fullerton was no longer an employee of CBS Musical Instruments. I was told he was forced out because they felt he was nonproductive. Not long after he left CBS, he was hired by Ernie Ball as the production manager of Earthwood. They manufactured acoustic-guitar–shaped basses.

In July 1969, I flew to CMI in Chicago and went to lunch with M. H. Berlin. He seemed very quiet, and that was unusual because he normally would be bubbling over with enthusiasm in asking how I was getting along at Asheville Industries. Finally he said, "Forrest, do you know how I got started in the music business?"

I answered, "Yes, you sold accordions door to door."

Tears were in his eyes when he said, "ECL just told me that they now own a stock majority and they will be taking over management of

CMI." ECL was a South American company that was in the cement and beer business. They had become interested in the music business and had been buying blocks of CMI stock. How I wished I could have done something or could have said the right words to comfort this great man. Neither one of us spoke for a minute or two and then he said, "ECL wants to consolidate the operation and they will dispose of Asheville Industries and move the manufacturing to Chicago." I told him I would resign as soon as he could find a replacement for me, because there was no way I would live in Chicago.

Mr. Berlin appointed a replacement for me and I left Asheville Industries and returned to California as soon as I possibly could. Joan and Curtis were still in Asheville because we had not sold our home there.

Within six months, I received a personal telephone call from M. H. Berlin. He asked, "Forrest, what are you doing?" I told him I was just resting. Actually I was waiting for Leo Fender's contract to run out with CBS. Mr. Berlin said, "There are a lot of problems at Asheville Industries. We have over 700 pianos with cracked sound-boards and our relationship with the dealers has never been so bad. Will you please come back and straighten things out and find us a buyer for the facility?"

Mr. Berlin had always treated me first-class, and there was no way I could refuse. I said, yes, I would help him. Fortunately, Joan had still not sold our home.

I drove back to Asheville, and within a relatively short period of time, I was able to have the problems corrected and was fortunate enough to find a quick buyer, Drexel Enterprises. I phased out the manufacturing operations and shipped all salvaged piano tooling and fixtures back to Chicago. I sold most of the material that was not worth shipping. M. H. Berlin was pleased with my effort.

The final agreement for merger between ECL and CMI was signed on Monday, July 28, 1969. This was the end of the Chicago Musical Instruments Co. It would now be called Norlin Corp. This was a terrible loss to a great giant in the musical instruments industry, my friend and former boss, Mr. M. H. Berlin. In 1970, he was with Norton Stevens of ECL at the music show in Chicago. When I met him, he took my hand in both of his and, with tears in his eyes, he said, "My boy, I have a very warm special

place in my heart for you." This was one of the high points of my life. Mr.
Berlin died after a brief illness on August 23, 1984, at the age of 89.

We sold our Asheville home in the summer of 1970 and moved back
to California. Our home in North Carolina was real close to the Blue Ridge
Parkway and it was beautiful country, but we were glad to be back in California and to see Leo and Esther Fender again.

I would like to move ahead a few years in order to continue the
story of the ECL acquisition of CMI. There was a very interesting article in
the January 1990 issue of *Music Trades* magazine written by editor Brian
T. Majeski, and reprinted with his permission:

NORLIN CORP.
How To Lose $158 Million

In 1970, ECL Corp. merged with Chicago Musical Instruments Corp.
to form Norlin. ECL operated an Ecuadorian Brewery, and CMI held claim
to being the largest U.S. music company, operating Lowrey, Gibson,
Olds, William Lewis, Krauth & Beninghofen, L.D. Heater, and several
other smaller divisions. Headed by the Harvard-educated Norton
Stevens, Norlin promised to revolutionize the music industry with MBA-
equipped "professional managers."

Stevens and his cadre of well educated professional managers did
revolutionize the music industry, unfortunately not for the better. After a
decade of chronic mismanagement, the '80s saw the once mighty CMI
disintegrate, awash in a sea of red ink and plagued by a loss of dealer
and consumer confidence. When the company ended its involvement in
music in 1986 by selling Gibson Guitar, its losses in music had reached a
record-breaking $158 million. No one had ever lost so much in the music
industry before, and no one has done so since.

In the 1975 Norlin annual report, Stevens proudly boasted, "Norlin
has led in the application of electronics to music, and is now, more than
ever, the nation's leading musical instrument company." Unfortunately,
between 1975 and 1985 Norlin reported music losses of $158 million, an
amount equal to twice the company's net worth in 1975! So much for the
professional managers.

CHAPTER **16**

LEO FENDER
KEEPS HIS
PROMISE

You will remember that when I told Leo I had resigned from CBS/
Fender Musical Instruments, he said, "What you need is your own company
and if CBS didn't have me tied up in a contract we would start tomorrow."

Leo Fender was very cautious about any infringement of his CBS
contract. He wanted to be sure that a full five years had elapsed before
anyone suspected he might become involved with the musical instrument
business again. So, to begin with, in the summer of 1971 Leo and I discussed possible options for me to consider before we began. He told me he
would design some amplifiers and guitars, and then something had to be
decided on for distribution.

I told Leo I would like Fred Martin, of Martin Guitar Co., to be the
distributor if he were interested. I remembered that Fred had told me he
didn't have electric solid-body guitars to sell, but if he did he would have
wanted me to be in charge of making them. Leo thought that was a good
idea. I asked Fred if he would be interested, and he was.

183

Please remember, Leo Fender came out of retirement to help me start a business of my own because of his promise to me on the day I resigned from CBS/Fender. Contrary to what some have claimed, he did not come out of retirement to start G & L, and he *would not have*, because of problems he faced with George Fullerton (his partner in G & L) in the Fender manufacturing operation during the very early years. I know this to be true concerning early years manufacturing problems because he told me so.

In the meantime, Don Randall quietly started to put things together that would eventually lead to his return to the musical instrument business. Tom Walker had worked for Don at Fender Sales during the early years as salesman for the Southern California area. He had left CBS Musical Instruments and was comparing notes with Don toward a business they would possibly be forming. But something happened and they stopped working together. Leo wondered if I would want Tom to take care of sales, to keep everything in-house so that we would not need an outside distributor. I talked to Tom and offered him equal interest in the preferred stock of the company. He agreed. He and I would each own 50% of the preferred stock and Leo would own 100% of the common stock.

Don Randall offered me the position of Vice President of Manufacturing in the company he was forming called Randall Instruments. I thanked Don for his offer but declined and told him I was planning to go into business for myself. It was a good feeling to have when Don offered me that position in his company. It proved to me that he believed I had done a good job at Fender.

I told Don that Tom was joining me in the proposed new company. He said, "I hate to tell you this but you may be sorry for that, if Tom acts the same way he did while he was with me. He seemed to think everything should be done his way and threatened to leave if it wasn't." And indeed, one day when Tom threatened to leave, Don accepted his resignation. I thanked Don, but told him I thought I could take care of any situation like that. Boy, was I ever wrong!

Toward the end of 1971, we were formulating plans and by March 7, 1972, we had formed Tri-Sonics, Inc. I came up with that name since there were three of us involved. The first year, I served as president and

Tom was vice president. My wife, Joan, had the title of secretary, even though I took care of those duties, and Tom's wife, Pat, served as treasurer. CLF Research, the company Leo formed (named, of course, for Clarence Leo Fender) for the consulting work he had planned to do for CBS/Fender, would make the stringed instruments for Tri-Sonics.

Leo and Tom were working on amplifier designs, and I started to work on a new look for the guitar and bass. I did not want our instruments to be confused with the Fender designs.

My design drawing for the bass head with 3 & 1 key configuration was completed on October 27, 1972, and the design drawing for the guitar head with 4 & 2 key configuration was completed in November of the same year. The trademark application for the bass was filed June 23, 1976, and was granted, Serial No. 699,032, showing me as the inventor/owner. I assigned the trademark to Music Man on April 29, 1977.

Western movie set, 1973, for *Guns of a Stranger* with Marty Robbins and Chill Wills. Dovie Beams, female lead, is shown between Forrest and Curtis White.

The name Tri-Sonics did not last long. We changed it to Musitek, Inc., on February 7, 1973. Tom served as president this year because we had previously agreed to rotate our positions. Leo was the vice president and I served as secretary/treasurer. The name Musitek was Leo's idea as short for Music Technology. This was fine if a person knew how to pronounce it. You have no idea what we were being called. Again, Leo came to the rescue. He said, "Why don't we use the name Music Man."

I said, "Leo, I don't think there is any way in the world we will be allowed to use that name." I was sure someone must have used Music Man, or a name sounding close to it, as their corporation name. It is difficult to select a corporation name that will be acceptable to the government. They will not allow you to use it if it looks, or sounds, like a name being used.

Forrest holding the first production model Music Man bass, serial #B001000 (photo: Curtis White). Early-years Fender employee Sam Hutton created this photo composite, with the background showing vintage Fender products.

We asked our attorney to run a check on the name, and sure enough, for some reason, the name was available.

On January 3, 1974, the State of California certified that we could call our company Music Man, Inc. Tom Walker was president, Leo Fender was vice president, and I was secretary/treasurer again.

I would like to explain what happened to the agreed rotation of officers between Tom Walker and myself. It was getting close to the time when I was to assume the title of president again. Tom said, "Forrest, I think that I should be president full-time since I am in charge of marketing. I will be dealing a lot with the Japanese and they always want to deal with the top man in a company."

I answered, "Tom, your being president full-time is not going to help you sell one additional guitar or amplifier, and we should keep our rotating system as agreed."

So he started. No matter what we were discussing from that time on, it would lead back to the old "I should be president full-time." He almost drove me crazy and, in desperation, I finally said, "Okay, be the president full-time and please shut up."

By January 1974, Ernie Ball had forced George Fullerton out of his job as the production manager at Earthwood for the same reason, I had been told, that CBS took like action earlier — for being nonproductive.

I felt sorry for George when I heard that he was no longer with Earthwood, and I asked him to dinner. I was shocked when I saw him; he had lost a lot of weight and looked as if he been ill for some time. I asked him what happened and if he would like to come to work at Music Man. He told me that it would be great to be working with me again. I said I would talk with Leo.

I told Leo I had dinner with George and that I would like to see him come in with us because I felt sorry for him. Here are Leo's exact words, "I don't want to go through that again." Nothing I said that day would cause him to change his mind. You will remember that Leo wanted me to fire George when I started to work at the Fender Electric Instrument Co. in 1954 and I refused, because it wouldn't look right.

My wife Joan and I invited George and his wife Lucille to have lunch with us the following Sunday. At that time, I told George I had talked to Leo and that he seemed to be upset with him for some reason. I suggested that he talk to Leo and see if he could get it straightened out. I knew exactly what was bothering Leo about hiring him but I couldn't tell George. My suggestion must have worked, because Leo called me and told me he had hired George as I had requested.

In 1975, Leo finally came out of hiding, and it was announced in the April issue of *Music Trades* that he was elected president of Music Man. You must understand that Tom gave up his position of president in favor of Leo because of the prestige he felt it gave the company. You see, 10 years had passed since CBS acquired Fender, and Leo now was no longer in fear of contract infringement.

In 1976, Leo and Esther moved from their large home, across the street from Joan and me, to a mobile home park on the outskirts of Fullerton. Leo did not believe a large home was necessary, and neither

Forrest White, Les Paul, Chet Atkins, and Leo Fender at the National Music Show in Atlanta, 1977. (photo: Fullerton)

Leo Fender, Forrest White, and M.H. Berlin at the National Music Show, Atlanta, 1977. (photo: Fullerton)

Dale Hyatt, Leo Fender, and Forrest White at the National Music Show, Atlanta, 1977. (photo: Fullerton)

Leo in his CLF research lab with Eddie Dean, former singing cowboy, 1978. (photo: White)

he nor Esther felt they had to impress anyone. Esther and Joan liked to pal around together and they enjoyed looking at new homes. One day they looked at some new homes which had been built on a hillside and told Leo how nice they were. Leo said those kind of homes cost too much and he would not want to even be associated with anyone who would pay those high ridiculous prices. That is the way he used to believe.

During the early years, Leo was able to keep his head above water only because Esther worked so hard to help pay the bills. Obviously, she didn't marry him for his money or position in life because he only had enough to barely get by, and he certainly was not the living legend he became later on in life. Esther loved Leo just for himself. She didn't have expensive diamonds, because in the early days Leo couldn't afford them. When he could afford them, she didn't want them. She was happy with what she had. They were as compatible as any couple you would ever meet because they were both content with the simple, no frills. They say there is usually a woman behind every successful man. Without a doubt, Esther, the one who helped him during those early years when the going was rough, deserves full credit for being the proverbial woman behind the successful Leo Fender.

Esther was not feeling well in 1978 and on August 1, 1979, passed away. Sadly enough, this was their 45th wedding anniversary. Leo, Joan, and I were the only ones at Esther's bedside at the end. She

did not want anyone else there, not even relatives. It is too bad that she did not live longer to enjoy the many benefits of the successful Fender operation which she had so faithfully helped build. Her death was a great loss to Leo.

It was during that time that Leo told me, "I know you are the best friend I have in this world." It was difficult for me to say anything after that.

Leo and Esther both liked to play pinochle, and each Saturday night Joan and I would meet with them to play. Leo and I were partners against Esther and Joan. Later on Leo told me how much he enjoyed and missed those happy days.

Almost every Sunday Leo and Esther would go down to their slip in the Balboa Harbor and play cards, or maybe just sit there and enjoy the scenery. They would not leave the slip all that often to go out on the ocean. Yachts were just plain "boats" to Leo. He preferred the Stevens boats which were made in Northern California. He would design his own floor plan for each boat, and have them custom-built to his specifications. He changed boats more often than a lot of people change cars. He would think of a floor plan change to make and...presto! Another new boat.

Leo and Esther had named all their boats the *Aquafen*, derived from the term Aqua for water, and, of course, the Fen from Fender. Their last boat was the *Aquafen IX*.

Leo could not think of using the boat again without Esther with him to enjoy it. He and I took all of his personal belongings off the boat on

Leo with friends at Knott's Berry Farm, 1978. L to R: (standing) Cliffie Stone, Dick Goodman, Leo Fender, Jerry Compton, Don Richardson, the Reinsmen; (front) Eddie Dean, Harold Hensley, Speedy West, Merle Moore. (photo: White)

Leo at lunch, Dana Point, 1979. (photo: White)

Another photo of Leo's last
day on the Aquafen IX.
(photo: White)

Leo's last day on the Aquafen
IX in 1979. This was his
favorite picture of himself.
(photo: White)

AQUAFEN IX
BALBOA

August 18, 1979, so it could be sold. This was
just 17 days after Esther passed away. He
never bought another boat. I took some pictures of him on *Aquafen IX* that last day,
and they appear in this book.

Esther had not been gone very long
when George Fullerton's wife, Lucille, introduced Leo to one of their close friends, a
younger woman, and Leo was married for
the second time in September 1980. He would
no longer live in a mobile home park. It was
a house on a hill.

I went to lunch with Leo some months
later and, for some reason that I am still
unsure of, he told me he didn't think a man
should marry more than once. Dale Hyatt
and Speedy West told me that Leo had mentioned the same thing to them on different
occasions. I wonder if the reason was because of the difference in their ages.

I am sorry to say that, after his second marriage, there seemed to be an invisible barrier separating Leo from Joan and me. Maybe it was because we had been too close to Leo and Esther in the past.

For many years I had been Leo's right-hand man, and now credit for that position seemingly was being changed by the marriage and his new wife's friendship with George and Lucille Fullerton. Some statements made were definitely not based on productive performance or factual early years Fender history. Later on, I asked Leo what company they were talking about when a reference was made concerning the early years of Fender. Certain individuals were taking, or being given, credit for things that never happened. Leo had tears in his eyes when he said, "I guess you know that I have some problems, and I have not been the source of those crazy stories." I had never known Leo to lie to me and I was satisfied that he did not approve of some of the things being written.

Shot Jackson and Merle Travis in Shot's Sho-Bud Service Center, Nashville, 1979. (photo: White)

One day Tom Walker said, "Being president is fine, but the Japanese only recognize the top man as being the person who owns the majority of stock."

That made me pretty upset and I answered, "That is the most stupid thing I ever heard of, and just forget it, because there is no way I will part with any of my stock."

Now Tom never would give up on a subject until he felt he had gained satisfaction, so he went to Leo with the same story. He must have driven Leo up the wall. Remember, Leo did not like confrontation. I went over to CLF Research to talk to Leo about something soon after my last encounter with Tom. When I was through, and about to walk out the door, Leo said, "Do me a favor. Sell Tom a couple shares of stock so he will get out of my hair. He is about to drive me crazy."

I answered, "Leo, I'm afraid to, because I don't know how he would treat me if he became the majority stockholder."

Leo said, "Look, I don't think there is any way he can hurt you. Do it for me so he will shut up." I told Leo I would think about it and I left for Music Man.

Now, what should I do? I didn't trust Tom. But there would be no Music Man without Leo's help. This was really what you would call being between a rock and a hard place.

Tom must have sensed that Leo said something to me. So he came to my office again, and ended up with the same line of bull: He should be the majority stockholder because he had to deal with the Japanese. I said, "Tom, how do I know what to expect from you if you become majority stockholder?"

He answered, "You should know there wouldn't be any difference in the way things are being done. You don't have anything to be afraid of."

I didn't believe him and I didn't trust him, but what was I supposed to do about Leo's request? Just what you would have expected me to do. I granted Leo's request. Tom and I each owned 50% of the preferred stock. I sold him the two shares Leo asked me too, and then—just as I was afraid of—things really changed.

By 1980, it was a toss-up in the race to destroy names. Would CBS destroy the name Fender before Tom Walker destroyed the name Music Man? It certainly was not CBS's intention to destroy the Fender name. Quite the contrary. They thought they were doing their best to try to save it. Sadly enough, they had not yet found the right person to save the Fender name from oblivion.

Tom Walker had no intention of destroying the Music Man name either. It was seemingly his misguided attempt to acquire the company by wearing Leo down. He probably thought he could get Leo to sell the company to him dirt cheap by constantly yakking at him, in the same way he had won his other victories. Leo told me that Tom almost drove him crazy by telling him something one day and swearing the next day that he had told him just the opposite. George agreed with Leo that Tom had been doing that. He had been there and had heard the conversations. Tom evidently did not realize at this time that Leo had almost run out of patience.

One day during the latter part of 1981 I received a very welcome telephone call from Freddie Tavares. He said, "Forrest, we finally have a fellow here who I think is capable of turning Fender around. He is a no-nonsense operator and a real stickler for insisting on good quality workmanship."

I said, "Well it's about time. What's his name, and where is he from?"

Freddie answered, "His name is Bill Schultz and he was with Yamaha." I told Freddie I had never heard of him. I thanked him for the call and asked him to keep me posted.

In the year 1981, I was no longer involved with management at Music Man. It was just as I expected. Tom Walker owned 51% of the controlling stock and was calling the shots quite opposite of what he had promised. I was still receiving the same amount of salary. Tom just did not want any competition or suggestions in running the company.

Leo in the CLF research lab, 1981. (photo: White)

Leo said Tom had been complaining about bad necks on the Music Man instruments. Tom told me he had dealers complaining about the inferior necks, and that he could not get replacements from CLF Research. Leo said that necks were not the only thing Tom had been complaining about.

In 1982, Leo told Tom he was starting another company and they would be selling instruments independently in competition with Music Man, but CLF would still make Music Man instruments. Dale Hyatt, who at various times had worked for Leo at Fender's Radio Service, sold cars, worked as a Fender salesman, and in recent years was a salesman for Randall Instruments, would head up the marketing. Needless to say, Tom hit the ceiling. Something had backfired. Leo would not sell the company to Tom. This proved to be the beginning of G & L and the continuation of a facility originally intended only for Music Man Instruments. The intials G & L were

for George and Leo. However, Leo told me that the name was not his idea.

Now, this is something I would like to make crystal clear. CLF Research was making the stringed instruments for Music Man, and the same tooling and machinery would now be used for making G & L instruments; contrary to what some have claimed, Leo Fender did *not* come out of retirement to organize G & L.

Eddie Miller, one of our employees in the early years of Fender, was one of the founders of the Academy of Country Music in Hollywood. I had the pleasure of serving

This 1979 photo of Leo was used on the ACM Pioneer Award Plaque he received in 1982. (photo: White)

Leo receiving the ACM Pioneer Award at Knott's Berry Farm in 1982.

on the ACM's Board of Directors from 1981 through 1985. The directors pick the person they feel is worthy to receive the Pioneer Award.

The Pioneer Award is a special award that was created in 1968 to recognize outstanding and unprecedented achievement in the field of country music. It is not bestowed on an annual basis and has had more than one recipient in a given year. In 1982, while serving as a member of the Board of Directors, I had the pleasure of presenting Leo's name to the Board.

On April 29, 1982, Leo Fender was presented the Academy of Country Music's Pioneer Award at the 17th annual awards show held at Knott's Berry Farm, Buena Park, California. The show was televised nationally. Many of Leo's friends praised him for his contribution to country music. Our friends Bill Boyd, Executive Director, and Fran Boyd, Executive Secretary of the Academy, helped make Leo's award possible by their support.

Leo is protecting his ears because his friend Dennis Zimmerman, tenor singer and manager for The Watchmen gospel quartet, is not playing a Fender instrument. (photo: White)

Leo was the first "non-performing artist" to receive the award since 1968, when it was given to Art Satherley. The award was presented to Leo for his achievements in revolutionizing the guitar and bass industry with the introduction of his electric solid-body designs in 1950. Leo was 72 years of age when he received the award.

By the latter part of 1982, Tom Walker was really having trouble with Music Man necks, and he had one cut open to check the adjusting truss rod. He found that it was absolutely straight. The truss rod is supposed to be installed with the bow down. When you tighten the nut on the threaded end, the adjusting truss rod then tries to return to its original straight position and, in doing so, it pulls the head end of the neck down to compensate for the uplifting pull from the string tension. Tom did not claim to be an engineer, but it does not require a lot of knowledge to know that a straight truss rod on a guitar cannot be adjusted.

Tom was really unhappy and he took the cut-open neck over to show Leo. He asked how they were making the necks for G & L instruments. Lloyd Chewning, who had made many Fender necks during the early years, brought in one of the G & L guitar necks. It had the proper bowed adjusting truss rod. Tom asked Leo why the Music Man necks were not being made in the conventional manner. Tom said Leo told him it was George Fullerton's idea. I personally don't care whose idea it was. It was wrong and whoever was responsible should have known better.

After the neck confrontation, communication between Leo and Tom was limited. Tom had a difficult time obtaining replacement necks from CLF because G & L production was being given preferential priority. This was not right. A lot of innocent dealers and customers were being hurt over the stupidity of using those straight truss rods. I still cannot believe it. Or the reason.

It was downhill now for Music Man financially. I was still drawing my regular salary but I didn't know for how long. Tom insisted on doing everything himself, and in a way, that was good. He had signed the last bank loan note himself as majority stockholder. We both signed when we owned equal shares of stock. He was becoming more concerned about the cash flow as the days went by. The bank was pressing him because they seemed to be worried. Dealers were becoming more dissatisfied as orders were not filled.

Tom Walker looked for a buyer for Music Man. But, there was this problem: He wanted the buyer to accept his services as part of the deal. I was told he had an offer from a Mr. Kojima, from Japan, but the sale was not consummated because Kojima planned to let Roger Balmer (formerly of CBS/Fender) have charge of all domestic sales and for Uschi Eastman (Tom's former employee and niece) to handle all export sales. My source said this was not acceptable to Tom because he was afraid he might not be offered a position.

Tom sold Music Man to Ernie Ball on March 7, 1984, and I was told it was for less than what Kojima would have paid because Tom would become an employee of Ernie Ball as part of the deal. There seemed to be no concern about my welfare as minority stockholder. Music

Man's remaining assets were sold to help satisfy the bank loan on Friday, June 1, 1984.

Music Man could have been a very successful company in those early years. We had everything going for us. I believe readers of this book can determine what caused the downfall.

Ernie Ball moved what was left of Music Man to San Luis Obispo, California, along with his guitar strings and musical accessory business. His new employee, Tom Walker, moved with him.

Well, my position with Music Man may have gone down the drain, but I was sure I could join up with Leo and George Fullerton and help build guitars at G & L, because I was the one who had persuaded Leo to hire George again. Right? Wrong! Do you suppose it had anything to do with Leo's second marriage? Leo Fender and I were still friends, and he had come out of retirement just to help me get started in a business he thought I should have—not to start G & L. What do you think happened along the way? Was it because of old resentments from the early Fender years, when I was George's boss and struggled with him over manufacturing problems?

I had lunch with Leo again and asked him why there was no room for me at G & L. Again, as I had heard before, he told me, "I think you know I have problems now." The tears were there as before. I understood there wasn't much Leo could do under the circumstances and still keep peace in his marriage.

That was when Leo told me that I should write a book about the history of the company and that I should not feel intimidated in telling exactly what happened. He told me many things he wanted people to know.

In the summer of 1984, I went to see my old friend F. C. Hall at Rickenbacker. Ward Deaton, the factory manager, wanted to retire, and I became the vice president and general manager of the factory.

There was much to do at Rickenbacker. I reworked the design of the guitar bridge assembly by adding a new channel and spring-loaded string length adjustments. The final assemblers had trouble adjusting the necks, which had double truss rods. I redesigned the double-truss rod system, and the necks were much easier to adjust. John Quarterman (formerly of Dobro, CLF Research, and Music Man) and Dick Burke, wood-shop foreman, suggested an easy way to install the wooden fill strip in the neck after the adjusting truss rods were inserted.

I had new routing plates made for routing out wood from the center core of the instrument bodies. The previous plates did not allow enough material around the section where the bridges were mounted. This change improved the tone of the instruments.

F. C. Hall and his son, John, both told me they thought we were making the best instruments in the history of Rickenbacker, with the design changes and improved manufacturing methods.

One day in August 1984, not too long after I had started with Rickenbacker, I had lunch with F. C. Hall. He told me he was going to retire and that John would be taking over the management of the company. I told him that I probably would not be there too long after John took over, because I thought John resented me.

F. C. retired in September 1984. John came to the factory not too long afterward. He had not had any experience in manufacturing musical instruments. He asked me to make a change in something that had to do with manufacturing, and I honestly do not remember what it was about. I told John that I didn't think it would work and he became very much upset.

I told F. C. about the encounter later on that day and said that I felt it would be just a matter of time now until I would be terminated. I was right. Not long after that, John fired me. He can say that he was the only one who ever fired Forrest White. F. C. and I are still very good friends.

I believe in giving credit where credit is due. From what I hear, John has been doing a commendable job with Rickenbacker. The company is growing and I wish him the very best of luck.

Finally, in 1985, CBS made the wise decision to get out of the musical instrument business. They put Fender up for sale. The Fender name had been plunging into oblivion until the year 1981, and then the downward trend started to level out a little. That was the year Freddie Tavares told me CBS had made the wise decision to hire Bill Schultz to take charge.

Bill really had a mess to clean up. It was no easy job to correct the many problems that had almost destroyed the Fender name. Slowly, he improved procedures in material control, manufacturing methods, and quality standards as the company began the long uphill climb in repairing the damage and regaining the former dealer and customer acceptance that had made Fender one of the leaders in the musical instrument business. By 1985 it was obvious that the company was going to survive, and CBS must have thought they had better get out while things were looking good.

Freddie called to tell me he was going to retire and that he had informed the company. I asked him how things were going, and that was when he told me CBS was going to sell. He said he thought Bill Schultz was trying to put a package together to make an offer for Fender, and he hoped he would be successful. I asked Freddie if he was still impressed with the job Bill was doing. He replied in the affirmative and said he thought Bill was the one who could restore Fender to its former position as king of the hill.

CHAPTER 17

FENDER MUSICAL INTRUMENTS— 1985

Bill Schultz and his associates were successful in buying Fender. Freddie Tavares said he could look forward to a happy retirement now that Fender was in good hands. Freddie was right. The Fender name would survive.

CBS Musical Instruments was no more. The name was changed back to Fender Musical Instruments. Bill Schultz moved the company out of the huge building CBS had built, because they didn't need that much room in 1985.

It was not long before Leo Fender's health started to fail. He was not one to give up easily, and many times through the years he would be working at the factory when he should have been home in bed. As stated previously, one of the reasons Leo sold the Fender Electric Instrument Co. was because, at that time, he had problems with a viral sinus infection.

George Fullerton sold his interest in G & L to Leo, at Leo's insistence, and the *G* was changed to Guitars. It was not George anymore. The company, however, was still called G & L but not "George & Leo." The operator would tell you that you had reached "Guitars *by* Leo" when you

In 1987, Leo had his name preserved, beside many of those of his peers in the music business, in a place of honor in front of the Guitar Center, a Fender dealer in Hollywood, CA. (photo: White)

called. I asked Leo if George had been willing to accept responsibility and make decisions any more than he had in Fender early years. Leo grinned and said, "Well, I guess he hasn't changed much."

Dale Hyatt called me in the latter eighties to tell me he was having manufacturing problems at G & L. He was trying to manage the operation by himself. I knew they were having financial problems so I told Dale I would help him at no charge if he wanted me to. Finally, he called to ask if I would help, so I started to work at G & L the following Monday. I thought I was finally back in the musical instrument business.

Leo went to lunch with us the first day. Dale had gone into the restaurant to get us a table and Leo told me, "I am having problems with the factory and I was going to call you if Dale hadn't." That explained the telephone call I had received. By now Leo was not physically able to drive, and you had to listen very carefully to understand what he was saying, as his speech was impaired by heavy medication.

Dale was not complimentary about the job George Fullerton had done as production manager at G & L. He thought George was more interested in how much bonus he made rather than using good judgment in scheduling the right production. Whatever the reason, poor scheduling was a loss to Leo, who was paying the bills.

I didn't stay at G & L very long to help because I did not like the working conditions. I was not given a proper office to work in, even though a room and desk were available. I left because I felt it was an impossible situation, and I was so sorry I was unable to help Leo with his problems.

My bowling buddy Ray Winchell left CBS Musical Instruments in 1984 to accept a position in the credit department at Rolandcorp US. Not long after going with the new company, Ray became the president of the music group's National Credit Managers' Association. Bill Schultz kept in touch with what Ray was doing, and in 1987, two years after Bill had acquired Fender, he asked Ray to come back to serve as national credit manager. After his return to Fender, Ray soon became chairman of the music group's Southern California Credit Managers' Association. I am proud to have hired him in the early Fender years.

The following article appeared in the January 1990 issue of *Music Trades* written by editor Brian Majeski and reprinted with his permission.

CBS MUSICAL INSTRUMENTS
Two Bad Quarters and You're Out

CBS entered the music industry in a big way in 1965, paying a whopping $13.5 million for Fender Musical Instruments. The same year, they bought the New York Yankees for a mere $11 million. Subsequent acquisitions included Electro Music, maker of the Leslie Speaker, Steinway & Sons, Gulbransen Organs, Gemeinhardt Flutes, Rodgers Organ, Lyon & Healy Harps, and the remnants of the ARP Synthesizer Company. Under the leadership of Robert G. Campbell, CBS Music's avowed goal was to surpass its archrival Norlin.

The CBS mode of operation was generally to pay an exorbitant price for a music company and then press management to deliver an impossible rate of return. Unreasonable demands prompted company managers to do outrageous things, like refusing to write off dead receivables or junk inventory, inflating sales, and cutting scores of untenable deals with music retailers.

If ever there was a company that operated with a short-term focus, it was CBS Music. Money was squandered on a lavish corporate office complex outside of Chicago, while only a pittance was allocated to capital investments in products and production equipment. As one former vice president explained, "The corporate brass doesn't care what you did to get the numbers, all they care about is seeing the numbers."

By 1980, CBS Music's management ran out of ways to postpone bad news, and the company began operating in the red. As the economy worsened managerial deficiencies at the company became more apparent, and the losses grew worse. In 1985, after having racked up losses of over $40 million, the company decided to get out of music. Regrettably, CBS's exit from the industry was as ungraceful as its 20 year presence: Gulbransen was liquidated at a cost of over $10 million; Fender was "shopped" to virtually every company in the guitar industry without any attempt at discretion; and Steinway, Rodgers, Lyon & Healy, and Gemeinhardt languished on the market for over a year due in large part to indecisive management. On a happy note, CBS's former music properties have all fared well under private ownership.

My friend Brian Majeski sure hit the nail on the head. I don't know how the other former CBS companies have succeeded, but by the time Brian wrote that article in 1990, Bill Schultz had done a remarkable job in bringing Fender back to its former position at the top of its industry. Freddie Tavares was right. The Fender name is in good hands.

I told you that Leo Fender's first business partner, Doc Kauffman, died June 26, 1990. Perhaps the Fender Telecaster, Stratocaster, and Precision Bass would not exist today if Leo had not met and worked with Doc during those early years. Soon after Doc passed away, Leo lost another good friend and former employee. Freddie Tavares passed away July 24, 1990. Freddie had worked by Leo's side in research and development during the golden early years at the Fender Electric Instrument Co. while the

Stratocaster was being conceived. He helped Leo with the development of all Fender products from 1953 until the company was sold in 1964.

Freddie was laid to rest in the Oahu Cemetery, Honolulu, Hawaii, his home state. My friend Jerry Byrd told me he played the steel guitar at the funeral service in Hawaii. I know Freddie would have approved, because of his appreciation of Jerry's talent. I am so thankful I had lunch and a nice visit with Freddie just before his illness. He was a wonderful person.

Leo Fender attended the memorial service for Freddie Tavares that was held in Anaheim on July 31, 1990. It was a beautiful service, and many of Freddie's friends were there, including George Fullerton, Dale Hyatt, Alvino Rey, Bill Shultz, and so many more that there was only standing room available.

Leo looked weak and he could hardly speak or walk. He acted like he was under very heavy sedation—absolutely lethargic. I sure hoped that he was not taking more medication than was necessary, because Leo was a proud man, and it must have been very embarrassing for him when he could not carry on an intelligible conversation with his friends.

I tried to talk to Leo briefly after Freddie's memorial service. I could hardly make out what he was saying to me most of the time. Just before we said good-bye he took my hand into both of his and it was so difficult to hear him. With tears in his eyes, he said, "Don't grow old...It isn't good for you." And he smiled very weakly. Those were the last words my close friend ever said to me and that was the last time I saw him.

Leo Fender passed away Thursday, March 21, 1991. The funeral service was held on Tuesday, March 26, and he was placed at rest beside his first wife, Esther. They were finally together. Somehow, somewhere, I believe they are aware of it.

George Fullerton called me just before noon on that day and said, "I hate to call you to give you bad news, but Leo died this morning." George and Dale Hyatt both lived close to Leo's home, and by then I lived 75 miles away. Either George or Dale had been picking Leo up each day to take him to lunch and then down to the lab where he would work for two or three hours. So they both knew how he was feeling, healthwise, on a day-to-day basis. I was shocked when George gave me the news, even though I had been anticipating such a call for a long time.

A memorial service was held for Leo at a local Fullerton church on Saturday, March 30, 1991. Many of his friends were there including Danny Michaels, Hank Penny, Alvino Rey, Eddie Dean, Harold Rhodes, Gene Galion, George Fullerton, and Dale Hyatt. Danny, Hank, Alvino, and I said a few words about our relationship with Leo. It was very hard for me to express how I felt about Leo in front of his many friends.

I will always remember the strumming sound across open guitar strings as Leo checked the amplifier's performance...the confidence he had in me when we had a problem and he would tell me to use my own judgment in taking care of it...the good times at lunch each workday...the many different diets he would start on, and would expect you to join him so you would not miss the benefits of his latest nutritional discovery...how we checked out the new cars when they came out each year...letting him out the side gate when he was ready to go home each workday evening... the pinochle games Joan and I had with Leo and Esther on Saturday nights...how he would laugh at Esther when she became upset and told him, "You're not down there at that fiddle factory now, you know!" There are so many things I will miss but, thank God, I still have the memories. This was the last good-bye to Leo Fender, the person who had the most influence on my life. He gave me the opportunity to become involved in the world of music. I will always be grateful.

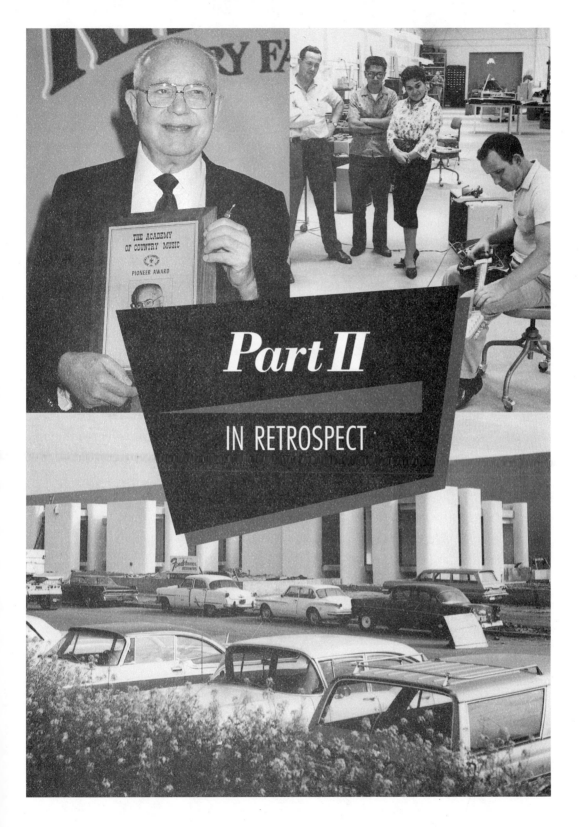

Part II

IN RETROSPECT

IN RETROSPECT

Maybe some people take things for granted, thinking that perhaps they deserve the good breaks that happen to them. Friend, I can tell you that I feel like the luckiest person in the world. Leo needed help, but to think of all the capable people who could have helped him…he chose me. Please forgive me for being a little proud that I was part of the early years history of Fender.

Perhaps I should tell you a little more about Leo's quest for the perfect diet and why I was fearful of what he would come up with next, knowing he would expect me to join him. One of his first experiments involved the use of cider vinegar as the sure cure for what ailed you. He would ask the waitress to bring us cider vinegar on the side, and we would then add a spoonful of that lurid liquid into our glass of drinking water. This concoction had to be downed before you dared take the first bite of your hamburger. You were expected to join this rigorous ritual during lunch, regardless of who you were.

Not long after the vinegar kick, he believed carrot juice was the answer. He then suggested (while twisting my arm) that I obtain a vegetable juice extractor. I drank carrot juice almost night and day for at least a month, then I noticed a change in my complexion. I showed Leo my arms and said, "Leo, I've got to quit drinking so much carrot juice because my complexion is becoming an orange color." Leo laughed so hard he almost became unglued.

Later on, he thought cabbage juice was the answer. I told him, "Leo, there is no way I'm going to drink cabbage juice. Turning orange was bad enough, and I am darn sure I am not going to take the chance of turning green." He was kind enough not to pressure me to drink cabbage juice but, you know, I would gladly join him on any diet he could think of if only the hands of time could be turned backward and he was with us once more. I just wish he could have found the proper diet to prevent the illness that took his life.

CHAPTER **18**

FROM A MANAGER'S
POINT OF VIEW

I mentioned earlier that I would try to explain why some employees did not like to work under my management. I would also like for you to know what I dislike about an employee's actions and their effect on productivity. I believe if any person accepts a position in a company which requires them to make practical and economical decisions, the company, in turn, has the right to expect a productive performance from that employee. It irritates me when one employee rides on the coattails of another. It irritates me even more when a company is successful and that same parasite employee is shameless enough to accept unearned credit for his limited contribution. Another thing that really irritates me is the employee who is habitually late for work.

A general manager has the responsibility to carry out many duties that are not very pleasant. Telling an employee that his performance isn't satisfactory, spelling out exactly how and why you expect him to do better, isn't a pleasant task. On the other hand, if his work is good, his effort should be recognized and appreciated. I am sorry to say that Leo Fender was not inclined to hand out compliments to his employees. Leo appreciated a good job being done but it was not his nature to tell an employee that he appreciated it. That is why his gift of the clock/barometer, with plaque, meant so much to me.

Employees knew that I expected them to do a good job in being productive but, above all, to maintain the excellent Fender quality workmanship. Those who worked under my direction might not all agree, but I tried at all times to be friendly, constructive, honest, and fair in my supervision. I hope they knew I always tried to give proper credit where credit was due.

It was not possible for me to know the names of all the employees as the Fender Company grew. I do hope they found our company to be a good place to work, and I wish they all could know how much I appreciated their help and cooperation during those wonderful early years.

Some employees appreciate their early years of employment at Fender so much that they are helping to retain that memory by making nostalgic memorabilia. Sam Hutton was one of the most outstanding employees we had in the amplifier cabinet covering department. Sam is presently making clocks that look like the front of Fender classic amplifiers. He is using the same kind of grill cloth and striped brown covering material we used on amplifiers during the early years. They may be available at some Fender dealers.

Charlie Hayes, you will recall, was one of the first Fender salesmen and one of the four partners when Fender Sales was formed in 1953. The day Charlie was killed he gave me a copy of what he used as his guide in selling Fender products and I would like to pass it on to you. Remember, the dealer is the customer, as well as the valued musicians who play Fender.

THE CUSTOMER

1. The customer is the most important person in our business.
2. He is not dependent upon us...we are dependent upon him.
3. He is not an interruption of our work...he is the purpose of it.
4. He does us an honor when he calls...we are not doing him a favor by serving him.
5. He is a part of our business, not an outsider...he is our guest.
6. He is not a cold statistic...he is a flesh and blood human being with feelings and emotions like our own.
7. He is not someone to argue or to match wits with.
8. He is one who tells us his requirements...it is our job to fulfill those requirements.

9. He is deserving of the most courteous and attentive treatment we can
   give him.
10. He is the lifeblood of this and every other business.

I wonder what Charlie Hayes would have thought if he could have heard what Speedy West told me recently. Speedy said that Elden Shamblen, who used to play guitar with Bob Wills and the Texas Playboys, sold his 1954 Stratocaster to Cain's Academy Ballroom in Tulsa, Oklahoma, for $12,500 in the spring of 1991. Wow! If I had only known this in 1954.

Another example of just how popular the Fender Stratocaster is: The founder of the Hard Rock Cafe has said he plans to build a $75 million hotel-casino in Las Vegas, Nevada, that he feels will be "a walk on the wild side," with guitar-shaped gaming tables and memorabilia. A press release stated that the gaming parlor will display a replica 130-foot Fender electric guitar smashed into the roof. Leo Fender would never have dreamed in the early years that one day, there would be a 130-foot Stratocaster sticking out of the roof of a hotel-casino in Las Vegas.

One of Webster's definitions for gambling is, "to take a risk in order to gain some advantage." If that's the meaning, then show me a person who has never gambled. Leo was not a Las Vegas–type gambler, but he was a gambler. A big gambler. He put all of his earthly possessions on the line when he started in business in those early years—all his money, his home. He went in debt. He took a risk to prove he could build the world's best electric guitars and amplifiers. Then, after a few years of hard work, he won. His risk had paid off—for personal financial security, for his employees, for the many Fender dealers, for thousands of musicians, for an honored place in history—because the Fender name will live on. Leo Fender became a true legend in his time.

I hope I have been able to give you a better idea of what really happened during the early years at Fender. This inside story was based on my personal documents and the fact that I was there when it happened while serving my friend, Leo Fender, as his vice president and general manager of the great Fender Electric Instrument Co., Fullerton, California.

I also hope you understand that I hold no malice toward any of those whom I worked with at Fender. I will admit I was terribly hurt by some of their actions, especially when I thought they were my friends. But life is too short to think negatively. I would much rather think of the good things that happened. And there were many.

I have been asked many times why I gave up a darn good job at Fender because I refused to approve the building of amplifiers that were not worthy of Leo's name. Well, Leo was my friend, and I knew he would not have approved of the amplifiers CBS expected me to build. I was unable to express my concern over the design to top management due to a failure in the communication system.

Leo told me he thought I was the best friend he had in this world. Just what kind of a best friend would I have been, and how could I have possibly justified his opinion of my friendship, by failing to stand up and defend the principles of design that he believed in? I was the only one who was loyal enough to Leo to resign rather than put the value of the greenback dollar ahead of our friendship. Think about this when any former early year employees, or their "cheering sections," make claims or infer that they were close friends of Leo's. Ask them how they showed their loyalty and friendship to Leo when the chips were down and they were asked to help build amplifiers he would have rejected. I consider loyalty to be a matter of honor.

I would make the same decision today that I made on the day of my resignation. I believe it would be the only way I could repay Leo's confidence in me. Perhaps my explanation clarifies any questions there may have been on this subject.

If you have enjoyed reading about Leo Fender, the man, and the inside story of the early years Fender history half as much as I have enjoyed writing it, then the effort was well worthwhile. Those who were there at the time will tell you I have been truthful in relating what actually occurred.

I hope you will also enjoy Part II of this book, as you read about the contribution Leo made to the wonderful world of music.

As I told my key personnel when I resigned from CBS, "Please protect and hold the name Fender as high as you possibly can."

CHAPTER **19**

LEO FENDER
TECHNOLOGY

TECHNOLOGY (*Webster's New World Dictionary*): 1.) The science or study of the practical or industrial arts, applied sciences, etc. 2.) The terms used in a science, art, etc ; technical terminology 3.) Applied science 4.) A method, process, etc. for handling a specific technical problem 5.) The system by which a society provides its members with those things needed or desired.

Leo Fender was not an engineer. His college education was limited to two years of junior college, where his major subject was accounting. Then he learned the technology of radio servicing and owned and managed Fender's Radio Service for a few years until he became interested in building amplifiers and guitars.

Let's see how well Leo complied with *Webster's* definition of technology. 1.), 2.), 3.) Self-explanatory. 4) Leo Fender excelled in developing methods and processing to handle specific technical design and tooling problems for manufacturing his musical instrument products. 5) No other person has done more than he to provide musicians with needed or desired superior musical instrument amplifiers and guitars, or enhanced the sound of music more for the listening pleasure of the general public.

There may be some with degrees in electronics or mechanical engineering who wonder why I would dare associate the name Leo Fender with the field of higher learning. May I respectfully suggest that they judge him on his success rather than on his lack of formal engineering education. Those of us who knew him can tell you of many times when he made "self-assumed know-it-alls" look foolish when they attempted to upstage him with their book-learning savvy.

I have the highest respect for formal education. However, I have hired some engineers with degrees who, in all fairness, did not seem to have as much know-how as Leo possessed in his little finger. He had God-given talent in knowing how to design, and tool for manufacturing, stringed musical instruments and amplifiers for those musicians who appreciate the highest quality in design, workmanship, and performance.

In the following pages you will be given examples of Leo Fender's creativity with these copies of original wiring diagrams and schematics, in addition to selective information regarding methods and procedures used in making these acclaimed musical instruments and amplifiers.

Leo's brand of technology may not have been the most advanced in its day but you can't argue with its margin of success. The name Fender will pass through the lips of outstanding musicians through the years, and much longer than many of them will remember, there was a person by the name of Leo who deserves the credit for the instruments they own and call the best. The quality and prestige of Fender Musical Instruments has been restored to assure its rightful leadership position in the music industry. Leo Fender can look down with pride, knowing that his brain-child is in good hands.

CHAPTER 20

THE SECRET
OF THE
FENDER SOUND

WHY FENDER INSTRUMENTS ARE SO ACCEPTABLE AND
HOW THE EARLY PICKUPS WERE MADE

If you would ask talented guitar players what they consider to be the best sounding present-day guitar, you may receive different answers. If you asked them what they consider to be the best all-time guitars, I'll bet you would hear "Fender" loud and clear. Why are these instruments different? What makes them so superior in sound and feel? Why haven't present-day competitors been able to duplicate their performance? I believe the answer is simply that the present-day Fender guitars are being manufactured by following basic guidelines that the founder, Leo Fender, established in the early glory years of his company.

But, you ask, what about the sound? Why do Fender guitars sound much better? The answer, of course, is the pickups. I will tell you how they were made in the early years using the material Leo Fender originally specified to achieve what he considered top performance at that time. He must have been right, because many of the top entertainers play Telecasters and

Stratocasters which are being duplicated by using the early year specifications to maintain the unmatched Fender sound.

EARLY YEARS FENDER INSTRUMENT PICKUP MATERIAL

(a) $^3/_{16}$"dia. Alnico Magnets — Length depends on the type pickup made for the particular instrument.

(b) Vulcanized Fiber — Used for coil form top and bottom pieces.

(c) Magnet Wire — #42 or #43 gauge, and P.E.(plain enamel) or S.T. (single teflon) coating, depending on the type pickup made for the particular instrument.

(d) Hook-Up Wire — Small gauge, stranded/tinned, used for leads. A single layer was wound around the pickup coils for protection of the magnet wire on the Broadcaster's and Telecaster's lead pickups. The rhythm pickup had a chrome-plated brass cover. The Stratocaster pickups, and the pickups on all the other model guitars which followed, were protected with plastic covers.

(e) Paraffin — Purchased in block form and melted in a deep fry-like container. Leo wanted the pickups dipped in the melted paraffin because he thought it would drive the moisture out and help to protect the pickups. This was done for years.

(f) Solder — Small dia. electronic rosin core (non-corrosive).

(g) Fiber Coil-Form Top Piece — We punched six slightly smaller holes than $^3/_{16}$"dia. into the fiber, with the use of a small punch press, to provide a snug fit for the magnets.

(h) Fiber Coil-Form Bottom Piece — Holes were punched for the magnets (as above) and, in addition, we punched two snug-fit holes for coil leads and two more that were used to slip the coil form onto the two prongs of the handmade coil-form holder.

The pickup forms were made by pressing the magnets into the six snug-fitting holes of the fiber top and bottom. We used an arbor press for this operation in the early years at Fender.

Leo used lightweight sewing machine motors for coil winding. The speed of the motors was controlled by the use of a foot control so that both of the operator's hands were free to hand-guide (scramble wind) the magnet wire onto the coil form. Leo mounted the handmade coil-form holder, along with the sewing machine–type motor, on a small board that was then placed on the workbench. The two units were positioned so that the small pulleys, mounted on the shaft ends of the motor and coil holder, were in alignment. A small rubber band was used for the belt to motor drive the coil holder. The use of the rubber band was very important for this particular purpose. Since it was soft and pliable, it helped to prevent breakage of the magnet wire. The coil-form holder was very simple, with just the means of supporting a small shaft with a pulley on one end and a two-pronged fork arrangement on the other end to slide the coil form onto while winding.

Now, to wind the coil. The inside lead wire (approximately 6" long) was inserted into the coil form through the snug-fitting hole provided, and then soldered to the end of the magnet wire to be wound. The coil form was then slipped carefully onto the prongs of the coil-form holder so that the solder joint would not separate. A method was devised to hold the magnet wire spool so that it turned freely during the winding of the coil. The magnet wire was then wound onto the coil form by the scramble-winding (hand-guided) method as mentioned before. There is a difference of opinion whether this method was better or worse than the layer-winding method that was possible with more expensive equipment. You must keep in mind, though, that we did not have a lot of money during those early years and could not afford the more sophisticated equipment that was available.

The number of turns required depended on the type of pickup being made. After the last turn on the coil, the operator would cut the magnet wire and solder it to the end of a long piece of hook-up wire. (Note that this lead wire had not been inserted through the coil-form bottom.) After soldering to the end of the magnet wire coil, the lead wire was carefully single-layer wound around the coil starting from the top down. When the coil magnet wire was completely covered, the end of the lead wire was then inserted down through the snug-fitting outside punched hole. The pickup magnet wire coil was now protected and ready to dip into the melted paraffin. After dipping, the pickup coil was placed onto a handmade chicken-wire frame so that it could drip and dry. And, friend, after that you had yourself a darn good pickup.

You may have guessed that the above procedure was used to make the lead pickups for the Broadcaster and early years Telecaster and Esquire. The lead wire single layer around the coil was not necessary for protection on the other early year pickups.

The magnet wire ends were soldered to the inside and outside lead wires onto Stimpson #A593 eyelets that had been fastened into the fiber for all of the pickups, except the early years Broadcaster, Telecaster, and Esquire.

Fender Musical Instruments has kept pace with new pickup technology through the years. There is none better today. Performance is assured for all discriminating musicians.

EARLY YEARS PICKUP SPECIFICATIONS

Year	Fender Electric Instruments	Coated Copper Magnet Wire	# of Turns	Ohm Reading Min.	Max.
1950	Telecaster Lead	#42 P.E.	1500	5200	5800
	Rhythm	#43 P.E.	1500	6200	6800
1950	Esquire	#42 P.E..	1500	5200	5800
1951	Precision Bass	#42 P.E.	2100	7300	8100
1954	Stratocaster	#42 P.E.	1600	5600	6200
1954	Stringmaster-6	#42 P.E.	1800	6200	7000
1954	Stringmaster-8	#42 P.E.	1800	8300	9300
1955	Deluxe 6 Steel	#42 P.E.	1600	5600	6200
1955	Deluxe 8 Steel	#42 P.E.	1600	7400	8300
1955	Champ 6 Steel	#42 P.E.	1500	5200	5800
1955	Studio Deluxe-6	#42 P.E.	1500	5200	5800
1955	White Studio-6	#42 P.E.	1500	5200	5800
1956	Musicmaster	#42 P.E.	1500	5200	5800
1956	Duo-Sonic	#42 P.E.	1500	5200	5800
1964	Mustang Standard	#42 P.E.	1500	5200	5800
1956	Mandolin-4 Strg.	#42 S.T.	1900	6600	7400
1957	Pedal 400/1000-8	#42 S.T.	1900	8800	9800
1958	Pedal 800/2000-10	#42 S.T.	1900	11000	12000
1958	Precision Bass	#42 S.T.	2100	5100	5800
1958	Prec. Fretless	#42 S.T.	2100	5100	5800
1958	Jazzmaster	#42 P.E.	1700	5900	6600
1960	Jazz Bass	#42 S.T.	1900	6600	7400
1961	Bass VI Guitar	#42 S.T.	1800	6200	7000
1962	Jaguar Lead	#42 P.E.	1800	6200	6800
	Rhythm	#42 S.T.	1800	6200	6800
1963	Musicmaster Bass	#42 P.E.	1800	6200	6800
1964	Mustang Bass	#42 P.E.	1900	4400	4900
1964	12-Strg. Standard				
	Split Pickup	#42 P.E.	2200	5100	5700
1965	5-String Bass				
	Lead	#42 P.E.	2400	4200	4600
	Rhythm	#42 P.E.	2600	6800	7300

CHAPTER 21

FRET
PLACEMENT

ACCURATE MUSICAL INSTRUMENT FRET POSITIONS
AND PROBLEMS WITH AN INACCURATE MUSIC SCALE

For many years, fret placement was not correct on some well-known brand fretted musical instruments. A few manufacturing corrections were made later on because of increasing competition. However, a problem still existed. Leo Fender never learned to play the guitar, but the ones he made were considered to be very accurate in intonation because he was so particular in the placement of frets. He told me that the following "Fret Placement Multiplier Guide," which I developed in the early years, was more accurate than what he used when he designed the Broadcaster, Telecaster, and Stratocaster. Coming from Leo, this was a compliment that I was extremely proud of.

The scale length of a fretted musical instrument is the measured distance between the nut and the center of the mounted bridge. The center of the bridge is used as the accurate measuring point for the scale length because adjustable bridges (with separate movable sections) are used to compensate for the difference in string gauges. The lighter the string gauge, the more the bridge is adjusted to shorten the string, to assure the correct intonation of the instrument. The heavier the gauge, the more the bridge is adjusted to lengthen the string. So, the bridge sections for the 1st, 2nd, and 3rd strings of a guitar, for example, are normally adjusted forward, toward the nut, and the bridge sections for the 4th, 5th, and 6th strings are normally adjusted backward toward the tail-end of the guitar. The most accurate measurement to determine the instrument scale length, then, would normally be from the nut to the average adjustment between the 3rd- and 4th-string bridge sections. It can be frustrating to try to correct a situation that is imperfect, since frets are straight across. I almost threw a good guitar away when I was learning to play because I did not know that the problem was not with me or the guitar. I had to learn to make compensation in the tuning. We should be thankful that most of us are not blessed with perfect pitch, because it is obvious that no fretted musical instrument that uses different string gauges can have perfect intonation. How can I make that statement and know that it is impossible for anyone to challenge it? Because it is quite simple: The music scale itself is not perfect. You can understand now that I have not challenged the superb accuracy of the fret placement on Fender instruments.

Any music major will tell you that what I have said is true—the music scale is not accurate. The term "equal temperament scale" actually means that a correction has been made to compensate for the inaccurate unequal intervals of the "natural" music scale. This is what the piano tuner has to do when he tunes your piano—he has learned to compensate for the inaccurate scale. This is also why you must learn to compensate when you tune your fretted musical instrument, even though the fret positions are accurate. Your guitar may sound great when you strum the C-chord, but then the E-chord may sound terrible. The answer? Learn to compensate and you will retain your sanity. If the problem bothers you too much, then purchase an "equal temperament scale" electronic tuner. I am sure that many of you professional musicians are aware of the problem. I just hope that I have helped those who have been faced with a tuning problem. Don't blame your instrument until you learn to compensate and live with the only music scale we have. You will have to ask someone with much greater knowledge than I why musicians have to live with this "blooper."

Fret placement is extremely important, and you will not find a fretted instrument more accurate than a Fender. The correct position of the 12th fret is exactly half way between the nut and the bridge. Banjo players should remember this. When they change strings, or the head of the banjo, they will know how to determine the correct bridge replacement.

The Telecaster and Stratocaster scale length is 25½". The Music Master, Duo-Sonic, and Mustang ¾-size guitars were available with a 22½" or 24" scale length. The Precision Bass scale length is 34". I mentioned that Leo Fender copied the scale length of a Gretsch archtop acoustic guitar when he designed the Broadcaster (Telecaster) guitar. It is quite obvious that he was lucky in choosing the 25½" scale length.

The Fret Placement Multiplier Guide that I have developed can be used to determine accurate fret positions for any fretted musical instrument scale length with ease. I will show how the first 12 frets of a 24" fretted musical instrument scale are located, as an example, with the use of the guide. I am sure it is easy enough to understand that frets #13 through #24 can be easily located by using the proper multiplier numbers.

FRET PLACEMENT MULTIPLIER GUIDE

Fret	Fret	24" Music Instrument Scale Fret Position From The Nut
#1 = .05613	#13 = .52806	#1 – 24" x .05613 = 1.347"
#2 = .10910	#14 = .55455	#2 – 24" x .10910 = 2.618"
#3 = .15910	#15 = .57955	#3 – 24" x .15910 = 3.818"
#4 = .20630	#16 = .60315	#4 – 24" x .20630 = 4.951"
#5 = .25085	#17 = .62542	#5 – 24" x .25085 = 6.020"
#6 = .29289	#18 = .64645	#6 – 24" x .29289 = 7.029"
#7 = .33258	#19 = .66629	#7 – 24" x .33258 = 7.981"
#8 = .37004	#20 = .68502	#8 – 24" x .37004 = 8.880"
#9 = .40540	#21 = .70270	#9 – 24" x .40540 = 9.729"
#10 = .43877	#22 = .71938	#10 – 24" x .43877 = 10.530"
#11 = .47027	#23 = .73513	#11 – 24" x .47027 = 11.286"
#12 = .50000	#24 = .75000	#12 – 24" x .50000 = 12.000"

Note: The 12th fret will always be located at one-half (50%) of any fretted musical instrument scale. You will also note that the 24th fret is three-fourths (75%) of scale length.

CHAPTER **22**

INSTRUMENT DIAGRAMS
AND SPECIFICATIONS

TELECASTER

Telecaster dual pickup guitar is entirely new in the electric Spanish guitar field. This instrument features a new style construction which vastly improves their usability. A new type one-piece neck is reinforced with an adjustable tension rod which provides a means for keeping the neck perfectly straight. This new slender neck is a great aid to easy fretting and fast action and it is replaceable by the owner in a matter of a few minutes, thus eliminating costly and time-consuming repairs. The body of this instrument is designed to provide easy accessibility to the entire length of the neck thereby making it possible to play full chords up to the very end of the fretboard. Because the body of this guitar is solid, there is no acoustic cavity to resonate and to cause the troublesome howl known as "freedback", and can be played at extreme volume for this reason. The pickups on this guitar are fully adjustable allowing a variable tonal response and, in addition to this, there is a full range tone control. A three-position tone change switch is provided which allows instantaneous changes from a sharp ringing "take-off" or "lead" tone to a very "soft" rhythm tone.

This instrument features the new adjustable Fender bridge which is the answer to every guitar player's desire. To be able to change the action and intonation of his instrument with this new bridge, the player can adjust each string for height from the fretboard and for length thereby obtaining perfect intonation and affording each player his own individual touch. The neck of the Telecaster Guitar is made of clear hard maple and the body is made of fine clear blonde hard wood. The instrument is trimmed with a white pickguard and all the metal parts are heavily chrome plated. Each guitar is furnished with a beautiful top grain adjustable leather strap.

PLASTILEATHER BAG
Full length zipper bag, padded, large side pockets for accessories.

CASE
Molded plush lined covered with striped airplane luggage linen.

TELECASTER

ADJUSTABLE SOLO-LEAD PICKUP
Beneath snap-on cover. Completely adjustable for best tone-balance by means of three elevating screws.

MICRO-ADJUSTABLE BRIDGE
Beneath snap-on cover Three longitudinal screws for adjusting string length for proper noting. Six elevating screws for adjusting height of each string.

MODERN STYLED HEAD
Places keys all on one side for better access. Provides straight pull for all strings.

FAST ACTION NECK
White maple neck with adjustable truss rod. The Fender neck is especially designed for fast comfortable playing. See Inset

ADJUSTABLE NECK TRUSS ROD
Remove pickguard. Turn slotted cap-screw in end of neck to level frets. Unique truss rod design makes adjustment seldom necessary. To adjust neck downward, turn slotted screw clockwise. To adjust neck upward, turn slotted screws counter-clockwise.

ADJUSTABLE RHYTHM PICKUP
Remove pickguard. Two elevating screws permit adjustment for proper tone balance.

MODERN CUTAWAY BODY
Permits easy playing of all twenty-one frets. Lighter weight solid body makes playing for longer periods less tiring.

LEVER SWITCH
Rear position for lead work modified by tone control. Middle position for straight rhythm work. Forward position for deep soft rhythm.

VOLUME CONTROL
Functions in all positions of lever switch and tone control.

TONE CONTROL
Functions as lead pickup modifer in lead position of lever switch.

PRECISION BASS

The new four string Precision Bass is one of the most revolutionary instruments to make an appearance in many years. It is the answer to every bass player's desire for a portable instrument of extremely fine tone quality, plus playing ease and comfort. This remarkable new instrument is infinitely easier to play than a conventional bass, inasmuch as the technique is like that used in playing a guitar. Very little string action is required to obtain full rich bass volume, thereby eliminating the effort that went in to playing the old style bass.

The neck of this instrument is slender and fretted, and the string adjustment is close to the frets, thus enabling the player to play with greatly increased speed. Most players find that their technique improves very rapidly with the use of this new instrument and that they can play considerably more difficult work than ever before.

With the Precision Bass, it is possible to obtain considerably more volume than with a conventional insrument. The space required for storage or carrying of this instrument is approximately 1/6 of that required for the old type bass.

The Fender Precision Bass opens an entirely new field of bass playing, and already they have become stock items in a great many of the nation's top musical organizations.

It is available in a DuPont Ducco color of the player's choice at an additional 5% cost.

CASE
   Rigidly constructed hard-shell case, plush lined, with striped airplane luggage linen covering.

PLASTILEATHER BAG
   Full length zipper bag, padded, large side pockets for accessories.

PRECISION BASS

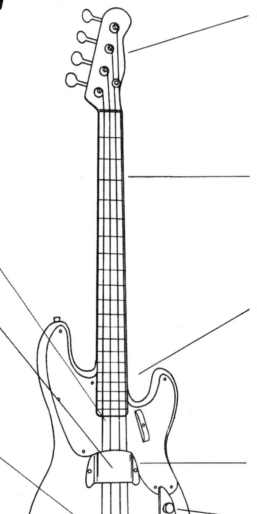

MODERN HEAD DESIGN
Places all keys on one side for easier access and straight string pull. Extra heavy tuning keys provide accurate tuning, easily turned.

ADJUSTABLE NECK TRUSS ROD
Remove pickguard. To adjust neck downward, turn slotted screw clockwise. To adjust neck upward, turn slotted screw counter clockwise. Unique truss rod design makes adjustment seldom necessary.

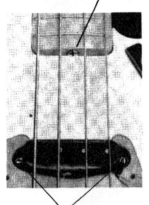

Slender neck of clear maple is fretted. Neck truss rod is adjustable providing a means for keeping the neck perfectly straight. See inset

Cutaway body design for access to all frets. Guitar body is comfort contoured.

Pickup elevating screws permit adjustment for any playing requirements.

Chrome plated hand rest positioned over adjustable pickup. See inset

VOLUME CONTROL

TONE CONTROL

MICRO-ADUSTABLE BRIDGE
Beneath chromed cover. Two longitudinal screws for adjusting string length for accurate noting. Four elevating screws for adjusting height of each string.

fine electric instruments

STRINGMASTER STEEL GUITARS

The STRING MASTER GUITAR represents the first major change and improvement in Hawaiian Steel Guitars, since they were first electrified. Many radically new improvements are incorporated in this instrument. New and easy to adjust key winds, dual counterbalanced pickups which eliminate hum and noise picked up from external sources and providing a wide range of sound, impossible to achieve in the single pickup type of guitar. It incorporates also, a new system of switching and mixing pickups which enables the player to obtain any tone from low bass to high staccato with one change of the tone control. This interconnection is a new development of the Fender engineers. The tone range of these instruments is far greater than anything else yet developed and must be played and heard to really be appreciated.

The pickups are fully adjustable so that any tone balance can be achieved suiting the player's needs. Each neck is elevated and the body is cut away along the side of the fret boards to provide ample playing clearance on all necks. The String Master is mounted on four telescoping legs which provide a playing height from a sitting position to a full standing position. In addition to all these features, it should be pointed out that all parts are precision built. The critical parts are case hardened and designed to prevent any ordinary wear from occurring.

In addition to these features, the instrument is fitted with an adjustable bridge in order that the intonation may be adjusted any time to compensate for different string gauges, assuring that the instrument will always be in perfect tune. One of the most outstanding and striking features of this instrument is the adjustable spacing bridge which allows the individual player a choice of narrow, average or wide string spacings.

Each neck is equipped with a balancing control which can be pre-set to balance the tone of the two pickups to the exacting requirements of each individual player. This is a most outstanding feature and one found only in the Fender String Master Guitar. It is possible to string one of the necks of the String Master Guitar with special bass strings, allowing a tuning an octive lower than the ordinary steel guitar tuning. Professional players who have used such a combination find that they can develop many new sounds and effects which heretofore have been impossible.

It is felt that this instrument completely obsoletes all other steel guitars and all professional performers will want one of these fine new instruments in order to compete on today's busy music market.

Stringmaster Guitars are available in 22½" and 24½" string lengths, dark or blonde finish.

CASE

Molded, plush lined case is covered with striped airplane luggage linen with leather bound, double stitched ends.

STRINGMASTER STEEL GUITARS

Single - Two - Three and Four Neck

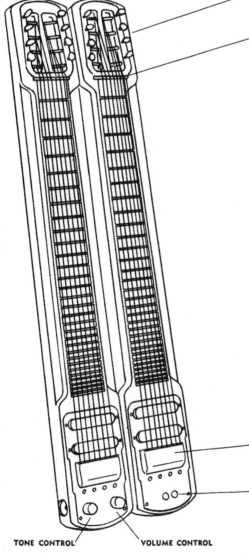

Precision made one-piece patent heads are chrome plated. Tuning keys with steel and brass gears, are made to take the tremendous string pull and hold string tuning at all times.

PRECISION GROOVED CASE HARDENED NUT

MICRO-ADJUSTABLE BRIDGE

Located beneath bridge cover of each neck. Two longitudinal screws permit bridge adjustment for accurate fretting and intonation. Bridges with variable string spacing are available to allow the player a choice of narrow, average or wide string spacing with variations from first to eighth string as follows:

		Distance from First to Eighth String
Narrow	- , -	2 7/16"
✽ Average	- -	2 5/8"
Wide	- -	2 3/4"

✽ (supplied with instrument)

PICKUP ADJUSTMENTS

Elevating screws are located at ends of the pickups. Pickups may be raised or lowered for proper tone balance.

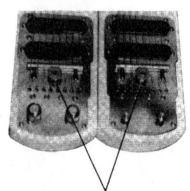

PICKUP BALANCE CONTROL

Located behind bridge of each neck, may be pre-set to balance the tone of the pickups.

BRIDGE COVER

Chromed swing-type bridge cover can be easily removed and snapped on whenever necessary. (See inset for string and tone adjusting units located under bridge cover).

NECK SELECTOR SWITCHES

Selector switches may be actuated simultaneously or individually. Inner-connections permit selected neck or necks to be actuated in any combination.

TONE CONTROL   VOLUME CONTROL

CHAMP GUITAR

Fender fine electric instruments

FENDER CHAMP GUITAR

The Champ Student Guitar is of an entirely new design that is distinctive and beautifully finished with Du Pont Ducco. The basic design of the guitar is such that is provides the beginning musicians with those advantages which facilitate rapid progress.

ONE-PIECE RECESSED PATENT HEAD

This completely new type patent head is chrome plated and is precision made to assure easier string tuning. The black pearl buttons attractively contrast with the guitar body.

PRECISION GROOVED NUT

Made of case hardened steel, this nut is grooved, thus, permitting the bar to pass over smoothly and quietly. In addition, its hardness prevents ordinary wear and string rattle.

ETCHED METAL FRETBOARD

This replaceable fretboard has raised fret markings with black finish between the frets to reduce glare.

ADJUSTABLE HIGH FIDELITY PICKUP

Adjusting screws at each end of the pickup permit string balance adjustments to suit the player.

VOLUME CONTROL

TONE CONTROL

RECESSED INPUT

This input accepts the Fender "cord-grip" plug. The cord extends away from the guitar and pivots freely for maximum convenience to the player.

The appearance of the Champ Guitar is enhanced by the chromed control mounting plate and bridge cover.

ADJUSTABLE BRIDGE

Corrections for string length are made with the two bridge adjusting screws, located beneath the bridge cover. This feature insures perfect intonation and string length for accurate fretting.

MUSICMASTER ³⁄₄ SIZE GUITAR

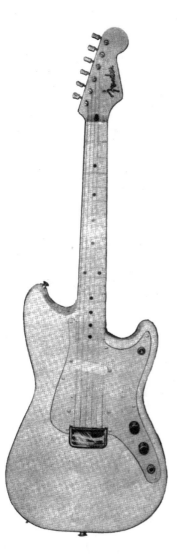

The Musicmaster Guitar has been designed to provide an instrument for those musicians with small hands who desire modern Spanish guitar design and the finest playing and tone qualities.

The Musicmaster is beautifully finished and incorporates the following features: The fast action Fender neck with adjustable truss rod and modern head design, the two-way adjustable bridge which affords variations of string height for playing ease and variable string length for perfect intonation and fretting. This guitar has excellent pickup with wide tone variations.

The body is of solid wood and features the cutaway design for full access to all twenty-one frets.

It has distinctive chrome plated metal parts with gold finished metal pickguard. It combines modern design and outstanding playing qualities to make it the finest three-quarter size guitar in its price range.

The case for the Musicmaster Guitar is attractively covered with brown leatherette and has genuine leather bound and stiched ends. It is lined with attractive crushed plush. Inset locks and hardware are solid brass.

MUSICMASTER ¾ SIZE GUITAR

ADJUSTABLE NECK TRUSS ROD

Remove Pickguard. Turn slotted cap-screw in end of neck to level frets. Unique truss rod design makes adjustment seldom necessary. To adjust neck downward, turn slotted screw clockwise. To adjust neck upward, turn slotted screw counter-clockwise.

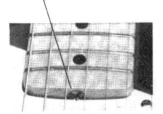

MODERN HEAD DESIGN

Places keys all on one side for better access. vides straight pull for all strings

FAST ACTION NECK DESIGN

Clear maple neck designed for fast action. Has adjustable truss rod. See inset "a". Neck is scientifically graduated and fretted to provide comfort and easier fretting for musicians with small hands.

MODERN CUTAWAY BODY

Permits easy playing of all twenty-one frets. Thinner body makes playing for long periods less tiring.

ADJUSTABLE PICKUP

Two elevating screws permit adjustment for proper tone balance.

VOLUME CONTROL

TONE CONTROL

Recessed jack receptacle accepts the new Fender "cord-grip" plug which pivots freely in all directions for maximum convenience to the player.

MICRO-ADJUSTABLE BRIDGE

Beneath snap-on cover. Three longitudinal screws for adjusting string length for proper noting. Six elevating screws for adjusting height of each string.

DUO-SONIC $3/4$ SIZE GUITAR

The Duo-Sonic Three Quarter Guitar is especially designed for adult and young musicians to provide a guitar that is both comfortable to play and one that incorporates the latest and advanced developments in guitar design.

This instrument has a scientifically graduated neck which is comfortable and affords fast action. It has twenty-one frets, all of which are easy to reach with the modern cutaway body design. In addition, the modern head design permits easy tuning and provides straight string pull for all strings.

The neck employs an adjustable truss-rod, easily adjustable if ever necessary. This rod assures perfect neck alignment and prevents warping.

Besides these features, the Duo-Sonic guitar uses two excellent pick-ups, both of which are adjustable. A conveniently located selector switch provides rapid changes from deep rhythm tones to lead tone, and in addition, the tone control will modify the playing tone with the selector switch in any of its three positions.

Playing action and string length are adjustments which can easily be made. These adjustments are located under the bridge cover. The string height may be varied for comfortable playing action, and the string length is adjustable insuring perfect intonation of each string.

The Duo Sonic guitar is beautifully finished and is striking in appearance. It has chromed controls and bridge cover and gold-finished pickguard.

DUO-SONIC CASE

The case for this instrument is of hard-shell construction, with rich plush lining and durable covering.

DUO-SONIC $\frac{3}{4}$ SIZE GUITAR

MODERN STYLE HEAD
Places keys all on one side for better access. Provides straight pull for all strings.

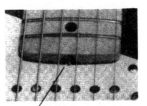

MICRO-ADJUSTABLE BRIDGE
Beneath snap-on cover. Three longitudinal screws for adjusting string length for proper noting. Six elevating screws for adjusting height of each string.

ADJUSTABLE NECK TRUSS-ROD
Remove pickguard. Turn slotted screw clockwise to pull neck upward. Turn screw counter-clockwise to adjust neck downward.

ADJUSTABLE RHYTHM PICKUP
Elevating screws at pickup ends permit adjustment for proper tone balance.

LEAD PICKUP
May also be adjusted to suit the player by means of the end adjusting screws.

PICKUP SELECTOR SWITCH
Forward position for soft rhythm tone. Middle position for straight rhythm tone. Rear position for lead tone.

VOLUME CONTROL
Volume Control functions in all positions of pickup selector switch.

TONE CONTROL
Functions in all pickup selector switch positions providing full range tone variation.

Surface-mount plug receptacle accepts "cord grip" plug which pivots freely and is out of the way at all times.

The Duo-Sonic guitar is beautifully finished with DuPont Duco. This finish is extremely durable and is easily kept new-looking.

ELECTRIC MANDOLIN

The Fender Electric Mandolin has been designed to meet the increasing demand for an instrument of its kind affording true mandolin tone and the design features which have made Fender instruments outstanding on todays musical market. This instrument affords not only the finest tone and playing qualities, but also incorporates the latest advancements known to the industry.

The Fender Electric Mandolin employs an excellent pickup which reproduces with fidelity of tone. In addition this pickup is fully adjustable to provide the string response to suit the individual player.

In addition, located under the chrome bridge cover are string adjusting screws which permit both adjustment of string length for perfect intonation and fretting and also adjustment of individual string height for string action to suit the individual playing requirements.

The modern solid body cut away design affords comfortable playing to the end of the fret board. The neck is scientifically graduated for playing comfort and each of the 24 frets are accurately positioned.

The Fender Electric Mandolin is an instrument which every player will want and one which provides all the playing qualities and outstanding design features assuring top performance.

CASE

Molded, plush lined case is covered with stripped airplane luggage linen with leather bound, double stitched ends.

fine electric
instruments

ELECTRIC MANDOLIN

**MICRO-ADJUSTABLE
BRIDGE**
Beneath chromed cover.
Two longitudinal screws
for adjusting string length
for accurate noting.
Four elevating screws for
adjusting height of each
string.

MODERN STYLED HEAD
Places keys all on one side for better access,
provides straight pull for all strings.

COMFORTABLE FAST ACTION NECK
Neck is expertly graduated for playing comfort. Each of the 24 frets are accurately
positioned for true noting.

MODERN CUT AWAY BODY
Cut away design permits easy playing all frets.
Thinner solid body styling makes playing for long
periods less tiring.

ADJUSTABLE PICKUP
Two elevating screws permit adjustment for
proper tone balance.

VOLUME CONTROL

TONE CONTROL

CONVENIENT CORD INPUT
Surface mount input permits cord to pivot in all
directions for maximum convenience to the
player.

STUDIO DELUXE GUITAR

- Fully Adjustable Bridge
- Chromed Swing Type Bridge Cover
- Precision Grooved Hardened Steel Nut
- Recessed One-Piece Patent Head
- Top-Mounted Input Receptacle
- Fender's Pivoting Right-Angle Plug

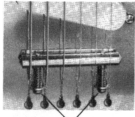

MICRO-ADUSTABLE BRIDGE
Beneath chromed cover. Two longitudinal screws for adjusting string length for accurate noting.

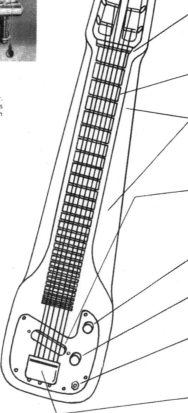

RECESSED PATENT HEAD
Recessed one-piece patent head is chrome plated. Pearl button tuning keys with brass gears give long dependable service, are easier tuning.

HARDENED STEEL NUT
Precision grooved nut of hardened steel will not wear, preventing string rattle.

ETCHED METAL FRETBOARD
Fret markings are etched in metal and the fretboard itself is finished so as to eliminate light reflection. It is easily replaceable in only a few minutes, if ever necessary.

NEW MODERN BODY DESIGN
The body design of the Studio Deluxe Guitar is such that the entire string length is free from obstruction permitting full use of the strings from the bridge to the nut. The body is of solid hardwood and is beautifully finished with DuPont Ducco.

ADJUSTABLE HIGH FIDELITY PICKUP
Adjusting crews for the pickup are located at each end of the pickup. This feature permits adjusting the pickup so that string tone balance meets the individual player's requirements. The Fender pickup gives instant response with fidelity of tone.

VOLUME CONTROL
Volume control is conveniently located for proper use for organ effects and other playing requirements.

TONE CONTROL
Wide tone variations are possible with the full range tone control.

RECESSED PLUG RECEPTACLE
One of the plugs on the cord supplied with this instrument is the new Fender "cord-grip" type. When used in this receptacle, the cord extends out away from the instrument and pivots freely in all directions allowing the player maximum freedom from the cord at all times.

ADJUSTABLE BRIDGE
Located beneath the swing type cover. Two longitudinal screws permit string length adjustment for perfect intonation at all times.

TELECASTER WIRING DIAGRAM 1/1/53

Lever Switch shown in deep rhythm position

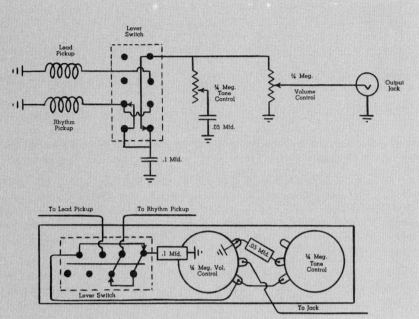

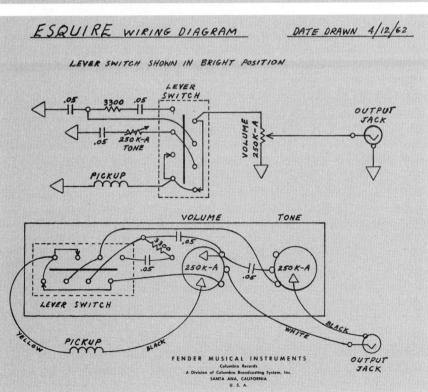

FENDER MUSICAL INSTRUMENTS
Columbia Records
A Division of Columbia Broadcasting System, Inc.
SANTA ANA, CALIFORNIA
U. S. A.

FENDER "STRINGMASTER" STEEL GUITAR
MODEL SM-5C-26

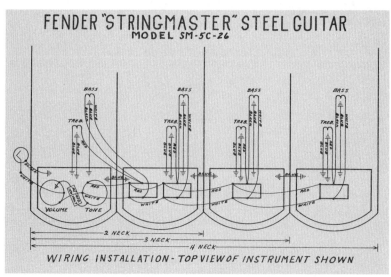

WIRING INSTALLATION - TOP VIEW OF INSTRUMENT SHOWN

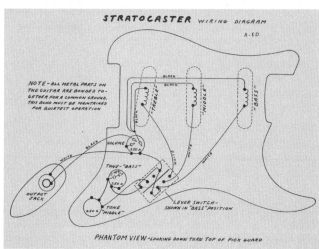

STRATOCASTER WIRING DIAGRAM

A-ED

NOTE - ALL METAL PARTS ON THE GUITAR ARE BONDED TOGETHER FOR A COMMON GROUND. THIS BOND MUST BE MAINTAINED FOR QUIETEST OPERATION

PHANTOM VIEW - LOOKING DOWN THRU TOP OF PICK GUARD

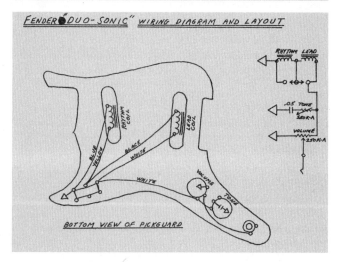

FENDER "DUO-SONIC" WIRING DIAGRAM AND LAYOUT

BOTTOM VIEW OF PICKGUARD

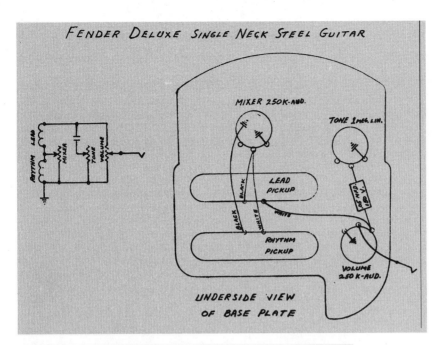

FENDER DELUXE SINGLE NECK STEEL GUITAR

MIXER 250K-AUD.

TONE 1 MEG. LIN.

LEAD PICKUP

RHYTHM PICKUP

BLACK

BLACK

WHITE

WHITE

.05 MFD. 150 V.

VOLUME 250 K-AUD.

RHYTHM
LEAD
MIXER
TONE
VOLUME

UNDERSIDE VIEW
OF BASE PLATE

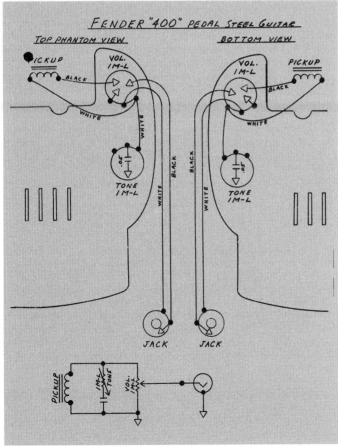

FENDER "400" PEDAL STEEL GUITAR

TOP PHANTOM VIEW

BOTTOM VIEW

PICKUP

VOL. 1M-L

VOL. 1M-L

PICKUP

BLACK

BLACK

WHITE

WHITE

WHITE

WHITE

BLACK

BLACK

.05

.05

TONE 1M-L

TONE 1M-L

JACK

JACK

PICKUP

1 MEG TONE

VOL. 1M-L

239

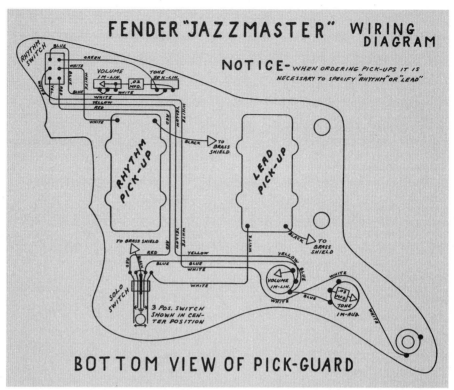

FENDER "JAZZMASTER" WIRING DIAGRAM

NOTICE— WHEN ORDERING PICK-UPS IT IS NECESSARY TO SPECIFY 'RHYTHM' OR 'LEAD'

BOTTOM VIEW OF PICK-GUARD

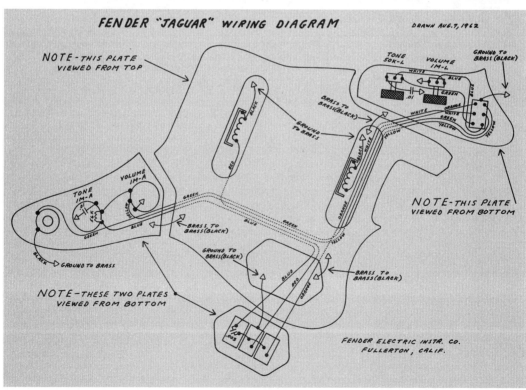

FENDER "JAGUAR" WIRING DIAGRAM

DRAWN AUG.7, 1962

NOTE— THIS PLATE VIEWED FROM TOP

NOTE— THIS PLATE VIEWED FROM BOTTOM

NOTE— THESE TWO PLATES VIEWED FROM BOTTOM

FENDER ELECTRIC INSTR. CO. FULLERTON, CALIF.

CHAPTER **23**

AMPLIFIER
SPECIFICATIONS

SUPER AMP

The Fender Super Amp is an extremely popular amplifier and has found widespread use among all classes of players, it being especially suited for broadcast and recording usage. It is a unit that combines excellent power characteristics along with extremely low distortion factor. It features the Fender ¾" solid wood lock jointed cabinet which is covered with the highest grade diagonal stripe brown and white airplane luggage linen. This material is extremely wear and scuff resistant and easy to maintain. The grill cloth is the latest style plastic material which not only adds to the beauty of the unit but is functional as well, inasmuch as its porocity allows considerably more sound to pass without being muffled and without the loss of high frequencies incurred with ordinary type grill cloth. The Super Amp features the Fender top mounted chassis which is beautifully chrome plated with white index markings and its overall appearance and excellent portability make it one of the favorites of the jobbing musicians. It employs two heavy duty 10" Jensen Concert Series speakers and features the latest in electronic development. Like other Fender amplifiers of professional qualifications, it features the parallel input circuits which allow the input stages of the amplifier to handle extreme surges of voltage without overloading the input tubes, thereby eliminating a primary source of distortion which is normal in all older type amplifiers.

The Super Amp tone control circuit is a Fender development employing both a bass and treble tone control which allows complete tone shading from the lowest bass to the highest treble without introducing distortion as is common in other types of tone controls. In addition to this, a presence control, which is an exclusive Fender feature is included which allows the delicate adjustment of the extremely high frequencies beyond those normally influenced by the regular treble control.

The regular panel equipment includes the on-and-off switch, the Fender developed stand-by switch, the bull's-eye type panel light, panel mount fuse holder, and a new and exclusive first—a ground switch which completely eliminates the problem of having to polarize the power plug. With this ground switch one can simply plug in the amplifier, turn it on, and if hum and line noise so frequently noticed in all amplifiers, is present, a flip of the ground switch completely eliminates this annoyance. It is no longer necessary to remove the plug from the wall and turn it over, which often is a considerable inconvenience.

An outstanding feature of this fine amplifier is the single unit parts panel, a feature which does not meet the eye of the ordinary buyer, but for those who are conscious of outstanding quality, this parts panel will be found to be extremely interesting. On it are mounted practically all of the small parts including the condensers and resistors, etc. These small parts are securely attached to the parts panel through brass eyelets into which they are soldered. Each is held securely in place and not allowed to vibrate or rattle around. This eliminates a great source of amplifier failure and guarantees that your Fender amplifier will give you long and faithful service without attention. In addition to these many features is the fact that this amplifier has an over-size power supply which guarantees extremely heavy duty power transformer for continuous duty operation.

The output transformer is also much heavier than is usually found in amplifiers of this size. All of these features are combined to provide the player with the finest piece of portable musical instrument amplification equipment ever developed and it is destined to set a standard which others will be seeking to attain for a long period in the future.

241

SUPER AMP

TECHNICAL CHARACTERISTICS

The Fender Super Amp is a compact, portable musical instrument amplifier conservatively rated, with all necessary controls for handling complete High Fidelity music reproduction.

Power Output: 20 Watts at less than 5% distortion.

Frequency Response: With optimum tone control setting ± 1 db 20 to 20,000 cycles per second at 16 Watts. Less than 0.5% harmonic distortion at rated 16 Watts output.

Hum and Noise Level: 80 db below rated output. Total feed back employed −30db.

Inputs: Four high impedence inputs interconnected to provide parallel input circuits when the first input jack of either the bright or the normal combination is used. This allows considerably more input voltage to be applied without introducing distortion.

Extension Speaker Jack: Mounted on under side of chassis.

Controls Appearing on Chassis: Ground Switch; Panel Extractor Fuse Post; Off-and-On Switch; Stand-by Switch; Bull's-Eye Pilot Light; Presence Control; Bass Control; Treble Control; two Volume Controls; four Input Jacks.

Number of Tubes: Six (three of these tubes are dual purpose tubes, giving the amplifier the equivalent of nine tubes).

Tubes Employed: Two 12AY7s; one 12AX7; two 6V6GTs; one 5U4G.

Speakers: Two heavy duty Jensen 10" Concert Series Speakers.

Power Consumption: 85 Watts.

Size: 22" wide, 10½" deep, 18" high; Shipping weight 42 lbs.
It will be noted from the accompanying photograph that practically all replacements can be made to the amplifier without removing the chassis. This includes all the condensers, resistors, tube sockets, controls, jacks, switches, etc. The only replacements for which it is necessary to remove the chassis are the power and output transformers and filter choke. This is a very important feature which must always be considered when time is important.

Cabinet: Solid ¾" wood with lock joint weldwood corners.

Covering: Highest grade, brown and white diagonal stripe airplane luggage linen. Highly wear and scuff resistant. Can be easily cleaned.
Safety codes for all states are equaled or exceeded. Fender Fine Electric Instruments are guaranteed to give complete customer satisfaction. This guarantee is backed by our many years of successful business relationship with all of our customers.

Photo shows back
cover removed

Specifications and prices subject to change without notice.

fine electric
instruments

PRO AMP

The Fender Pro Amp is one which has become a standard in the musical world. It has been in use for many years and has proven itself by its many durable performances under the most drastic conditions. This amplifier has been constantly changed and improved to present day standards until today it represents the most modern circuitry possible. It is capable of excellent power and fidelity and has proven itself as a long time favorite among all classes of players. The Pro Amp features the ¾" solid wood lock jointed cabinet and is covered with the highest grade diagonal stripe brown and white airplane luggage linen which is extremely wear and scuff resistant. The grill cloth is the latest style plastic material which is not only very attractive but functional as well inasmuch as its porosity allows considerably more sound to pass without muffling and without the loss of high frequencies incurred when using ordinary grill cloth. The Pro Amp features the Fender top mounted chassis which is beautifully chrome plated with white index markings and its overall appearance is one of outstanding balance and symmetry. It employs an extremely heavy duty 15" Jensen Concert Series speaker and features the latest principles in electronic design, inasmuch as the inputs are so arranged that tremendous surge of input voltage can be accommodated without overloading the input tubes, thereby eliminating a great source of distortion which is normal in all older type amplifiers.

The Pro Amp tone control circuit is a Fender development employing both a bass and treble tone control which allows complete tone shading from the lowest bass to the highest treble without introducing distortion as is common in other types of tone controls. In addition to this, a presence control, which is an exclusive Fender feature is included which allows the delicate adjustment of the extremely high frequencies beyond those normally influenced by the regular treble control.

The regular panel equipment includes the on-and-off switch, the Fender developed stand-by switch, the bull's-eye type panel light, panel mount fuse holder, and a new and exclusive first—a ground switch which completely eliminates the problem of having to polarize the power plug. With this ground switch one can simply plug in the amplifier, turn it on, and if hum and line noise so frequently noticed in all amplifiers, is present, a flip of the ground switch completely eliminates this annoyance. It is no longer necessary to remove the plug from the wall and turn it over, which often is a considerable inconvenience.

An outstanding feature of this fine amplifier is the single unit parts panel, a feature which does not meet the eye of the ordinary buyer, but for those who are conscious of outstanding quality, this parts panel will be found to be extremely interesting. On it are mounted practically all of the small parts including the condensers and resistors, etc. These small parts are securely attached to the parts panel through brass eyelets into which they are soldered. Each is held securely in place and not allowed to vibrate or rattle around. This eliminates a great source of amplifier failure and guarantees that your Fender amplifier will give you long and faithful service without attention. In addition to these many features is the fact that this amplifier has an over-size power supply guaranteeing continuous duty.

The output transformer is also much heavier than is usually found in amplifiers of this size. All of these features are combined to provide the player with the finest piece of portable musical instrument amplification equipment ever developed and it is destined to set a standard which others will be seeking to attain for a long period in the future.

TECHNICAL CHARACTERISTICS

The Fender Pro Amp is a compact, portable musical instrument amplifier conservatively rated, with all necessary controls for handling complete High Fidelity music reproduction.

Power Output: 30 Watts at less than 5% distortion.

Frequency Response: With optimum tone control setting ± 1 db 20 to 20,000 cycles per second at 26 Watts. Less than 0.5% harmonic distortion at rated 26 Watts output.

Hum and Noise Level: 80 db below rated output. Total feed back employed —30db.

Inputs: Four high impedence inputs interconnected to provide parallel input circuits when the first input jack of either the bright or the normal combination is used. This allows considerably more input voltage to be applied without introducing distortion.

Extension Speaker Jack: Mounted on under side of chassis.

Controls Appearing on Chassis: Ground Switch; Panel Extractor Fuse Post; Off-and-On Switch; Stand-by Switch; Bull's-Eye Pilot Light; Presence Control; Bass Control; Treble Control; two Volume Controls; four Input Jacks.

Number of Tubes: Six (three of these tubes are dual purpose tubes, giving the amplifier the equivalent of nine tubes).

Tubes Employed: Two 12AY7s; one 12AX7; two 5881s or 6L6Gs; one 5U4G.

Speakers: One heavy duty Jensen 15" Concert Series Speaker.

Power Consumption: 125 Watts.

Size: 22" wide, 10½" deep, 20" high; Shipping weight 44 lbs.
It will be noted from the accompanying photograph that practically all replacements can be made to the amplifier without removing the chassis. This includes all the condensers, resistors, tube sockets, controls, jacks, switches, etc. The only replacements for which it is necessary to remove the chassis are the power and output transformers and filter choke. This is a very important feature which must always be considered when time is important.

Cabinet: Solid ¾" wood with lock joint weldwood corners.

Covering: Highest grade, brown and white diagonal stripe airplane luggage linen. Highly wear and scuff resistant. Can be easily cleaned.
Safety codes for all states are equaled or exceeded. Fender Fine Electric Instruments are guaranteed to give complete customer satisfaction. This guarantee is backed by our many years of successful business relationship with all of our customers.

Photo shows back cover removed

Specifications and prices subject to change without notice.

Fender
fine electric instruments

TWIN AMP

The Fender Twin Amp is probably the finest musical instrument amplifier ever offered to the buying public. It is a unit that combines tremendous power, low distortion factor and beauty of design in such a package that it is completely portable and easily handled. Heavy duty dual speakers give it outstanding advantages over any single speaker amplifier and it actually produces more audio power than any other portable musical instrument amplifier up to this time. The Fender Twin Amp is housed in a beautiful cabinet made of ¾" solid stock with lock jointed corners. It is covered with the highest grade diagonal stripe brown and white airplane luggage linen, which is extremely wear resistant. The grill cloth is the latest style plastic material, which is not only very attractive, but functional as well, inasmuch as its porosity allows considerably more sound to pass without being muffled and without the loss of high frequencies incurred with ordinary grill cloth. The Twin Amp features the Fender top mounted chassis which is beautifully chrome plated with white index markings and its overall appearance is one of sleek modern lines. It employs two heavy duty Jensen Concert Series speakers and features the latest in electronic design, inasmuch as the inputs are so arranged that tremendous surges of voltage can be accommodated without over-loading the first tubes, thereby eliminating a great source of distortion which is normal in all older type amplifiers.

The Twin Amp tone control circuit is a Fender development employing both a bass and treble tone control which allows complete tone shading from the lowest bass to the highest treble without introducing any distortion as is common in other types of tone controls. In addition to this, a presence control, which is an exclusive Fender feature is included which allows the delicate adjustment of the extremely high frequencies beyond those normally influenced by the regular treble control.

The regular panel equipment includes the on-and-off switch, the Fender developed stand-by switch, the bull's-eye type panel light, panel mount fuse holder, and a new and exclusive first—a ground switch which completely eliminates the problem of having to polarize the power plug. With this ground switch one can simply plug in the amplifier, turn it on, and if hum and line noise so frequently noticed in all amplifiers, is present, a flip of the ground switch completely eliminates this annoyance. It is no longer necessary to remove the plug from the wall and turn it over, which often is a considerable inconvenience.

An outstanding feature of this fine amplifier is the single unit parts panel, a feature which does not meet the eye of the ordinary buyer, but for those who are conscious of outstanding quality, this parts panel will be found to be extremely interesting. On it are mounted practically all of the small parts including the condensers and resistors, etc. These small parts are securely attached to the parts panel through brass eyelets into which they are soldered. Each is held securely in place and not allowed to vibrate or rattle around. This eliminates a great source of amplifier failure and guarantees that your Fender amplifier will give you long and faithful service without attention. In addition to these many features is the fact that this amplifier has an over-size power supply employing an extremely heavy duty power transformer and two 5U4G rectifier tubes, instead of the usual one.

The output transformer is also much heavier than is usually found in amplifiers of this size. All of these features are combined to provide the player with the finest piece of portable musical instrument amplification equipment ever developed and it is destined to set a standard which others will be seeking to attain for a long period in the future.

TECHNICAL CHARACTERISTICS

The Fender Twin Amp is a compact, portable musical instrument amplifier conservatively rated, with all necessary controls for handling complete High Fidelity music reproduction.

Power Output: 60 Watts at less than 5% distortion.

Frequency Response: With optimum tone control setting ± 1 db 20 to 20,000 cycles per second at 50 Watts.
Less than 0.5% harmonic distortion at rated 50 Watts output.

Hum and Noise Level: 80 db below rated output. Total feed back employed -30db.

Inputs: Four high impedence inputs interconnected to provide parallel input circuits when the first input jack of either the bright or the normal combination is used. This allows considerably more input voltage to be applied without introducing distortion.

Controls appearing on Chassis: Ground Switch; Panel Extractor Fuse Post; Off-and-On Switch; Stand-by Switch; Bull's-Eye Pilot Light; Presence Control; Bass Control; Treble Control; two Volume Controls; four Input Jacks.

Number of Tubes: Eight, four of these tubes are dual purpose tubes, giving the amplifier the equivalent of twelve tubes.

Tubes Employed: Three 12AY7s; one 12AX7; two 5881s or 6L6Gs; two 5U4Gs.

Speakers: Two heavy duty Jensen 12" Concert Series Speakers.

Power Consumption: 180 Watts.

Size: 24½" wide, 10½" deep, 16" high; Shipping weight 54 lbs.
It will be noted from the accompanying photograph that practically all replacements can be made to the amplifier without removing the chassis. This includes all the condensers, resistors, tube sockets, controls, jacks, switches, etc. The only replacements for which it is necessary to remove the chassis are the power and output transformers and filter choke. This is a very important feature which must always be considered when time is important.

Cabinet: Solid ¾" wood with lock joint weldwood corners.

Covering: Highest grade, brown and white diagonal stripe airplane luggage linen. Highly wear and scuff resistant. Can be easily cleaned.
Safety codes for all states are equaled or exceeded. Fender Fine Electric Instruments are guaranteed to give complete customer satisfaction. This guarantee is backed by our many years of successful business relationships with all of our customers.
Specifications and prices subject to change without notice.

Photo shows back cover removed

TREMOLUX AMP

The Fender Tremolux Amplifier is one of the newest of the Fender amplifier family. It incorporates the latest type electronic tremolo circuit. This tremolo circuit should not be confused with others of the past inasmuch as it provides greater ranges of both speed and depth than any previous type. It is a most remarkable performer in its price class. It includes the following outstanding features: the durable solid stock Fender cabinet with diagonal stripe brown and white airplane luggage linen. It has the top mounted chrome plated chassis with the following controls: "On" and "Off" swith, tremolo depth control, tremolo speed control, full range tone control, two volume controls, and four imput jacks. It also has the "Bulls-Eye" pilot light and the extractor type panel mounted fuse holder. It features an extremely heavy duty 12" Jensen speaker and comes complete with a tremolo foot control switch. One must hear this amplifier in use to appreciate its versatility and wonderful tone.

An outstanding feature of this fine amplifier is the single unit parts panel, a feature which does not meet the eye of the ordinary buyer, but for those who are conscious of outstanding quality, this parts panel will be found to be extremely interesting. On it are mounted practically all of the small parts including the condensers and resistors, etc. These small parts are securely attached to the parts panel through brass eyelets into which they are soldered. Each is held securely in place and not allowed to vibrate or rattle around. This eliminates a great source of amplifier failure and guarantees that your Fender amplifier will give you long and faithful service without attention. In addition to these many features is the fact

that this amplifier has an over-size power supply employing an extremely heavy duty power transformer and a 5U4G rectifier tube.

The output transformer is also much heavier than is usually found in amplifiers of this size.

An outstanding feature of the Tremolux Amplifier and one which must be experienced to be appreciated is the absence of the heavy pulsing sensation when the volume is turned up and no signal being fed to the unit. Most tremolo type amplifiers give off a heavy beat or pulse under the same conditions which can be very annoying, and this feature alone elevates the Tremolux Amp head and shoulders above anything else on the market today.

Fender

TREMOLUX AMP

TECHNICAL CHARACTERISTICS

The Fender Tremolux Amp is a compact, portable musical instrument amplifier conservatively rated, with all necessary controls for handling complete High Fidelity music reproduction.

Power Output: 18 Watts at less than 5% distortion.

Frequency Response: With optimum tone control setting ± 1 db 20 to 20,000 cycles per second at 16 Watts. Less than 0.5% harmonic distortion at rated 16 Watts output.

Hum and Noise Level: 80 db below rated output. Total feed back employed −30db.

Inputs: Four high impedence inputs interconnected to provide parallel input circuits when the first input jack of either the bright or the normal combination is used. This allows considerably more input voltage to be applied without introducing distortion.

Controls Appearing on Chassis: Panel Extractor Fuse Post; Off-and-On Switch; Bull's-Eye Pilot Light; two Volume Controls; four Input Jacks; Full Range Tone Control; Tremolo Depth Control; and Tremolo Speed Control.

Number of Tubes: Six (three of these tubes are dual purpose tubes, giving the amplifier the equivalent of nine tubes).

Tubes Employed: Two 12AY7s; one 12AX7; two 6V6-GTs; one 5U4G.

Speakers: One heavy duty Jensen 12" Concert Series Speaker.

Power Consumption: 80 Watts.

Size: 22" wide, 10½" deep, 20" high; Shipping weight 35 lbs.
It will be noted from the accompanying photograph that practically all replacements can be made to the amplifier without removing the chassis. This includes all the condensers, resistors, tube sockets, controls, jacks, switches, etc. The only replacements for which it is necessary to remove the chassis are the power and output transformers and filter choke. This is a very important feature which must always be considered when time is important.

Cabinet: Solid ¾" wood with lock joint weldwood corners.

Covering: Highest grade, brown and white diagonal stripe airplane luggage linen. Highly wear and scuff resistant. Can be easily cleaned.
Safety codes for all states are equaled or exceeded. Fender Fine Electric Instruments are guaranteed to give complete customer satisfaction. This guarantee is backed by our many years of successful business relationship with all of our customers.

Photo shows back cover removed

Specifications and prices subject to change without notice.

BANDMASTER AMPLIFIER

The Fender Bandmaster Amplifier is another high performance musical instrument amplifier. It is a unit that combines high power, low distortion factor and beauty of design in such a package that it is completely portable and easily handled. Three heavy duty speakers give it outstanding advantages over any single speaker amplifier. The Fender Bandmaster Amplifier is housed in a beautiful cabinet made of ¾" solid stock with lock jointed corners. It is covered with the highest grade diagonal stripe brown and white airplane luggage linen, which is extremely wear resistant. The grill cloth is the latest style plastic material, which is not only very attractive, but functional as well, inasmuch as its porosity allows considerably more sound to pass without being muffled and without the loss of high frequencies incurred with ordinary grill cloth. This unit features the Fender top mounted chassis which is beautifully chrome plated with white index markings and its overall appearance is one of sleek modern lines. It employs three heavy duty Jensen Concert Series speakers and features the latest in electronic design, inasmuch as the inputs are so arranged that tremendous surges of voltage can be accommodated without overloading the first tubes, thereby eliminating a great source of distortion which is normal in all older type amplifiers.

The Bandmaster Amplifier tone control circuit is a Fender development employing both a bass and treble tone control which allows complete tone shading from the lowest bass to the highest treble without introducing distortion as is common in other types of tone controls. In addition to this, a presence control, which is an exclusive Fender feature is included which allows the delicate adjustment of the extremely high frequencies beyond those normally influenced by the regular treble control.

The regular panel equipment includes the on-and-off switch, the Fender developed stand-by switch, the bull's-eye type panel light, panel mount fuse holder, and a new and exclusive first—a ground switch which completely eliminates the problem of having to polarize the power plug. With this ground switch one can simply plug in the amplifier, turn it on, and if hum and line noise so frequently noticed in all amplifiers, is present, a flip of the ground switch completely eliminates this annoyance. It is no longer necessary to remove the plug from the wall and turn it over, which often is a considerable inconvenience.

An outstanding feature of this fine amplifier is the single unit parts panel, a feature which does not meet the eye of the ordinary buyer, but for those who are conscious of outstanding quality, this parts panel will be found to be extremely interesting. On it are mounted practically all of the small parts including the condensers and resistors, etc. These small parts are securely attached to the parts panel through brass eyelets into which they are soldered. Each is held securely in place and not allowed to vibrate or rattle around. This eliminates a great source of amplifier failure and guarantees that your Fender amplifier will give you long and faithful service without attention. In addition to these many features is the fact that this amplifier has an over-size power supply which guarantees continuous duty performance.

The output transformer is also much heavier than is usually found in amplifiers of this size. All of these features are combined to provide the player with a fine piece of portable musical instrument amplification equipment and it has set a standard which others are constantly trying to duplicate.

BANDMASTER AMPLIFIER

TECHNICAL CHARACTERISTICS

The Fender Bandmaster Amplifier is a compact, portable musical instrument amplifier conservatively rated, with all necessary controls for handling complete High Fidelity music reproduction.

Power Output: 30 Watts at less than 5% distortion.

Frequency Response: With optimum tone control setting ± 1 db 20 to 20,000 cycles per second at 26 Watts. Less than 0.5% harmonic distortion at rated 26 Watts output.

Hum and Noise Level: 80 db below rated output. Total feed back employed −30db.

Inputs: Four high impedence inputs interconnected to provide parallel input circuits when the first input jack of either the bright or the normal combination is used. This allows considerably more input voltage to be applied without introducing distortion.

Extension Speaker Jack: Mounted on under side of chassis.

Controls Appearing on Chassis: Ground Switch; Panel Extractor Fuse Post; Off-and-On Switch; Stand-by Switch; Bull's-Eye Pilot Light; Presence Control; Bass Control; Treble Control; two Volume Controls; four Input Jacks.

Number of Tubes: Six (three of these tubes are dual purpose tubes, giving the amplifier the equivalent of nine tubes).

Tubes Employed: One 12AY7; Two 12AX7s; Two 5881s or 6L6Gs; Two 5U4Gs.

Speakers: Three heavy duty Jensen 10" Concert Series Speakers.

Power Consumption: 130 Watts.

Size: 22¼" wide, 10¼" deep, 22½" high; Shipping weight 50 lbs.
It will be noted from the accompanying photograph that practically all replacements can be made to the amplifier without removing the chassis. This includes all the condensers, resistors, tube sockets, controls, jacks, switches, etc. The only replacements for which it is necessary to remove the chassis are the power and output transformers and filter choke. This is a very important feature which must always be considered when time is important.

Cabinet: Solid ¾" wood with lock joint weldwood corners.

Covering: Highest grade, brown and white diagonal stripe airplane luggage linen. Highly wear and scuff resistant. Can be easily cleaned.
Safety codes for all states are equaled or exceeded. Fender Fine Electric Instruments are guaranteed to give complete customer satisfaction. This guarantee is backed by our many years of successful business relationship with all of our customers.

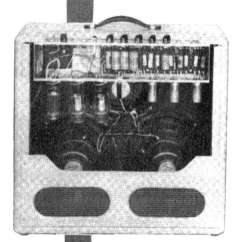

Photo shows back cover removed

Specifications and prices subject to change without notice.

DELUXE AMP

This amplifier is as modern as tomorrow and will give long lasting satisfaction to the user. It is beautifully styled and covered in the finest airplane luggage linen. The case is particularly rugged, yet exceptionally pleasing in appearance. This amplifier, in its size and price class, is an outstanding performer and one which will provide excellent volume without distortion and capable of handling any job where medium power amplification is required. One need only compare this amplifier with other units in the similar price bracket to realize its vast superiority. The Deluxe Amp features the Fender top mounted chassis and utilizes the heavy duty Jensen 12" Concert Series speaker. The same high grade airplane luggage linen covering and special plastic grill cloth is used in the Deluxe Amp as is used in the higher priced Fender amplifiers.

The Deluxe Amplifier features a full range tone control which allows complete tone feeding from the lowest bass to the highest treble. And, in addition, the regular panel equipment includes the on-and-off switch, the Fender developed stand-by switch, bull's-eye pilot light, panel mounted fuse holder, two volume controls and four input jacks.

An outstanding feature of this fine amplifier is the single unit parts panel, a feature which does not meet the eye of the ordinary buyer, but for those who are conscious of outstanding quality, this parts panel will be found to be extremely interesting. On it are mounted practically all of the small parts including the condensers and resistors, etc. These small parts are securely attached to the parts panel through brass eyelets into which they are soldered. Each is held securely in place and not allowed to vibrate or rattle around. This eliminates a great source of amplifier failure and guarantees that your Fender amplifier will give you long and faithful service without attention. In addition to these many features is the fact that this amplifier has an over-size power supply employing an extremely heavy duty power transformer.

The output transformer is also much heavier than is usually found in amplifiers of this size. All of these features are combined to provide the player with a fine piece of portable musical instrument amplification equipment and it has set a standard which others are constantly trying to duplicate.

TECHNICAL CHARACTERISTICS

The Fender Deluxe Amp is a compact, portable musical instrument amplifier conservatively rated, with all necessary controls for handling practically any amplified music problem.

Power Output: 18 Watts at less than 5% distortion.

Frequency Response: With optimum tone control setting + 1 db 40 to 15,000 cycles per second at 15 Watts. Less than 0.5% harmonic distortion at rated 15 Watts output.

Hum and Noise Level: 80 db below rated output. Total feed back employed −30db.

Inputs: Four high impedence inputs interconnected to provide parallel input circuits when the first input jack of either the bright or the normal combination is used. This allows considerably more input voltage to be applied without introducing distortion.

Extension Speaker Jack: Mounted on under side of chassis.

Controls Appearing on Chassis: Ground Switch; Panel Extractor Fuse Post; Off-and-On Switch; Bull's-Eye Pilot Light; Two Volume Controls; Four Input Jacks; and Full Range Tone Control.

Number of Tubes: Five (two of these tubes are dual purpose tubes, giving the amplifier the equivalent of seven tubes).

Tubes Employed: Two 12AX7s; two 6V6-GTs; one 5U4G.

Speakers: One heavy duty Jensen 12" Concert Series Speaker.

Power Consumption: 85 Watts.

Size: 20" wide, 10½" deep, 16" high; Shipping weight 26 lbs.
It will be noted from the accompanying photograph that practically all replacements can be made to the amplifier without removing the chassis. This includes all the condensers, resistors, tube sockets, controls, jacks, switches, etc. The only replacements for which it is necessary to remove the chassis are the power and output transformers and filter choke. This is a very important feature which must always be considered when time is important.

Cabinet: Solid ¾" wood with lock joint weldwood corners.

Covering: Highest grade, brown and white diagonal stripe airplane luggage linen. Highly wear and scuff resistant. Can be easily cleaned.
Safety codes for all states are equaled or exceeded. Fender Fine Electric Instruments are guaranteed to give complete customer satisfaction. This guarantee is backed by our many years of successful business relationship with all of our customers.

Photo shows back
cover removed

Specifications and prices subject to change without notice.

BASSMAN AMP

The Fender Bassman Amp is one of the finest musical instrument amplifiers ever offered to the buying public. It is a unit that combines tremendous power, low distortion factor and beauty of design in such a package that it is completely portable and easily handled. Four Heavy Duty 10" Speakers give it outstanding advantages over any single speaker amplifier and it produces tremendous audio power without distortion. The Fender Bassman Amp is housed in a beautiful cabinet made of ¾" solid stock with lock jointed corners. It is covered with the highest grade diagonal stripe brown and white airplane luggage linen, which is extremely wear resistant. The grill cloth is the latest style plastic material, which is not only very attractive, but functional as well, inasmuch as its porosity allows considerably more sound to pass without being muffled and without the loss of high frequencies incurred with ordinary grill cloth. The Bassman Amp features the Fender top mounted chassis which is beautifully chrome plated with white index markings and its overall appearance is one of sleek, modern lines. It employs four heavy duty 10" Jensen Concert Series Speakers and features the latest in electronic design, inasmuch as the inputs are so arranged that tremendous surges of voltage can be accommodated without overloading the first tubes, thereby eliminating a great source of distortion which is normal in all older type amplifiers.

The Bassman Amp tone control circuit is a Fender development employing both a bass and treble tone control which allows complete tone shading from the lowest bass to the highest treble without introducing any distortion as is common in other types of tone controls. In addition to this, a presence control, which is an exclusive Fender feature is included which allows the delicate adjustment of the extremely high frequencies beyond those normally influenced by the regular treble control.

The regular panel equipment includes the on-and-off switch, the Fender developed stand-by switch, the bull's-eye type panel light, panel mount fuse holder, and a new and exclusive first—a ground switch which completely eliminates the problem of having to polarize the power plug. With this ground switch one can simply plug 'n the amplifier, turn it on, and if hum and line noise so frequently noticed in all amplifiers, is present, a flip of the ground switch completely eliminates this annoyance. It is no longer necessary to remove the plug from the wall and turn it over, which often is a considerable inconvenience.

An outstanding feature of this fine amplifier is the single unit parts panel, a feature which does not meet the eye of the ordinary buyer, but for those who are conscious of outstanding quality, this parts panel will be found to be extremely interesting. On it are mounted practically all of the small parts including the condensers and resistors, etc. These small parts are securely attached to the parts panel through brass eyelets into which they are soldered. Each is held securely in place and not allowed to vibrate or rattle around. This eliminates a great source of amplifier failure and guarantees that your Fender amplifier will give you long and faithful service without attention. In addition to these many features is the fact that this amplifier has an over-size power supply employing an extremely heavy duty power transformer and two 5U4G rectifier tubes, instead of the usual one.

The output transformer is also much heavier than is usually found in amplifiers of this size.

The Bassman Amplifier is excellent for amplification of any type of string bass, either electric bass or amplified acoustic bass. At the same time, it has been designed in such a way that it is outstanding as an amplifier for all other electric music instruments. It will be found that the Bassman Amplifier is especially effective when used with an accordion, providing the low, feathery bass and the balance of tone that all accordion players are seeking.

All of these features are combined to provide the player with the finest piece of portable musical instrument amplification equipment ever developed and it is destined to set a standard that others will be seeking to attain for a long period in the future.

Fender

BASSMAN AMP

Photo shows back cover removed

TECHNICAL CHARACTERISTICS

The Fender Bassman Amp is a compact, portable musical instrument amplifier conservatively rated, with all necessary controls for handling complete High Fidelity music reproduction.

Power Output: 60 Watts at less than 5% distortion.

Frequency Response: With optimum tone control setting + 1 db 20 to 20,000 cycles per second at 50 Watts. Less than 0.5% harmonic distortion at rated 50 Watts output.

Hum and Noise Level: 80 db below rated output. Total feed back employed -30db.

Inputs: Four high impedence inputs interconnected to provide parallel input circuits when the first input jack of either the bright or the normal combination is used. This allows considerably more input voltage to be applied without introducing distortion.

Controls appearing on Chassis: Ground Switch; Panel Extractor Fuse Post; Off-and-On Switch; Stand-by Switch; Bull's-Eye Pilot Light; Presence Control; Bass Control; Treble Control; two Volume Controls; two Input Jacks.

Number of Tubes: Seven. Three of these tubes are dual purpose tubes, giving the amplifier the equivalent of ten tubes.

Tubes Employed: Two 12AY7s; one 12AX7; two 5881s or 6L6Gs; two 5U4Gs.

Speakers: Four heavy duty ten inch Jensen Concert Series Speakers.

Power Consumption: 180 Watts.

Size: 22½" wide, 10½" deep, 23" high.

Shipping Weight: 50 lbs.

It will be noted from the accompanying photograph that practically all replacements can be made to the amplifier without removing the chassis. This includes all the condensers, resistors, tube sockets, controls, jacks, switches, etc. The only replacements for which it is necessary to remove the chassis are the power and output transformers and filter choke. This is a very important feature which must always be considered when time is important.

Cabinet: Solid ¾" wood with lock joint weldwood corners.

Covering: Highest grade, brown and white diagonal stripe airplane luggage linen. Highly wear and scuff resistant. Can be easily cleaned.

Safety codes for all states are equaled or exceeded. Fender Fine Electric Instruments are guaranteed to give complete customer satisfaction. This guarantee is backed by our many years of successful business relationships with all of our customers.

Specifications and prices subject to change without notice.

INDEX

  Forrest White, with a background in business management and industrial engineering, built guitars as a hobby before joining the Fender Electric Instrument Company as General Manager on May 20, 1954. Later he served as Vice President of Fender, as well. He also has worked for CMI, Rickenbacker, and Music Man.

  "Forrest White was among the most talented industrial engineers and business managers in musical instrument manufacturing," according to guitar expert Richard Smith. In Forrest's own words, "Leo Fender became a true legend in his lifetime and he allowed me to work by his side along the way. It just so happens my education and experience in business management and industrial engineering, and the fact that I had also built guitars as a hobby, was what Leo Fender needed at a given time."